MARINE BIOPROSPECTING, BIODIVERSITY AND NOVEL USES OF OCEAN RESOURCES

Human use of marine resources is changing, as is the marine environment itself, and our understanding of marine ecosystems and biodiversity is developing. This open access book explores the challenges this raises for legal regimes pertaining to the oceans and their domestic implementation. It engages with developments in areas such as bioprospecting, fisheries, deep-sea mining and shipping.

Several case studies discuss genetic resources and the implications of the new UN Agreement on marine biological diversity of areas beyond national jurisdiction. A team of experts suggest new approaches to questions of interpretation, established management principles, and institutional relationships. Not limiting their scope to the international law of the sea, they also examine international environmental law, intellectual property rights, and domestic law.

The book broadens the scholarly debate and provides a timely reflection on the dramatic policy developments currently happening in the field of marine resource governance. It will be welcomed by lawyers, NGOs and policymakers.

The ebook editions of this book are available open access under a CC BY-NC-ND 4.0 licence on bloomsburycollections.com. Open access was funded by the University of Gothenburg, Department of Law and the Nordic Council of Ministers.

Volume 92 in the series Studies in International Law

Studies in International Law

Recent titles in this series

Intervention in Civil Wars: Effectiveness, Legitimacy, and Human Rights
Chiara Redaelli

General Principles as a Source of International Law: Art 38(1)(c) of the Statute of the International Court of Justice
Imogen Saunders

The Law of Humanity Project: A Story of International Law Reform and State-making
Ukri Soirila

Extraterritoriality and Climate Change Jurisdiction: Exploring EU Climate Protection under International Law
Natalie L Dobson

International Law and the War with Islamic State: Challenges for Jus ad Bellum and Jus in Bello
Saeed Bagheri

Private Actors as Participants in International Law: A Critical Analysis of Membership under the Law of the Sea
Armando Rocha

Truth and Transitional Justice: Localising the International Legal Framework in Muslim Majority Legal Systems
Alice Panepinto

State Responsibility for Non-State Actors: Past, Present and Prospects for the Future
Richard Mackenzie-Gray Scott

International Agreements between Non-State Actors as a Source of International Law
Melissa Loja

Judicial Decisions in International Law Argumentation: Between Entrapment and Creativity
Letizia Lo Giacco

South-South Migrations and the Law from Below: Case Studies on China and Nigeria
Oreva Olakpe

Territorial Status in International Law
Jure Vidmar

Marine Bioprospecting, Biodiversity and Novel Uses of Ocean Resources: New Approaches in International Law
Edited by Niels Krabbe and David Langlet

For a complete list of titles in this series see www.bloomsbury.com/uk/series/studies-in-international-law/

Marine Bioprospecting, Biodiversity and Novel Uses of Ocean Resources

New Approaches in International Law

Edited by
Niels Krabbe
and
David Langlet

•HART•
OXFORD • LONDON • NEW YORK • NEW DELHI • SYDNEY

HART PUBLISHING

Bloomsbury Publishing Plc

Kemp House, Chawley Park, Cumnor Hill, Oxford, OX2 9PH, UK

1385 Broadway, New York, NY 10018, USA

29 Earlsfort Terrace, Dublin 2, Ireland

HART PUBLISHING, the Hart/Stag logo, BLOOMSBURY and the Diana logo are trademarks of Bloomsbury Publishing Plc

First published in Great Britain 2024

A catalogue record for this book is available from the British Library.

A catalogue record for this book is available from the Library of Congress.

ISBN: HB: 978-1-50996-827-5
ePDF: 978-1-50996-829-9
ePub: 978-1-50996-828-2

Typeset by Compuscript Ltd, Shannon

Contents

List of Contributors

Niels Krabbe is a Postdoctoral Researcher at the University of Gothenburg School of Business, Economics and Law.

David Langlet is Professor of Law at Uppsala University.

Richard Barnes is Professor of International Law at the University of Lincoln, and Adjunct Professor of Law at the Norwegian Centre for the Law of the Sea at the University of Tromsø.

Aleke Stöfen-O'Brien is Assistant Professor at the Sasakawa Global Ocean Institute of the World Maritime University.

Christian Prip is a Senior Researcher in international environmental policy and law at The Fridtjof Nansen Institute.

Aldo Chircop is Professor of Law based at the Marine & Environmental Law Institute, Schulich School of Law, Dalhousie University.

Alfonso Ascencio-Herrera is Legal Counsel and Deputy to the Secretary-General of the International Seabed Authority.

Fredrik Haag is the Head of the Office for London Convention & Protocol and Ocean Affairs at the Marine Environment Division of the International Maritime Organization.

Ekaterina Antsygina is a Postdoctoral Fellow at the University of Hamburg.

Nkeiru Scotcher is a Solicitor of the Supreme Court of England and Wales and Research Fellow of International and European Law at the Vrije Universitiet Brussel.

Peter Gottschalk is Senior Lecturer in business law at Lund University School of Economics and Management.

Snjólaug Árnadóttir is Associate Professor of Public International Law and director of the Centre for Law on Climate Change and Sustainability at Reykjavik University.

Valeria Eboli is Professor of International Law at the Italian Naval Academy and Chair of the IWG on Fair Treatment of Seafarers of the Comité Maritime International.

1

Novel Uses of Ocean Resources – An Introduction

NIELS KRABBE AND DAVID LANGLET

THE UNITED NATIONS has declared 2021 to 2030 as the Decade of Ocean Science for Sustainable Development. This highlights the profound importance of the oceans, of increasing our understanding not only of how oceans and marine ecosystems function, but also of our own interactions with the oceans, and of enhancing the governance structures that should enable us to use the riches of the oceans without degrading or destroying them. We know that many ocean ecosystems are put under immense pressure by a multitude of human activities. At the same time, oceans remain a vital source of resources and ecosystem services for an expanding world population. Increasingly, humanity derives benefits from the oceans not only from traditional activities such as capture fisheries and a growing marine aquaculture, but also from novel uses such as the exploration of marine genetic resources and potentially from exploring the mineral and other resources of the deep sea. These novel uses are associated with important potential benefits, but also with risks and challenges of an ecological as well as social nature. Also, more well-known ways of using ocean resources, such as certain fishing practices, are increasingly being recognised as putting marine ecosystems in peril due to expanding scientific knowledge.

Recent decades have seen great advances in science and technology that enable us – or, rather, those who have the requisite financial and technological resources – to explore and derive ever more benefits from the marine realm. In some ways, technological developments risk making legal frameworks obsolete, addressing problems that are no longer pertinent or facilitating activities that are no longer relevant. If regulatory and institutional structures do not keep pace with technological developments and changing practices in the scientific and commercial sector, they can also become obstacles to desirable activities and hamper progress towards sustainable development. The story told by the contributions to this volume is to a large extent one of fragmentation and path dependencies that make the law and its institutions less than fit for addressing many current challenges. It also strongly calls for innovative thinking and, perhaps more than anything else, effective collaboration and cross-fertilisation between branches of law, institutions, scholarly disciplines and industry. To many, the elaboration of a legal instrument under the United Nations Convention on the Law of the Sea (UNCLOS) on the conservation and sustainable use of marine biological diversity of areas beyond national jurisdiction (ABNJ) offers a rare opportunity to advance the law in these regards. Fortunately, this instrument was finally adopted after lengthy negotiations in March 2023, which enabled consideration of the finally adopted text by the contributing authors dealing with topics relating to the so-called BBNJ Agreement.[1]

By looking at how legal and institutional structures address, or fail to address, core sustainability dimensions of novel ocean uses or uses that are being re-evaluated in the light of increasing scientific understanding, this volume aims to support the objectives of the Ocean decade, ie to deliver solution-oriented research needed for a well-functioning ocean in support of the UN 2030 Sustainable Development Agenda (Agenda 2030).

In the first chapter after this introduction, Richard Barnes explores the concept of stewardship and how it could be fruitfully applied to the regulation of marine genetic resources in ABNJ. Stewardship, he argues, could aid the urgently needed rethink of our relationship with the natural world. By stating in the preamble to the BBNJ Agreement that they are 'Desiring to act as stewards of the ocean in areas beyond national jurisdiction on behalf of present and future generations', the parties open the way for a more transformative approach to defining our relationships with resources in ABNJ. Barnes provides a typology of stewardship concepts, including stewardship as an intellectual construct, as a form of conduct and as practical arrangement. He then goes on to suggest parameters for an analytical framework for stewardship and explores how stewardship could apply to the governance of ABNJ through the BBNJ Agreement.

In the third chapter, Niels Krabbe evaluates the debate on marine genetic resource in ABNJ and identifies important shortcomings in terms of pre-existing legal principles and structures being used to address novel challenges for which they are not well suited. Krabbe suggests that distinctive characteristics of genetic resources are being disregarded. This may be due to the dominant role played by ideas and rationales of the law of the sea to the detriment of other relevant regimes of international law, such as intellectual property law, as well as practical and business perspectives. Krabbe sees a risk that a rigorous framework for physical access to genetic resources in the marine environment is established while actual biotechnological development is largely based in collections far from the sea. To prevent new rules from becoming irrelevant, states and observers involved

[1] Agreement under the United Nations Convention on the Law of the Sea on the Conservation and Sustainable Use of Marine Biological Diversity of Areas beyond National Jurisdiction (adopted 19 June 2023) www.un.org/bbnj/.

must look beyond the confined perspective of the law of the sea and consider how genetic resources are actually used.

In the fourth chapter, Aleke Stöfen-O'Brien takes a somewhat similar approach to that of Krabbe by exploring the impact of existing and dominant legal frameworks on the governance of the marine environment in ABNJ. However, rather than looking specifically at the negotiations concerning marine genetic resources, Stöfen-O'Brien explores a topic which has not been dealt with at depth even in the scientific literature, namely the interrelationship between trade law, the law of the sea and international environmental law at the nexus of ABNJ. The chapter explores how these regimes may work together to develop suitable measures for the protection and conservation of the marine environment as a whole and in particular focusing on ABNJ. While this is not necessarily an easy thing, it does not require the establishment of new treaties or formal institutions. In fact, Stöfen-O'Brien concludes, improved cooperation between the environment, the law of the sea and trade regimes can already be implemented in the short to medium term.

The fifth chapter, by Christian Prip, takes a close look at the emergence of digital sequence information (DSI) and its implications for the regulation of access to marine genetic resources and bioprospecting. By making it possible to download DNA sequences from public databases and reconstruct the DNA, DSI challenges the underlying assumptions for the regulation of access to genetic resources and the sharing of benefits from their use. As technological developments have drastically reduced the demand for physical genetic material, new controversies and complexity have arisen. The use of DSI takes place without applying the concept of benefit sharing of the Nagoya Protocol, and it is often extremely difficult to identify the original source of the sequences or pinpoint the benefits arising from their use. Prip sees the BBNJ Agreement as a platform to explore alternative ways of achieving fair and equitable benefit sharing from marine bioprospecting through a multilateral system decoupled from transactions of physical samples.

In the sixth chapter, Aldo Chircop, Alfonso Ascencio-Herrera and Fredrik Haag analyse the interface of the competencies of the International Seabed Authority (ISA) and the International Maritime Organization (IMO) in relation to activities in the international seabed area (the Area), ie the seabed and subsoil in ABNJ. Although currently only seabed exploration activities are underway, exploitation may commence soon. Activities in the Area and those supporting shipping will be inextricably interlinked because the remoteness of the deep seabed requires ships to serve as platforms for mineral recovery and transportation. Since the IMO is the competent international organisation for international shipping and navigation, the mandates of the ISA and the IMO require coordination. The authors demonstrate that ISA and IMO competencies are highly complementary. However, as the regulatory regime for seabed mining continues to develop, regulatory overlaps might emerge. The analysis also raises further questions, including how ISA regulations depend and rely upon IMO regulations as well as how maritime security in seabed mining should be regulated.

In chapter seven, Ekaterina Antsygina explores the limits of the protection of biodiversity of the sedentary species of continental shelves. More specifically, she discusses whether coastal states can base a prohibition on bottom trawling on the high seas on rights over extended continental shelves to protect eg the corals and sponges that create structural habitats for many other species. While this is an issue that has divided scholars, Antsygina's conclusion is that coastal states have the right to impose measures protecting sedentary species on the high seas superjacent their extended continental shelves according to Parts VI and XII of UNCLOS coupled with the provisions of the Convention on Biological Diversity (CBD). Such measures can be necessary to protect sedentary species from the adverse effects of bottom trawling and would constitute a precautionary step beneficial for the preservation of the marine environment.

This is followed by a chapter in which Nkeiru Scotcher looks at tensions in the governance of fisheries and marine biodiversity in ABNJ. She does so by combining a more traditional international law perspective with an analysis of the development of norms and associated practices using the English school theory of international relations. In this way, the chapter offers a legally informed system analysis of fisheries management, highlighting the tension between institutional structures governing fisheries and marine biodiversity. By historically following the emergence of inter alia UNCLOS, the UN Fish Stocks Agreement and the CBD, Scotcher sheds light on issues with applying concepts of sovereignty and territoriality to a resource that does not fit into the same spatial parameters. Encouragingly, she finds that although institutional interactions with respect to fish, fisheries and marine biodiversity developed separately, they are increasingly converging.

In the book's ninth chapter, Peter Gottschalk asks how policy and law for marine bioprospecting should be formulated and designed to achieve sustainability. A challenge in this regard is to achieve integration and coherence across several different legal regimes, including the law of the sea, the rules on access and benefit sharing, and intellectual property law. Using sustainability as expressed through the Sustainable Development Goals (SDGs), Gottschalk explores synergies and conflicts between goals and how the SDG framework can aid in promoting coherence of the diverse legal framework relating to marine bioprospecting. While Agenda 2030 is largely detached from the international legal system, it relies on international law for its implementation. Achieving its goals in relation to marine bioprospecting requires extensive international cooperation. Paying close attention to ways to achieving policy coherence across relevant legal regimes and their national implementation is imperative.

Chapter 10 is dedicated to a case study on the regulation of marine bioprospecting in Iceland, a country where the use of marine genetic resources has developed into a major industry. Snjólaug Árnadóttir explores Icelandic activities relating to marine bioprospecting and looks at the existence of applicable Icelandic law as well as how it relates to the most relevant international obligations under the CBD, the Nagoya Protocol and UNCLOS. Based on this, she suggests key components for new Icelandic legislation governing marine bioprospecting. She also identifies a number of principles that should guide the process of codifying new rules governing marine bioprospecting at the national level, including equitable sharing of benefits, legal certainty and predictability, and the ecosystem approach.

The rights of indigenous peoples in relation to bioprospecting in the Arctic is discussed by Valeria Eboli in chapter eleven. More specifically, Eboli looks at the rights or interests of indigenous communities in the Arctic in relation to marine genetic resources and how far they are entitled to participate in the decision-making processes related to the exploitation of such resources and to bioprospecting activities. She discusses the CBD, the Nagoya Protocol and UNCLOS with a view to elucidating their implications for the rights and interests of indigenous peoples in relation to marine genetic resources. Eboli finds that the right of indigenous peoples to participation in access and benefit sharing is undermined by several factors, including a fragmented legal framework that does not guarantee a proper involvement of local communities. Here the BBNJ Agreement offers some opportunity for an improved legal situation.

In the twelfth and final chapter, the editors Niels Krabbe and David Langlet attempt to provide a synthesis of the findings of the different contributions. They highlight how recent developments in international negotiations connect to the changing human uses of marine resources. In addition to the BBNJ Agreement, the recently concluded Global Biodiversity Framework represents an important and historic step in adapting international law to new perspectives of the oceans and their resources. Of similarly high relevance to this theme, the ongoing negotiations at the International Seabed Authority are at a crucial crossroads. In the development of the mining code, states appear increasingly polarised between conservationist and resource exploitation interests. Furthermore, other areas are suggested, in particular relating to the role of the oceans in the climate, where scientific discoveries and an increasing awareness of potential conflicts between different objectives call for further developments of law and policy.

2

Stewardship Beyond the State: Implications for the Regulation of Marine Genetic Resources in Areas Beyond National Jurisdiction

RICHARD BARNES

I. INTRODUCTION

MARINE GENETIC RESOURCES (MGRs) are natural resources with potentially significant intellectual and commercial value for use in medical and industrial processes. International regulation of MGRs ranges across a variety of regimes and instruments: the law of the sea (United Nations Convention on the Law of the Sea 1982[1] (UNCLOS)), biodiversity law (Convention on Biological Diversity 1992[2] and the Nagoya Protocol 2010[3]) and intellectual property regimes (ie the TRIPS Agreement 1994[4]). Each of these regimes may govern aspects of MGRs, but as yet we lack a holistic approach to their regulation.[5] Fundamentally, though, MGRs are a natural resource. As such, they fall into long-established patterns of contested use and control over valuable resources.

For most of human history, the natural world has been treated as a resource available for some of us to exploit in one form or another; it is regulated as the object of competing human claims. The uneven legacy of this approach is a natural environment that is heavily depleted and despoiled as we take and take, or pile use upon use for generation after generation. Whether it is through

[1] The United Nations Convention on the Law of the Sea 1982, 1833 UNTS 3.

[2] Convention on Biological Diversity 1992, 1760 UNTS 79.

[3] Nagoya Protocol on Access to Genetic Resources and the Fair and Equitable Sharing of Benefits Arising from their Utilization to the Convention on Biological Diversity 2010, UN Doc UNEP/CBD/COP/10/27, 29 October 2010.

[4] Agreement of Trade-Related Aspects of Intellectual Property, 1869 UNTS 299.

[5] Krabbe, *Bioprospecting and Deep-Sea Genetic Resources in a Fragmenting International Law* (University of Gothenburg, 2021).

individual tools of ownership or collective regimes of sovereignty, humanity has devised ways to rework the natural world to varying degrees, and with varying degrees of responsibility, in its own image. As some describe our situation, we live in the Anthropocene, a geological era defined simply by mankind's impact on the planet. We live in a failing environment of our own making.[6] In the face of a self-inflicted existential crisis, we are striving to rethink our fundamental relationship with the natural world. However, although we share a common concern in this endeavour, we lack a common language, common values and common solutions. For example, at that critical nexus between human and environment, only recently have some states committed to the idea that there should be a human right to a healthy environment.[7] This approach introduces into the language of rights the idea that human life depends not merely upon use of resources, but upon a healthy environment, and that human life and natural systems are mutually dependent notions. This points to the need to change the way we think of human–nature relationships. However, change is slow, and it is often resisted because it must occur against the backdrop of the deeply rooted structures and strictures of the law, and against the values that are embodied therein.

The challenge of redefining our relationship with the natural environment is brought into sharp relief in respect of the legal status of MGRs of the deep seabed. As a space that lies beyond the limits of national jurisdiction, the deep seabed is necessarily the domain of international law-making enterprises, in part under UNCLOS, in part under the 1994 Implementation Agreement and in part through the activities of the International Seabed Authority. As noted above, it is also shaped by international law more generally. In this law-making enterprise, individual human concerns are typically subordinated to those of the state. Although the international seabed area (the Area) is designated the common heritage of mankind, and activities therein must not cause harm to human life or the environment, the totality of rules is otherwise focused upon the rights and duties of states. In this regime, these rights and duties are the immediate focus of law, with humans and the environment relegated to mere objects of interstate relationships. At the same time, the heterogeneity of state interests and the fragmented forms of authority that exist in the Area generate new differences and fault lines that we must strive to overcome in the development of suitable governance regimes. In these circumstances, law becomes overly focused on the interests of states and not enough on the purposes or consequences of granting states some combination of rights and duties. Thus Articles 140–49 UNCLOS, on the common heritage of mankind, are left as a thin veneer of purpose on a body of rules otherwise concerned

[6] Cloutier de Repentigny, 'To the Anthropocene and Beyond: The Responsibility of Law in Decimating and Protecting Marine Life' (2020) 11 *Transnational Legal Theory* 180.

[7] Human Rights Council, Resolution Recognising a human right to a healthy environment, UN Doc A/HRC/48/L.32/Rev.1, 8 October 2021.

with the distribution of legal authority, and the commercial exploitation of ocean resources.[8] In the decades following the adoption of UNCLOS, we have struggled to develop fair, effective and appropriate governance frameworks for international spaces,[9] let alone frameworks that define human–natural environment relationships in marine spaces in any meaningful way. The point I wish to make is that when considering the regulation of deep seabed resources, we need to understand the deeper-lying normative structures that shape the law and understand these against the wider challenges facing the governance of the environment. As such, this chapter is concerned with exploring options for reimagining our relationship with the natural environment, and what implications this may have for the regulation of MGRs.

In recent years, this struggle to better articulate our relationship with the natural environment has been very evident in the developing regime for the conservation and use of marine biodiversity in areas beyond national jurisdiction (ABNJ).[10] This was manifest in the negotiation of a legally binding instrument on conservation and sustainable use of marine biodiversity in ABNJ, commonly referred to as the Biodiversity Beyond National Jurisdiction (BBNJ) Agreement.[11] Originally conceived of as a space where potentially valuable mineral rights could be exploited, the Area became the focus of debates about how to govern access to and use of the valuable MGRs derived from species that have evolved chemical and physiological properties that enable them to withstand the extreme conditions of heat and pressure that exist at great ocean depths. Access to and use of such resources may have profound effects on the development of medicines and other industrial products, and their consequent distribution across societies. Exploitation of such resources may also have a profound impact on poorly understood rare and vulnerable ecosystems.

One of the core issues that divided states during the BBNJ negotiations was that of determining which overarching principle(s) should govern the ABNJ regime. On the one hand, freedom of the high seas favours a more decentralised, liberal approach, where individual states are entitled to freely conduct research

[8] Ranganathan, 'Ocean Floor Grab: International Law and the Making of an Extractive Imaginary' (2019) 30 *European Journal of International Law* 573.

[9] See 'Symposium: International Law and Economic Exploitation in the Global Commons' (2019) 30 *European Journal of International Law* 541.

[10] Freestone, 'International Governance, Responsibility and Management of Areas Beyond National Jurisdiction' (2012) 27 *International Journal of Marine and Coastal Law* 191; Warner, 'Conserving Marine Biodiversity in Areas Beyond National Jurisdiction: Co-evolution and Interaction With the Law of the Sea' (2014) 1 *Frontiers in Marine Science* Art 6; Blanchard, Durussel and Boteler, 'Socio-ecological Resilience and the Law: Exploring the Adaptive Capacity of the BBNJ Agreement' (2019) 108 *Marine Policy* 103612; De Santo et al, 'Protecting Biodiversity in Areas Beyond National Jurisdiction: An Earth System Governance Perspective' (2019) 2 *Earth System Governance* 100029; Frank, 'Options for Marine Protected Areas Under a New Agreement on Marine Biodiversity of Areas Beyond National Jurisdiction' in Heidar (ed), *New Knowledge and Changing Circumstances in the Law of the Sea* (Brill, 2021) 101–23.

[11] Mandated in UNGA Res 69/292, UN Doc A/Res/69.292, 6 July 2015. For developments, see www.un.org/bbnj/.

and exploit the genetic potential of resources in the deep seabed unilaterally subject to some limits on reasonable use and due regard to the interests of other states. This follows a broadly liberal and exploitative tradition in the law of the sea. On the other hand, the common heritage of mankind favours a more robust institutional framework that seeks to ensure the benefits of exploitation are shared according to predetermined distributive benchmarks. It differs principally in that it favours community interests over individual state interests. Of course, both principles are framed exclusively in anthropocentric terms and concerned with some mode of exploitation. There are other principles potentially applicable to ABNJ, such as precautionary and ecosystem-based approaches, but these penetrate less deeply to the core of the issue as to whether we have more inclusive or exclusive forms of governance prevail. Freedom of the high seas or common heritage concern the basic status of the space, with subsequent principles providing guidance about how such space is to be used. Understanding how the Biodiversity Beyond National Jurisdiction negotiations addressed this point is important because the BBNJ Agreement will shape our future and fundamental relationship with the natural environment of the Area.

On 4 March 2023, states agreed the text of a binding agreement on the conservation and sustainable use of marine biological diversity of areas beyond national jurisdiction.[12] Significantly, the BBNJ Agreement refers to the notion of 'stewardship' in its Preamble and this may open the way for a more transformative approach to defining our relationships with resources in ABNJ. This reference to stewardship provides the point of departure for the present chapter because it invites reflections on new ways of constructing our relationship with the natural environment and its resources in ABNJ. The draft text has already sparked some academic interest in exploring the meaning and content of stewardship as a legal principle.[13] Recently, Riding has advanced stewardship as a way of thinking about the governance of ABNJ – arguing that it can be used to reconcile the principles of common heritage and freedom of the seas.[14] She defines stewardship as a form of individual and collective responsibility to protect and preserve the environment for present and future generations, based upon principles of responsible use, cooperative management and equity.[15] Riding uses stewardship to synthesise and help frame existing environmental responsibilities. Whilst this has the advantage of grounding it in accepted rules and principles of international law, it does not interrogate more fundamentally

[12] Agreement under the United Nations Convention on the Law of the Sea on the Conservation and Sustainable Use of Marine Biological Diversity of Areas beyond National Jurisdiction (adopted 19 June 2023) www.un.org/bbnj/ (BBNJ Agreement).

[13] Harden-Davies, 'Deep-Sea Genetic Resources: New Frontiers for Science and Stewardship in Areas Beyond National Jurisdiction' (2017) 137 *Deep Sea Research Part II: Topical Studies in Oceanography* 504; Harden-Davies et al, 'Rights of Nature: Perspectives for Global Ocean Stewardship' (2020) *Marine Policy* 104059.

[14] Riding, 'Redefining Environmental Stewardship to Deliver Governance Frameworks for Marine Biodiversity Beyond National Jurisdiction' (2018) 75 *ICES Journal of Marine Science* 435, 439.

[15] ibid 439.

how stewardship might be used to reframe our relationship with the natural world. If stewardship is to be of value, it must be more than the sum of its parts. To collapse stewardship back into existing rules and principles begs the question: so what? If those rules and principles exist anyway, then what value does stewardship add? In this chapter, I argue that more needs to be done to understand the content of stewardship. In other words, how can stewardship offer a better way of framing our relationship with the natural world, specifically in areas beyond national jurisdiction?

Whilst the broad line of argument in this chapter is that stewardship has the potential to transform how we frame our relationship with the natural world, this entails several steps. Most obviously, we need to consider more carefully the precise meaning of stewardship. Whilst it is novel for the concept to feature in an international agreement, stewardship does have some intellectual heritage and legal significance, so it is essential that we understand what this entails. To this end, I provide a brief typology of stewardship concepts, which shows some of the challenges of using such a value-laden term as stewardship (section III). To address such concerns, I then provide the parameters for an analytical framework for stewardship (section IV), which can be used to explore how stewardship could apply to the governance of ABNJ through the BBNJ Agreement (section V). This provides a guide to how the Agreement might usefully frame our relationship with resources in ABNJ. Before developing the notion of stewardship, I explain why this approach should be considered. In short, stewardship is a relationship that elevates the interests of the beneficiary (eg a person or the environment) above those of the steward (ie the state).

II. WHY STEWARDSHIP?

The horizontal structure of international law means it is ill-suited to advancing non-state interests. International law's primary social reality is one based upon sovereignty of the state, and the law is immediately concerned with the rights, duties and interests of states.[16] Any other human or environmental interests are only conveyed into international social reality through the medium of the state. Some form of domestic process of government feeds sub-national interests into the machinery of the state and this is indirectly fed into the international system. International interests are then formed through the interactions of states (and other international actors) in international fora, eg treaty negotiations. In this way, the creation of international norms is the product of the double aggregation of domestic and then state interests, and one where the international social reality takes on a life of its own. International law may service individual human interests (or environmental interests), but this is rarely

[16] Allott, '*Mare Nostrum*: A New International Law of the Sea' (1992) 86 *American Journal of International Law* 764.

done directly. Thus, rules on the protection of human rights or environmental goods are invariably framed in terms of interstate rights and responsibilities – rather than as direct commitments by states to individuals or the environment. For the most part, humans and the environment are the object of laws. This makes them subordinate to state interests since the benefit of any such entitlements or protections will usually depend upon the intermediary acts of states.

The prescription of environmental rights and duties in this tradition serves only to reaffirm the structural bias towards state-centred interests. Every time a new rule is agreed upon the use of some natural resource, the rule reinforces the state's pivotal role in determining the use of that resource. The Rio Declaration might have boldly stated that 'Human beings are at the centre of concerns for sustainable development',[17] but this does nothing to change the fundamental structure of international legal commitments.

Recognising the failure of traditional state-centric approaches to addressing environmental harm, there have been innovative efforts to reconceive our relationship with the natural environment that seek to subvert or move away from state-based approaches. For example, we have the idea of environmental rights, which seek to draw upon the structural and rhetorical power of human rights to drive the protection of environment. Human rights are rights that exists vis-à-vis the state and so seek to constrain sovereign power in accordance with fundamental moral considerations.[18] These rights may be defined as 'individual or group based human rights that afford protection to the environment, either directly or indirectly'.[19] Another approach is to vest nature or natural entities with rights of their own. Originating in academic debates,[20] this approach is gaining traction in many legal systems around the world. The Report of the United Nations Secretary General on Harmony with Nature 2019 provides both international recognition of this movement and a telling survey of legal and policy initiatives across the globe.[21] More recently, Harden-Davies et al advanced this approach as offering fresh insights into the challenges of governing BBNJ – linking this to the idea of ocean stewardship.[22] Arguably operating at a more ambitious scale is the Earth Systems Law movement, an approach to governance that responds to the fundamental role that humans play as part of a natural system (rather than its master).[23] Scholars in this tradition advance

[17] Principle 1, Rio Declaration on Environment and Development, A/CONF.151/26, 12 (Vol 1), 12 August 1992.

[18] Raz, 'Human Rights Without Foundation' (2007) Oxford Legal Studies Research Paper 14/2007.

[19] Barnes, 'Environmental Rights in Marine Spaces' in Bogojevic and Rayfuse (eds), *Environmental Rights in Europe and Beyond* (Hart Publishing, 2018) 53.

[20] This was the object of Christopher Stone's seminal article of 1972, 'Should Trees Have Standing?' (1972) 45 *Southern California Law Review* 450.

[21] UN Doc A/74/236, 26 July 2019.

[22] Harden-Davies et al (n 13).

[23] Biermann et al, 'Earth System Governance: A Research Framework' (2010) 10 *International Environmental Agreements: Politics, Law and Economics* 277; Kim and Mackey, 'International Environmental Law as a Complex Adaptive System' (2014) 14 *International Environmental Agreements:*

an idea of law that accounts for the interdependence of humans and natural systems and the complexity of such systems as factors that should shape how we govern human affairs. This more radically challenges the complicity of international law in environmental harm, taking the view that international law 'shuts out any meaningful involvement, incentivization and promotion of non-state actors in earth system governance at a time when such involvement is in fact critically required'.[24]

If nothing else, these approaches show the direction of travel and a move away from simplistic state-centric ways of thinking. They show the importance of holistic, cooperative approaches that view natural systems as intimately connected to human and social systems. Of course, this begs the question: why add stewardship to the list? Does this not complicate things? The response to this question is twofold.

First, given the diversity of natural conditions across the globe and the diversity of human experience, a diverse response to rethinking our relationship with the natural world should come as no surprise. Indeed, this diversity of approaches seems appropriate. In the absence of a grand unified theory of socio-ecological harmony, we should be open to a plurality of approaches. Pluralism leaves space for new ideas and creativity, leaves space for competing values to interact and play out, and allows space for adapting and calibrating solutions to fit different circumstances. Diversity is an important feature of modern pluralist societies.[25] This flexibility is particularly important in areas beyond national jurisdiction. Within the state, we might condition or structure how this plurality of approaches comes together. Structures of government, systems of law and the relatively lower scale of diversity in natural and social conditions might result in the scale of debate being easier to circumscribe. Beyond the state, in shared spaces such as the high seas, there is less homogeneity and so more complexity in interactions that construct social and legal relationships. Yet it is reasonable to infer that a higher degree of diversity within a society will make it more difficult to agree common ways of doing things. Thus, diversity is particularly important in creating space for compromise in ABNJ.

Second, stewardship as a concept operates at a deeper structural level than specific rules or principles. Stewardship has a long heritage and there is a rich and largely untapped body of scholarship that can be drawn upon to inform debates about how we can redefine our relationship with the natural world. Whilst scholarship is increasingly used to frame relationships with natural resources within states,[26] it is relatively untouched in international law

Politics, Law and Economics 5; Kotzé (ed), *Environmental Law and Governance for the Anthropocene* (Hart Publishing, 2017); Kotzé and Kim, 'Earth System Law: The Juridical Dimensions of Earth System Governance' (2019) 1 *Earth System Governance* 100003.

[24] Kotzé and Kim (n 23) 5.

[25] Rawls, 'The Idea of an Overlapping Consensus' (1987) 7 *OJLS* 1, 4–5.

[26] See, eg Leopold, *A Sand County Almanac* (Oxford University Press, 1949); Worrell and Appleby, 'Stewardship of Natural Resources: Definition, Ethical and Practical Aspects' (2000) 12 *Journal of*

literature. This is perhaps surprising, because stewardship is fundamentally concerned with the relationship between humans and natural resources, so it is unsurprising that it became a point of reference for resource-related issues during the BBNJ negotiations – ie responsible management of vulnerable, finite or shared natural resources. This is beginning to happen more widely. Thus, some initiatives in ABNJ are being framed in terms of stewardship – such as the Deep Ocean Stewardship Initiative.[27] However, these are not yet subject to mainstream legal analyses.

So, can stewardship be used to frame and direct the governance of ABNJ? Even if one sees value in alternative approaches or questions the need for a pluralistic approach, there are more mundane reasons to consider stewardship. Significantly, stewardship is a framing concept in the Preamble to the BBNJ Agreement, with states parties

> *[d]esiring* to act as stewards of the ocean in areas beyond national jurisdiction on behalf of present and future generations by protecting, caring for and ensuring responsible use of the marine environment, maintaining the integrity of ocean ecosystems and conserving the inherent value of biodiversity of areas beyond national jurisdiction.[28]

Stewardship is now part of the language of the BBNJ regime, so it will be a point of reference for future legal and policy initiatives.

III. WHAT IS STEWARDSHIP?

There is a growing literature on stewardship but it uses the term in quite different ways and in quite different contexts, so it is important to have a working concept of stewardship if we are to test its use in ABNJ. Stewardship operates as a concept at multiple levels;[29] it is at once an ethic, an approach, a principle and a way of framing legal obligations. This enables stewardship to work in different ways according to context. And since stewardship has a common thread of responsible use, this enables a flow of related ideas and values to move across discourse at different levels. Of course, these points require further articulation, so the next two sub-sections consider the typology of stewardship and the analytical structure of the legal concept of stewardship. The former explains the different conceptualisations of stewardship, whereas the latter advances a specific legal structure for stewardship.

Agricultural and Environmental Ethics 263; Mathevet et al, 'The Concept of Stewardship in Sustainability Science and Conservation Biology' (2018) 217 *Biological Conservation* 363.

[27] DOSI is a network of experts from across disciplines and sectors who collaborate to inform and advise on sustainable deep-ocean governance and management of resources. See www.dosi-project.org.

[28] BBNJ Agreement, Preamble, para 11.

[29] Nassauer, 'Care and Stewardship: From Home to Planet' (2011) 100 *Landscape and Urban Planning* 321.

A. A Typology of Stewardship

There are several useful reviews of the literature on stewardship. In broad terms, Welchman finds that stewardship has a long history associated with wise or responsible use.[30] More recently, Enqvist et al conducted a qualitative systematic literature review of stewardship in an environmental context, showing a significant growth in interest in the concept as some combination of an ethic, motivation, action or outcome.[31] The literature on stewardship is deepening and increasingly coalescing around specific challenges, such as the protection of landscapes[32] or ecosystems,[33] or governance of planetary systems.[34] Some of the literature is focused on practical initiatives, such as certification schemes for forestry or fisheries.[35] This diversity brings its own challenges, with some criticism being levelled at stewardship for its ambiguity.[36] Others have criticised stewardship for failing to deliver its promised benefits,[37] for representing an instance of greenwashing[38] or for carrying problematic intellectual baggage.[39] Critiques based on ambiguity can be found in legal analyses of stewardship and it is perhaps this line of criticism that is most harmful to stewardship since the doubt raised casts a shadow over the concept as a whole.[40] Although stewardship

[30] Welchman, 'A Defence of Environmental Stewardship' (2012) 21 *Environmental Values* 297.

[31] Enqvist et al, 'Stewardship as a Boundary Object for Sustainability Research: Linking Care, Knowledge and Agency' (2018) 179 *Landscape and Urban Planning* 17, 20.

[32] Plieninger and Bieling, 'The Emergence of Landscape Stewardship in Practice, Policy and Research' in Bieling and Plieninger (eds), *The Science and Practice of Landscape Stewardship* (Cambridge University Press, 2017) xiii–xiv.

[33] von Zharen, 'Ocean Ecosystem Stewardship' (1998) 23 *William and Mary Environmental Law and Policy Review* 1; Folke, Chapin and Olsson, 'Transformations in Ecosystem Stewardship' in Folke, Kofinas and Chapin (eds), *Principles of Ecosystem Stewardship* (Springer, 2009) 102–25.

[34] Steffen et al, 'The Anthropocene: From Global Change to Planetary Stewardship' (2011) 40 *Ambio* 739; Folke et al, 'Reconnecting to the Biosphere' (2011) 40 *Ambio* 719; Stuart Chaplin II et al, 'Earth Stewardship: A Strategy for Social–Ecological Transformation to Reverse Planetary Degradation' (2011) 1 *Journal of Environmental Studies and Sciences* 44.

[35] On forestry, see Pattberg, 'What Role for Private Rule-Making in Global Environmental Governance? Analysing the Forest Stewardship Council (FSC)' (2005) 5 *International Environmental Agreements* 175; Marx and Cuypers, 'Forest Certification as a Global Environmental Governance Tool: What Is the Macro-effectiveness of the Forest Stewardship Council?' (2010) 4 *Regulation & Governance* 408. On fisheries, see Constance and Bonanno, 'Regulating the Global Fisheries: The World Wildlife Fund, Unilever, and the Marine Stewardship Council' (2000) 17 *Agriculture and Human Values* 125; Jacquet et al, 'Seafood Stewardship in Crisis' (2010) 467 *Nature* 28; Gray and Hatchard, 'Environmental Stewardship as a New Form of Fisheries Governance' (2007) 64 *ICES Journal of Marine Science* 786.

[36] Roach et al, 'Ducks, Bogs, and Guns: A Case Study of Stewardship Ethics in Newfoundland' (2006) 11 *Ethics and the Environment* 43, 46–48.

[37] Christian et al, 'A Review of Formal Objections to Marine Stewardship Council Fisheries Certifications' (2013) 161 *Biological Conservation* 10.

[38] Dryzek, *The Politics of the Earth: Environmental Discourses* (Oxford University Press, 2005) 110.

[39] Palmer, 'Stewardship: A Case Study in Environmental Ethics' in Ball et al (eds), *The Earth Beneath: A Critical Guide to Green Theology* (SPCK, 1992) 67–86; Beavis, 'Stewardship, Planning and Public Policy' (1991) 31 *Plan Canada* 75.

[40] Lucy and Mitchell, 'Replacing Private Property: The Case for Stewardship' (1996) 55 *CLJ* 566, 584; Barnes, *Property Rights and Natural Resources* (Hart Publishing, 2009) 156; Barritt,

scholarship is maturing, as Bennett et al show, there remains a critical need to pin down and reflect upon the developing constructs of stewardship.[41] By way of trying to help clear up the conceptual ambiguity, a typology of stewardship approaches is presented, which can then better inform how we construct stewardship as a legal analytic concept.

From the wider academic literature on stewardship, it is possible to identify three ways of categorising stewardship, though noting that each category may relate to, or be influenced by, the others. These are outlined briefly, before noting what is distinctive about a legal concept of stewardship.

(i) Stewardship as an Intellectual Construct

Under this category, we can group a range of approaches that consider stewardship in the broad sense of an idea, be it within the framework of religious belief, philosophical or political thought, or potentially scientific commitments. Arguably, the oldest tradition of stewardship is that rooted in religious doctrines. Thus, man is 'given dominion over nature', and mandated to exploit land and other natural resources for his own benefit.[42] In Christian doctrine, man is not the owner of the powers; rather, he is a steward on behalf of God.[43] Although often seen in a Christian tradition, the underlying notions of responsibility to nature are not exclusive to particular belief systems, and notions of guardianship or respect for nature are found in several religions and in many indigenous cultures.[44] Some have sought to reconnect modern notions of stewardship to its religious or spiritual origins.[45] Stewardship in this tradition has occasionally received recognition by courts of tribunals.[46] However, most approaches tend to subsume this within broader moral or ethical accounts. The difficulty in drawing upon stewardship in this tradition is that it resists

'Conceptualising Stewardship in Environmental Law' (2014) 16 *Journal of Environmental Law* 1, 2; Riding (n 14) 438.

[41] Bennett et al, 'Environmental Stewardship: A Conceptual Review and Analytical Framework' (2018) 61 *Environmental Management* 597.

[42] Genesis I:28.

[43] Shelton, 'Dominion and Stewardship' (2015) 109 *AJIL Unbound* 132.

[44] Attfield, 'Environmental Sensitivity and Critiques of Stewardship' in Berry (ed), *Environmental Stewardship. Critical Perspectives – Past and Present* (T&T Clark, 2006) 76; Kawharu, 'Kaitiakitanga: A Maori Anthropological Perspective of the Maori Socio-environmental Ethic of resource Management' (2000) 109 *Journal of the Polynesian Society* 349; Appiah-Opoku, 'Indigenous Beliefs and Environmental Stewardship: A Rural Ghana Experience' (2007) 24 *Journal of Cultural Geography* 79; Ross et al, *Indigenous Peoples and the Collaborative Stewardship of Nature: Knowledge Binds and Institutional Conflicts* (Left Coast Press, 2011).

[45] Enderle, 'In Search of a Common Ethical Ground: Corporate Environmental Responsibility From the Perspective of Christian Environmental Stewardship' (1997) 16 *Journal of Business Ethics* 173; Patterson, 'Conceptualizing Stewardship in Agriculture Within the Christian Tradition' (2003) 25 *Environmental Ethics* 43.

[46] The Government of the State of Eritrea and The Government of the Republic of Yemen, Award of the Tribunal in the Second Stage of the Proceedings (Maritime Delimitation), 17 December 1999, para 92.

universalisation as a value or approach since its form and function are rooted in particular belief systems.

Stewardship is often framed as an ethical or moral imperative. Typical of this approach is Welchman, who treats stewardship as an ethic, a set of moral principles that affect a person's behaviour or how they conduct their activities.[47] For Welchman, the 'steward must possess and act from dispositions such as loyalty, temperance, diligence, justice and integrity, as well as intellectual virtues or technical skills such as prudence and practical rationality'.[48] The influence of the ethic is dependent upon the coherence and reception of those underlying values. But this is not uncontentious. As critics of stewardship argue, its pedigree includes religious, patriarchal, elitist or anthropocentric forms of control in varying degrees.[49]

(ii) Stewardship as a Form of Conduct

Here, stewardship is a form of observable behaviour whereby an individual acts in the best interests of a principal or collective cause, rather than out of immediate self-serving interests.[50] The behaviour may be connected to an underlying moral or ethical position. In this sense, the behaviour is ethically informed action. Hernandez defines stewardship as 'attitudes and behaviors that place the long-term best interests of a group ahead of personal goals that serve an individual's self-interests'.[51] Similarly, David et al observe that a steward is someone 'whose behavior is ordered such that pro-organizational, collectivistic behaviors have higher utility than individualistic, self-serving behavior'.[52] Of course, behaviours cannot simply be posited or assumed to exist; they are the product of social and institutional contexts, and we must think about how behaviours are informed and changed through legal, social or other conditions. As Hernandez argues, stewardship is fundamentally an other-regarding perspective, so there is a close connection between the individual psychological motivations to act and external circumstances that shape other-regarding values.[53]

Related to this is the idea of stewardship as an occupation. According to this approach, a steward is employed to look after a thing in return for financial or other benefits. Here, stewardship would be a specific legal or practical arrangement determined by the terms of a contract, employment or agency

[47] Welchman (n 30). See also Palmer (n 39) 63.

[48] Welchman (n 30) 299.

[49] Palmer (n 39) 67–86.

[50] Di Paola, 'Environmental Stewardship, Moral Psychology and Gardens' (2013) 22 *Environmental Values* 503.

[51] Hernandez, 'Promoting Stewardship Behavior in Organizations: A Leadership Model' (2008) 80 *Journal of Business Ethics* 121.

[52] Davis, Schoorman and Donaldson, 'Toward a Stewardship Theory of Management' (1997) 22 *Academy of Management Review* 20, 24.

[53] Hernandez (n 51) 181.

agreement. Typical examples include environmental stewardship schemes that pay landowners to enhance the quality of land or resource systems.[54] This may be contrasted with voluntary stewardship, as informed by a personal ethic, as described above.

(iii) Stewardship as a Practical Arrangement

The third way of framing stewardship is as practice. Although there may be overlaps with stewardship as a way of thinking or acting, stewardship as practice is distinct in that it aims to establish a practical arrangement for the pursuit of stewardship values. Stewardship as practice focuses on practical or institutional arrangements that are intended to deliver stewardship. It is not possible to exhaustively map such stewardship arrangements, but some examples are provided.

Stewardship may take the form of a policy, either as a specific goal or a broad set of objectives. There are many examples of stewardship policies, at the global, national or local level.[55] At the global level, the United Nations Millennium Declaration resolves 'to adopt in all our environmental actions a new ethic of conservation and stewardship'.[56] An example of national policy is the US Stewardship of the Ocean, Our Coasts, and the Great Lake.[57] This presidential policy sought to enhance the quality of the natural environment, with related benefits for the security and prosperity of current and future generations. This, in turn, was fleshed out according to the Recommendations of the Interagency Oceans Policy Task Force.[58] Here, policy sets out a guide to action for public decision-makers, as opposed to a specific set of binding legal requirements. There may be little to distinguish stewardship from its use as an idea, although it is clear that specific policy statements will articulate the content of stewardship in greater detail. Thus, US policy advances 10 objectives and articulates four modes through which stewardship will be promoted. Although this policy approach seems to have languished in recent years, it will be reinvigorated through the establishment of the Ocean Policy Committee as a permanent, statutory, inter-agency cooperative body.

Stewardship arrangements may take specific legal forms. For example, in the UK, a regime of Environmental Stewardship agreements for managing land is established under statute. Under such agreements, a person with an interest in land or landholder is required to carry out specified activities to further

[54] Dobbs and Pretty, 'Agri-environmental Stewardship Schemes and "Multifunctionality"' (2004) 26 *Applied Economic Perspectives and Policy* 220; Courtney et al, 'Investigating the Incidental Benefits of Environmental Stewardship Schemes in England' (2013) 31 *Land Use Policy* 26.

[55] See, eg Bennett et al (n 41).

[56] UN General Assembly Resolution 55/2, 8 September 2000, para 23.

[57] Executive Order 13547, 19 July 2010, https://obamawhitehouse.archives.gov/the-press-office/executive-order-stewardship-ocean-our-coasts-and-great-lakes.

[58] https://obamawhitehouse.archives.gov/files/documents/OPTF_FinalRecs.pdf.

environmental protection in return for payments.[59] Thus, stewardship is advanced through a contractual arrangement. In Australia, the Product Stewardship Act 2011 establishes a system that seeks to reduce the environmental impact of manufactured products. Such statutory regimes develop specific rules governing the use of things and may combine regulatory incentives with voluntary arrangements that advance a broader set of environmental objectives. In a marine context, stewardship is most frequently associated with product certification schemes designed to enhance the traceability and good environmental province of seafood.[60] There also exist more general arrangements that can be accommodated within the category of stewardship although they are often designated otherwise. For example, in the USA, public trust doctrine establishes a form of public property holding that renders certain resources (usually waterways or coastal areas) inalienable and subject to certain governmental responsibilities.[61] At a more general level, the legal concept of trust is perhaps the best analogue for stewardship. Here, a person holds property as a nominal owner for the benefit of others.[62] This provides some of the conceptual underpinnings to the common heritage of mankind. It is stewardship as a legal arrangement in respect of natural resources that is of most interest to us because it is this form of stewardship that is being advanced as a way of reframing our relationship with the oceans.

B. Instrumentalising Stewardship

Although stewardship may be viewed in different ways, a common thread running through the different approaches is the idea that the steward acts responsibly – either in respect of the environment or others or in collective concerns – which may include the environment. The origins of stewardship beliefs or values may be diverse, but they can shape both individual action (through cognitive influences) and collective action through public policy and law. A key point is that if stewardship is to be delivered, then this will in part be through legal regimes, since this provides part of the institutional capacity to deliver stewardship.[63] This is not to deny the relevance of other enablers of stewardship, but it is important to focus on its specific legal attributes particularly if we are to respond to the criticism that stewardship lacks a meaningful content.

When we look at stewardship as a legal arrangement, then it is helpful to consider it in terms of specific legal relationships. This is because stewardship is

[59] The Environmental Stewardship (England) Regulations 2005.

[60] Blasiak, 'Evolving Perspectives of Stewardship in the Seafood Industry' (2021) 8 *Frontiers in Marine Science* 676.

[61] Sax, 'The Public Trust Doctrine in Natural Resources Law: Effective Judicial Intervention' (1970) 68 *Michigan Law Review* 471; Klass, 'Modern Public Trust Principles: Recognizing Rights and Integrating Standards' (2006) 82 *Notre Dame Law Review* 699.

[62] For an international law perspective, see Redgwell, *Intergenerational Trusts and Environmental Protection* (Manchester University Press, 1999).

[63] See Bennett et al (n 41) 600 and 608.

not a monolithic concept. As a form of holding, like other forms of property, it is a bundle of variable interests and so can be adapted to suit different circumstances. This is considered in the next section.

IV. ANALYTICAL STRUCTURE OF STEWARDSHIP

The typology above shows that stewardship can be understood in terms of subject matter, actors, motivations and capacity. This draws upon Barritt's elegant conceptual framework for understanding stewardship.[64] Barritt shows that stewardship has four core dimensions: the object of stewardship; the duty holder; the beneficiary; and the nature of the duty. Specific applications of stewardship may vary or qualify these dimensions to achieve different ends, but they must exist to some degree for stewardship to retain some functionality. Underpinning this is a set of values that influence the content and intensity of the duty.

It is not clear that this is a complete structure, since it does not explicitly account for the institutional context within which stewardship arises. However, this could be regarded as an exogenous constraint on how stewardship functions, rather than something inherent in the structure of stewardship as a legal relationship. More importantly, the fourfold account does not say to whom the steward is accountable – as distinct from the beneficiary. For this reason, we should add another dimension to Barritt's approach: the account holder. Who ensures that the steward acts responsibly? When we elevate stewardship concepts to the international level, this raises important challenges, particularly if it is the state individually or collectively that is the duty holder. Who, then, holds the state as steward to account? I return to this question below in section IV.E.

A. Object of the Duty

In theory, stewardship can be applied to anything: land, natural resources, intangible assets, people. It can apply to a part of the environment, such as a river or an ocean, or the planet as a whole.[65] It might apply to an individual species or a habitat, or some combination of these. Stewardship is a socially constructed relationship between people in respect of a thing. Whilst this suggests that whilst the social element is critical, one cannot ignore the influence the material object of stewardship has on the construction of the stewardship relationship.[66]

[64] Barritt (n 40).

[65] Brown Weiss, 'In Fairness to Future Generations and Sustainable Development' (1992) 8 *American University Journal of International Law and Policy* 19, 20.

[66] ibid 4.

The determination of a thing – defining it or its boundaries – is a critical issue to working out a stewardship regime. Imprecision in the object of stewardship will make it difficult to determine the impact of any rule or policy of stewardship. If we look at a couple of examples, this becomes clear. Stewardship is often framed in terms of land. However, what is land? It may be viewed as a geographic space, but equally it may be viewed as a composite of different physical features, such as surface soils, subsoils, minerals, buildings, flora and fauna located on the land. Most things can be disaggregated into their component parts – so this begs the question: should the object be the whole or its component parts? The converse is also true: some natural resources can be aggregated into larger resource systems. Thus, a protected natural habitat may comprise a range of natural features, including bodies of water or land and resident species of flora and fauna. An ecosystem might also be viewed as the object of stewardship. Here, we are focused on a 'functional entity or unit formed locally by all the organisms and their physical (abiotic) environment interacting with each other'.[67] Yet this also involves definitional challenges, because the functional unit may be defined according to its functional processes (ie means) or the services those means deliver (ends).[68] For example, pollination or photosynthesis are means to an end (food production). How such factors are used to define the ecosystem impacts upon how we determine the boundaries of a system and how we determine any stewardship responsibilities.

Closely related to this is the question of how social and equitable values influence the determination of ecosystems. It is common to understand ecosystems in terms of a range of provisioning, cultural, regulating and supporting services, each of which may involve value judgement about their significance. In short, our constructs of ecosystems are produced knowledge and so are influenced by sites, traditions and practices of knowledge construction.[69] This, in turn, influences how stewardship is constructed. In simple terms, the more complex and large scale the object of stewardship, the more challenging any claim to define it as the proper object of stewardship.

The fact that there is an object of stewardship entails prior questions about how the boundaries of that object are drawn. As Barritt observes, we should also reflect on the explicit and implicit choices that we make about how we define the object of stewardship.[70] It is perhaps impossible to account for all the different objects of stewardship. Instead, we should be explicit in accepting this, and instead focus on how different attributes of a thing may impact upon the way stewardship can or should be constructed. The following variables need to be carefully considered to fully understand and analyse the impact of the

[67] Tirri et al, *Elsevier's Dictionary of Biology* (Elsevier, 1998).

[68] Wallace, 'Classification of Ecosystem Services: Problems and Solutions' (2007) 139 *Biological Conservation* 235.

[69] Schutter and Hicks, 'Speaking Across Boundaries to Explore the Potential for Interdisciplinarity in Ecosystem Services Knowledge Production' [2021] *Conservation Biology* 1198.

[70] Barritt (n 40) 6. See also Palmer (n 39) 63.

nature of a thing on the construction of stewardship: the location, size, precision and physical attributes of the thing, and the limits of our knowledge of it. This has consequences for how stewardship would apply to ABNJ.

At present, the object of stewardship duties is not precisely delimited in the BBNJ Agreement text. Stewardship is initially framed in the Preamble in terms of 'the ocean in areas beyond national jurisdiction'. This includes both the high seas and the Area – and is suggestive of a holistic approach. Stewardship so defined would demand the involvement of all states since the oceans are common to all states. It could also entail responsibilities for numerous other actors that have competence to govern parts of ABNJ, such as the International Seabed Authority and regional fisheries management organisations. It would potentially include other actors with an interest in ABNJ to the extent that they are able to participate in the proposed BBNJ regime. However, the BBNJ Agreement text also asserts a more limited remit, so applies to the conservation and sustainable use of marine biological diversity in ABNJ.[71] Marine biological diversity is not actually defined in the Agreement's text, but if one looks at wider definitions, then this includes not just the components of diversity, but also the quality of variability within a system.[72] This entails wider consequences for stewardship since variability depends upon connections and qualities between components of systems. So, even a more limited object of stewardship may entail quite complex responsibilities for the stewards. Although the Preamble refers to oceans, the BBNJ Agreement text also has more specific points of focus, with provisions focusing only on 'marine genetic resources'. MGR is defined as 'any material of marine plant, animal, microbial or other origin containing functional units of heredity of actual or potential value'.[73] It includes resources both in situ and ex situ, but does not include fish as a commodity. It does not apply to pure research – only to resources for utilisation purposes, resources collected or accessed. As a result, the BBNJ Agreement may provide greater focus and perhaps more limited responsibilities of stewardship. In any event, greater clarity on the scope of stewardship duties would improve the effectiveness of the proposed regimes. It is possible that stewardship may operate at different scales, from the global ocean level down to the specific location and use of an individual component of genetic resource. If this is the case, then care is needed to ensure that stewardship duties reflect these nested objects of stewardship.

B. Duty Holder

If stewardship is a duty, then who is the duty holder? Much of the literature on stewardship is concerned with land and the resources thereon, so it is no

[71] BBNJ Agreement, Art 2.
[72] Barnes, *Property Rights* (n 40) 136.
[73] BBNJ Agreement, Art 1(8).

surprise that landowners are most often addressed as the potential holders of a duty of stewardship. However, this is too narrow a category of persons responsible for stewardship. If stewardship is about some form of responsible use of a thing, then stewardship should extend to a wider category of persons who may enjoy control over the object of stewardship. This could include any category of property owner, or anybody with authority to exercise control over a thing. As discussed below, ownership is a complex set of legal relationships, and more than one person may have a legal interest and ability to use a thing. Accordingly, all of these persons can in principle be subject to certain responsibilities in respect of the use of that thing. If we remember that property is a bundle of incidents, which may vest in one or more persons, then any person having some degree of authority over one or more of the incidents of ownership may be considered as a potential steward. Indeed, if stewardship is framed in terms of how we use or interact with the environment, then stewardship touches upon any person who may use or interact with the environment. For example, I may have the right to use a piece of land belonging to another person for the purpose of exercising a right of way. This right of way not only limits the rights of the landowner – but also imposes a wider set of responsibilities to not disturb wildlife or interrupt the amenity interests of others. This shows that duties may be varied and contextual, and may correlate with the other dimensions of stewardship.

Within states, the steward can include landowners and any other property owner, as well as individuals and other legal persons enjoying rights or use of a thing. This includes the state, but it also extends to public authorities, companies, communities, indigenous peoples and other forms of social organisation. This wider category of stewards is reflected in practice. For example, landowners may enter into stewardship agreements with the state concerning the use of their land.[74] In some states, oil companies are required to manage their assets in accordance with a set of stewardship expectations.[75] Forest stewardship plans and contracts have been used between government bodies and landowners or service providers to direct resource use towards public benefits.[76] Indigenous peoples may act as stewards over land.[77] Private companies can establish stewardship schemes that introduce checks on the quality of products entering supply chains, such as for seafood.[78] Local communities have established

[74] eg UK Environmental Stewardship scheme, www.gov.uk/guidance/environmental-stewardship.

[75] www.ogauthority.co.uk/exploration-production/asset-stewardship/expectations/.

[76] See www.fs.usda.gov/managing-land/forest-stewardship/program. See also Mattor et al, 'Assessing Collaborative Governance Outcomes and Indicators Across Spatial and Temporal Scales: Stewardship Contract Implementation by the United States Forest Service' (2020) 33 *Society & Natural Resources* 484.

[77] See Hasteh, 'Analysis of the Duty of the State to Protect Indigenous Peoples Affected by Transnational Corporations and Other Business Enterprises' (23 February 2012) E/C.19/2012/3; Dawson et al, 'The Role of Indigenous Peoples and Local Communities in Effective and Equitable Conservation' (2021) 26 *Ecology and Society* article 19.

[78] See, eg the work of the Marine Stewardship Council, www.msc.org. See further Karavias, 'Interactions Between International Law and Private Fisheries Certification' (2018) 7 *Transnational Environmental Law* 165.

water stewardship programmes.[79] Coastal state responsibilities in the exclusive economic zone (EEZ) are often cast as stewardship responsibilities, blending use rights with conservation and management duties.[80] Stewardship has also been used to frame marine protected area responsibilities,[81] and the use of ocean space more generally.[82]

A state's stewardship responsibilities may also operate beyond the state in respect of any things in which the state enjoys a use interest. As noted above, stewardship features in the Preamble of the BBNJ Agreement. It is also used to frame other responsibilities, such as for the Arctic region[83] or Antarctica.[84] In 2014, five governments signed the Hamilton Declaration on Collaboration for the Conservation of the Sargasso Sea, an area of the high seas that provides a critical habitat for many vulnerable species.[85] The Declaration established the Sargasso Sea Commission (the Commission), with a mandate to 'exercise a stewardship role for the Sargasso Sea and keep its health, productivity and resilience under continual review'.[86] As Balton has observed, the Commission has a limited mandate and so cannot adopt binding decisions,[87] and this limits its ability to act as a steward. This points to the importance of better developed legal mechanisms to support stewardship. This challenge, as well as the risk of unaccountable stewardship, is echoed in critiques of other international spaces. For example, Henricksen notes that stewardship appears to have been used as a means of legitimising the intervention of the Arctic coastal states, rather than as a device to frame a special set of legal responsibilities.[88] Of course, this opens important questions about the basis of responsibilities in law, since these will generally depend upon the existence of a recognised competence to act, so duties may entail some prior authority to act. Logically, one cannot be expected to act in a way which exceeds one's competence or capacity to act.

The BBNJ Agreement text is clearly intended to place primary responsibility for stewardship upon states. Each obligation in the agreement text is directed

[79] See, eg Isundwa and Mourad, 'The Potential for Water Stewardship Partnership in Kenya' (2019) 12 *Arabian Journal of Geosciences* 389.

[80] See Clingan Jr, 'The Law of the Sea Convention: International Obligations and Stewardship Responsibilities of Coastal Nations' (1992) 17 *Ocean & Coastal Management* 201.

[81] Sand, 'Marine Protected Areas and Ocean Stewardship: A Legal Perspective' (2018) 19 *Biodiversity* 1.

[82] Steinberg, 'Lines of Division, Lines of Connection: Stewardship in the World Ocean' (1992) 89 *Geographical Review* 254.

[83] Henricksen, 'The Arctic Ocean, Environmental Stewardship, and the Law of the Sea' (2016) 6 *UC Irvine Law Review* 61.

[84] Vanstappen, 'Legitimacy in Antarctic Governance: The Stewardship Model' (2019) 55 *Polar Record* 358.

[85] Adopted 11 March 2014 by the Azores, Bermuda, Monaco, the UK and the USA. See www.sargassoseacommission.org/storage/documents/Hamilton_Declaration_on_Collaboration_for_the_Conservation_of_the_Sargasso_Sea.with_signatures.pdf.

[86] ibid Annex II, para A.

[87] Balton, 'Strengthening the Stewardship of the Sargasso Sea' in Barnes and Long (eds), *Frontiers of International Environmental Law: Oceans and Climate Challenges* (Brill, 2021) 490.

[88] Henricksen (n 83) 82.

at states. However, the text also implicates other actors. First, it is intended that the Agreement 'does not undermine relevant legal instruments and frameworks and relevant global, regional, subregional and sectoral bodies'.[89] Whilst this preserves existing competences, by implication it draws them into the orbit of the Agreement since cooperation will be required to ensure integrated and coordinated governance of ABNJ. There are 19 intergovernmental bodies with some governance responsibility for the high seas or the Area.[90] However, none has cross-cutting governance competence, so duties cannot be the sole responsibility of states individually, nor of sectoral bodies. Effective stewardship will need to have cooperative arrangements between different actors. Second, there are references in the text to collaboration or coordination with international organisations.[91] Other provisions provide for consultation or cooperation with a range of bodies, including Indigenous Peoples and local communities, civil society, the scientific community and the private sector.[92] The clearing-house mechanism for making research and data available shall be managed by a number of possible bodies, including specialised mechanisms or

> the Intergovernmental Oceanographic Commission of the United Nations Educational, Scientific and Cultural Organization, in association with relevant organizations, including the International Seabed Authority and the International Maritime Organization, and shall be informed by the Intergovernmental Oceanographic Commission Criteria and Guidelines on the Transfer of Marine Technology.[93]

Again, given the range of potential actors involved in governing aspects of ABNJ, this will require careful delineation of responsibilities and coordination of any stewardship responsibilities.

C. The Beneficiary of Stewardship

If stewardship is responsibility, then this responsibility is owed to someone or something. In the wider literature on stewardship, the beneficiaries are usually identified as groups or communities rather than individuals, since the aim of stewardship is to counter some of the individualistic tendencies that give rise to environmental degradation. However, there is the potential for stewardship to be wider than this. For example, recent developments in thinking about rights of nature, as well as legal developments in some states, show that the environment can be the beneficiary of duties. This has only begun to be used as a template for rethinking human–ocean relationships.

[89] BBNJ Agreement, Art 4(2).

[90] PEW, *Mapping Governance Gaps on the High Seas (Chartbook)* (August 2016) www.un.org/depts/los/biodiversity/prepcom_files/PEW_MappingGovernanceGapsontheHighSeas_final.pdf.

[91] See BBNJ Agreement, Arts 51(4), 52(5) and 52(8).

[92] ibid Arts 7(J) and (k), 13, 19(2), (3) and (4), 21, 24(3), 26(5), 31, 32(3), 35, 37(4), 4192), 44(1)(b), 48, 49(2) and 51(3)(c).

[93] ibid Art 51(4).

There are three categories of beneficiary of stewardship: current generations; future generations; and the environment. The first category, current generations, is the one that is most commonly recognised in law. In principle, this might extend to some categories of persons who possess legal agency: states, non-state actors, public authorities, companies, communities, indigenous peoples, and other forms of social organisation and individuals. There are many examples of such persons being regarded as beneficiaries of duties. For example, we might refer to a quite extensive range of legal duties owed by states to other states or persons in respect of the environment.[94] Although this focuses on states, there are examples of other beneficiaries in international instruments. Peoples are recognised as the beneficiaries of responsibilities to use natural resources.[95] Indigenous peoples are the beneficiaries of states' commitments under Articles 29 and 32 of the UN Declaration on the Rights of Indigenous Peoples to establish environmental rights as well as to provide mechanisms to mitigate adverse environmental impacts.[96] Individuals are increasingly the object of environmental rights. This is reflected in Principle 1 of the Stockholm Declaration,[97] Principle 7 of the Rio Declaration[98] and Article 24 of the African Charter on Human and Peoples' Rights.[99] Recently, the Human Rights Council adopted a resolution recognising for the first time a general human right to a clean, healthy and sustainable environment.[100] There is no general standard of responsibility towards such beneficiaries. The extent of any such beneficial interests will be determined according to content.

As a matter of international law, it useful to distinguish between beneficiaries that are subjects of the law and those that are objects, since the latter frequently do not enjoy the capacity to secure the protection of their beneficial interests. Also, not all beneficiaries will be treated in the same way. For example, differential commitments may entail greater or lesser degrees of responsibility towards different beneficiaries.[101] Thus, developing states may enjoy varying degrees of support according to need.

The second category of beneficiary is that of future generations. Future generations have always posed a challenge in law since present obligations to future generations constitute obligations for which there are no correlative

[94] See generally Birnie, Boyle and Redgwell, *International Law and the Environment*, 3rd edn (Oxford University Press, 2009) ch 3.

[95] UN General Assembly Resolution on Permanent sovereignty over natural resources, Resolution 1803 (XVII), 14 December 1962.

[96] UN General Assembly Resolution 61/295, UN Doc A/RES/61/295, 13 September 2007.

[97] Declaration of the United Nations Convention on the Human Environment 1972, UN Doc A/CONF/48/14/REV.1.

[98] Declaration of the United Nations Convention on Environment and Development 1992, UN Doc A/CONF/151/26/Rev.1.

[99] African Charter on Human and Peoples Rights 1981, (1982) 21 ILM 52.

[100] HRC, The human right to a safe, clean, healthy and sustainable environment, Resolution 48/12, UN Doc A/HRC/48/L.23/Rev.1, 5 October 2021.

[101] French, 'Developing States and International Environmental Law: The Importance of Differentiated Responsibilities' (2000) 49 *ICLQ* 35.

rights, because there are no determinate persons to whom the right attaches. Also, adding future generations into the mix of interests entails new challenges of weighting different interests.[102] However, this has not prevented commitments to future generations emerging in law. For example, Principle 3 of the Rio Declaration, Article 1 of the Aarhus Convention[103] and Article 3 of the United Nations Framework Convention on Climate Change[104] all speak to the interests of future generations. More generally, legal commitments to conserve or manage a resource will have some unarticulated future-looking dimension, since this is inherent in the temporal nature of legal commitments. The category of future generations tends to exist as a group and there appear to be no examples of differentiation between categories of future generations in the same way that present generations are considered. One critical issue is a lack of representation in legal fora, especially judicial proceedings, which makes the implementation of duties to future generations more problematic.[105] Interestingly, this barrier is being overcome in the context of rights of nature, as will be discussed next.

The third category of beneficiaries is the environment. At least originally, stewardship was conceived as an anthropocentric value, focusing on how humans can use things for their benefit. This has led to criticism of the concept for separating out a necessary relationship between human and environment, and for devaluing the environment in this relationship.[106] Rights of nature have emerged as an alternative way of framing environmental protection. Such rights recognise the legal standing of some natural features or ecosystems, and require steps to be taken to protect those features from harm or to restore those features if degraded. A number of states have recognised rights of nature within their constitutions or domestic legislation, including Ecuador,[107] Bolivia[108] and New Zealand.[109] There has also been some litigation giving effect to such rights, most recently by the Constitutional Court of Ecuador, which ruled that plans to mine in a protected forest violated rights of nature.[110] In 2010, Bolivia hosted the World People's Conference on Climate Change and the Rights of Mother Earth, which resulted in the adoption of the Universal Declaration of

[102] Posner, 'Agencies Should Ignore Distant-Future Generations' (2007) 74 *University of Chicago Law Review* 139.

[103] Convention on Access to Information, Public Participation in Decision-Making, and Access to Justice in Environmental Matters 1998, (1998) 38 ILM 517.

[104] United Nations Framework Convention on Climate Change 1992, (1992) 31 ILM 581.

[105] Birnie et al (n 94) 121.

[106] Palmer (n 39) 70–74.

[107] See Constitution of Ecuador 2008, ch 7, https://pdba.georgetown.edu/Constitutions/Ecuador/english08.html.

[108] See Ley de Derechos de la Madre Tierra 2010, https://bolivia.infoleyes.com/norma/2689/ley-de-derechos-de-la-madre-tierra-071.

[109] Te Urewera Act 2014, www.legislation.govt.nz/act/public/2014/0051/latest/whole.html.

[110] Caso No 1149-19-JP/20, 10 November 2021. See also, Opinion STC4360 of the Supreme Court of Columbia of 12 April 2018, www.cortesuprema.gov.co/corte/wp-content/uploads/2018/04/STC4360-2018-2018-00319-011.pdf.

the Rights of Mother Earth.[111] The Report of the United Nations Secretary General on Harmony with Nature 2019 provides both international recognition of this movement and a telling survey of legal and policy initiatives across the globe.[112] Recently, Harden-Davies et al advanced this approach as offering fresh insights into the challenges of governing BBNJ – linking this to the idea of ocean stewardship.[113] Notably, the authors point to how the benefits from exploitation of MGRs should be used to contribute to conservation and sustainable use.[114]

These three categories of beneficiary are not necessarily discrete categories. This means stewardship of an ocean resource may be simultaneously directed at some or all of these types of beneficiaries. Frequently, instruments are silent on the actual beneficiary of a duty. For example, in Article 194 UNCLOS, it is written that states

> shall take, individually or jointly as appropriate, all measures consistent with this Convention that are necessary to prevent, reduce and control pollution of the marine environment from any source, using for this purpose the best practicable means at their disposal and in accordance with their capabilities.

States are implicit as the beneficiaries of a duty – since the commitment is contained within a multilateral agreement. The environment benefits from protective measures, although only as the target of actions. Future generations are not mentioned, nor do they feature as part of the text of the convention. However, they are at least passive recipients of a healthier marine environment since protective measures are inevitably prospective. The use of the threefold distinction is to draw attention to the structural and practical implications of stewardship for different beneficiaries.

As noted above, beneficiaries are usually identified as groups, rather than as individuals. Thus, Lynton Caldwell insists that in order to embrace stewardship, 'society must shift its focus from the rights of the … [individual] to the communal rights of society'.[115] This is an important dimension to stewardship because it points to the ideas of connectivity of human/ecological systems that underpin the reasons for enhanced environmental protection. Protection is not merely about individual interests, it is about the disaggregate but interdependent interests that exist between humans, and also between humans and natural systems.

The beneficiaries of the BBNJ Agreement are clearly identified upfront to include both present and future generations.[116] Many benefits are indirect,

[111] https://pwccc.wordpress.com/programa/.
[112] UN Doc A/74/236, 26 July 2019.
[113] Harden-Davies et al (n 13).
[114] ibid 8.
[115] Caldwell, 'Land the Law: Problems of Legal Philosophy' (1986) *University of Illinois Law Review* 319, 323.
[116] BBNJ Agreement, Preamble.

resulting from the broader public benefits of improving governance in ABNJ. One specific area of defined benefits includes those resulting from the use of MGRs.[117] Part of the BBNJ Agreement sets out quite detailed provisions explaining how such benefits include a range of monetary and non-monetary benefits.[118] They should be shared equitably.[119] However, these are proving to be difficult issues to resolve.[120] Interestingly, such resources should be used to build 'the capacity of Parties, particularly developing States Parties, in particular the least developed countries, landlocked developing countries, geographically disadvantaged States, small island developing States, coastal African States, archipelagic States and developing middle-income countries'.[121] This opens up the possibility for differentiated benefit sharing through an access and benefit-sharing committee whose composition will take account of gender and equitable geographic distribution, including from least developed countries.[122] However, we should be cautious about this because experience suggests that the law of the sea has not done enough to properly advance differentiated responsibilities.[123]

The Preamble of the BBNJ Agreement appears to frame the environment as a beneficiary of 'stewardship duties'. However, it is generally treated as an indirect beneficiary of commitments that states undertake vis-à-vis other states. There are few specific references to the environment as being an immediate objective of protective measures. The most important of such commitments relate to the use of marine protected areas. Thus, Article 17 includes in the objectives for area-based management the aim to 'Conserve and sustainably use areas requiring protection, including through the establishment of a comprehensive system of area-based management tools, with ecologically representative and well-connected networks of marine protected areas'.[124] It further provides for the objective to 'Protect, preserve, restore and maintain biodiversity and ecosystems, including with a view to enhancing their productivity and health, and strengthen resilience to stressors, including those related to climate change, ocean acidification and marine pollution'.[125] The Preamble refers to 'maintaining the integrity of ocean ecosystems and conserving the inherent value of biodiversity of areas beyond national jurisdiction'. This is potentially important since it focuses less on any instrumental value of nature and more on its intrinsic value. Similarly, Article 14(1) provides that benefits from MGRs may

[117] ibid Art 9(a).
[118] ibid Art 14.
[119] ibid Part II and Art 14(1).
[120] See Riding (n 14) 441.
[121] See BBNJ Agreement, Art 9(b).
[122] See also ibid Art 15(2).
[123] See further Barnes, 'Global Solidarity, Differentiated Responsibilities and the Law of the Sea' (2020) *Netherlands Yearbook of International Law* 107.
[124] BBNJ Agreement, Art 17(a).
[125] ibid Art 17(c).

'contribute to the conservation and sustainable use of marine biological diversity of areas beyond national jurisdiction'. This could be used to reinvest gains back in nature. However, the challenge here will be representing such interests. Whilst there is an access and benefit-sharing committee, this is focused on the distribution of benefits between states, such as monetary payments, and not on reinvesting benefits back into environmental improvements per se. The BBNJ Agreement falls short of establishing strong rights of nature when compared to some terrestrial regimes.[126] Given the lack of connection that specific communities or peoples have with spaces or resources in ABNJ, there is likely to be weaker protection of such interests than for terrestrial spaces where people have much stronger cultural and material bonds.[127]

Beyond the provision on marine protected areas, there are some other references to direct responsibilities to protect the environment. The Preamble refers to the obligation to protect and preserve the marine environment contained in UNCLOS, and Article 27(b) provides that the objectives of Part IV, on environmental impact assessments, is to 'Ensure that activities covered by this Part are assessed and conducted to prevent, mitigate and manage significant adverse impacts for the purpose of protecting and preserving the marine environment'. However, beyond these provisions, there is no general duty to protect the marine environment to be found in the text; there is merely the preambular reference back to UNCLOS duties. The approach of the Agreement is to focus on conservation-sustainable use, rather than preventing harm per se.

D. The Content of the Stewardship Duty

The analysis so far reveals stewardship to be a highly contextual concept and that the responsibilities of a steward will depend upon the object of the stewardship, the extent of the steward's rights or interests in a thing and the range of beneficiaries. It will also depend upon the supporting legal regime – domestic or international law. This means that a complete account of stewardship duties is not possible. Instead, a schematic account of stewardship duties is provided. This draws upon the typology of stewardship discussed in section III above. Stewardship, broadly speaking, is a duty to look after something. To help explain this, Barritt organises stewardship into three categories: custodial, managerial and proprietorial duties. However, she accepts that there is some overlap between these approaches.[128] Stewardship duties exist on a spectrum ranging from the minimum content of custody to more strongly framed proprietary duties. These three modes of stewardship are considered in turn.

[126] See text accompanying nn 107–15 above.

[127] On the limits of environmental rights in marine spaces, see Barnes, 'Environmental Rights' (n 19).

[128] Barritt (n 40) 15.

Custody is defined as 'keeping, guarding, care, watch, inspection, preservation or security of a thing'.[129] The impetus for custody is to act for the benefit of a thing (eg children or the environment), rather than as a matter of self-interest. There are legal templates for custodial duties in existing legal systems, both domestic and international. For example, the legal concept of bailment entails a duty to take reasonable care of things that are given into your possession.[130] In the USA, the public trust doctrine, which applies inter alia to coastal areas, establishes a fiduciary relationship by the state over certain resources.[131] It does not depend upon ownership, and hence can explain stewardship in the absence of property rights. Notably, arguments to extend the public trust to the EEZ have been made by some commentators.[132] At a larger scale, Brown Weiss has called for planetary trust.[133] Arguably, the idea of trust can be used to frame commitments such as that found in the Convention on Biological Diversity to 'conserve and sustainably use biological diversity for the benefit of present and future generations'.[134] Interestingly, Barritt uses the idea of trust to frame such commitments because it is able to reflect the other-regarding-type responsibilities to the environment that exist at all levels, from the individual to the state. At the international level, this is reflected in a turn towards conceiving of the state as a fiduciary of those who are in its care.[135]

Such an approach is compellingly advanced by Benvenisti, who argues that other-regarding responsibilities are part of the normative justifications for the exercise of sovereign power. Thus, sovereigns (states) are global trustees of humanity.[136] At a minimum level, other-regarding obligations entail consideration of the interests of other states or actors because individual states can rarely act alone or without consequence for others in a world based upon material and political interdependence.[137] A stronger account of other-regarding

[129] ibid 15.

[130] See *Coggs v Barnard* (1703) 92 ER 107. See further Autor, 'Bailment Liability: Toward A Standard of Reasonable Care' (1987–88) 61 *Southern California Law Review* 2117.

[131] Sand, 'Public Trusteeship for the Oceans' in Ndiaye and Wolfrum (eds), *Law of the Sea, Environmental Law and Settlement of Disputes: Liber Amicorum Judge Thomas A Mensah* (Martinus Nijhoff, 2007) 521.

[132] Nanda and Ris Jr, 'The Public Trust Doctrine: A Viable Approach to International Environmental Protection' (1976) 5 *Ecology Law Quarterly* 291; Jarman, 'The Public Trust Doctrine in the Exclusive Economic Zone' (1986) 65 *Oregon Law Review* 1; Osherenko, 'New Discourses on Ocean Governance: Understanding Property Rights and the Public Trust' (2007) 21 *Journal of Environmental Law and Litigation* 317.

[133] Brown Weiss, 'The Planetary Trust: Conservation and Intergenerational Equity' (1984) 11 *Ecology Law Quarterly* 495.

[134] United Nations Convention on Biological Diversity 1992, 1760 UNTS 79, Preamble.

[135] Peters, 'Humanity as the A and Ω of Sovereignty' (2009) 20 *European Journal of International Law* 513; Waldron, 'Are Sovereigns Entitled to the Benefit of the International Rule Of law?' (2011) 22 *European Journal of International Law* 315, 325; Fox-Decent, *Sovereignty's Promise: The State as Fiduciary* (Oxford University Press, 2011); Criddle and Fox-Decent, *Fiduciaries of Humanity: How International Law Constitutes Authority* (Oxford University Press, 2016).

[136] Benvenisti, 'Sovereigns as Trustees of Humanity: On the Accountability of States to Foreign Stakeholders' (2013) 107 *American Journal of International Law* 295.

[137] ibid 298, 303.

commitments entails a duty to act in a way that not only refrains from harming the interests of others, but also actively includes such interests, including that of global welfare.[138] Thus, harm is defined as omissions that fail 'to move the current status quo towards an increase in global welfare'.[139] There are examples of international tribunals upholding such duties, but Benvenisti is cautious about reading too much into such interventions, given the questions of legitimacy that this raises when tribunals review and intervene in the policy decisions of sovereigns.[140]

Managerial stewardship entails more active responsibilities towards others or the environment.[141] It means actively caring for or managing a resource in a particular way. It describes not just the duty, but the quality of that duty. Thus, it is *careful* management of resources or *conservative* use of things. This may, for example, entail using no more than is necessary of a resource rather than fully exploiting it. Management dictates how things are used and so can provide a more directed way of meeting others' needs.[142] This allows for a more flexible application of management stewardship. Typically, management is applied to the use of things that are owned, but, as Welshman argues, management may also focus on how individuals or other actors conduct themselves, and so it need not depend upon a proprietary interest in the thing being used.[143] However, the specific nature of management duties means that it depends upon such duties being expressly stated. Whereas custody of things can be inferred from a fundamental need to be other-regarding, management entails specific responsibilities and so will depend upon the existence of specific legal mechanisms to articulate and deliver stewardship.

The managerial approach has its counterpart in international law. Chayes and Chayes advance it as part of their New Sovereignty, where they argue that compliance with law is predicated on an interactive process of justification, discourse and persuasion.[144] In this sense, sovereignty is not freedom, but rather a product of these interactions. The 'manager' is the regime of international law (typically a treaty regime), and it plays an active role in modifying preferences, generating options, directing the normative development of the law and shaping compliance.[145] Interestingly, non-compliance in such a regime is frequently the result of ambiguity and indeterminacy in legal texts, pointing to the importance of clearly delimited responsibilities.[146]

[138] ibid 328.
[139] ibid 329.
[140] ibid 332.
[141] Barritt (n 40) 17. See also Roach et al (n 36) 50.
[142] Lucy and Mitchell (n 40) 597.
[143] Welchman (n 30) 302.
[144] Chayes and Chayes, *The New Sovereignty: Compliance with International Regulatory Agreement* (Harvard University Press, 1998).
[145] ibid 110.
[146] ibid 15, 123.

The third form of stewardship is proprietary stewardship.[147] Stewardship in this tradition focuses on the idea that certain responsibilities are inherent in the ownership of things. What distinguishes stewardship from private property is its emphasis on other-regarding duties. More specifically, stewardship is a form of holding subject to overriding duties of conservation and preservation.[148] Conservation is the keeping of resources for posterity, as distinct from preservation, which is the saving of resources from harm.[149] Most legal systems entail limits on the use of property to ensure harm is not caused to others or so that certain public interests are met. A recent example of whether this can be structured towards distinct public benefits is the regime of conservation covenants under the UK's Environment Act 2021, which enables landowners to agree with a responsible body to introduce use conditions on their land for the public benefit.[150] Where difficulties arise is in explaining the nature of such duties. As I asked in some earlier research: is stewardship 'merely something that is grafted onto existing property structures, or is [it] a distinctive form of holding?'[151] The former view is reflected in the work of scholars like Yannacone,[152] Karp,[153] Hunter[154] and Rodgers.[155] The latter is seen in the work of Lucy and Mitchell, who argue that stewardship cannot be reconciled with private ownership because it fundamentally challenges the idea that the owner possesses the full extent of rights of exclusivity, enforceability and transferability that inhere in private property.[156] We need not be detained by this debate too long. If we recall that property is a variable bundle of interests, then it is possible to weigh and construct forms of property in different ways. This flexibility allows for different forms of holding to be adapted to different situations, and it is compatible with the idea that stewardship operates in a highly contextual way.

The proprietary model of stewardship can be extended to international law.[157] Redgwell has shown that international law structures and limits the control of resources in terms analogous to property.[158] This echoes the earlier

[147] Barritt (n 40) 18.

[148] ibid 157–59.

[149] Passmore, *Man's Responsibility for Nature*, 2nd edn (Duckworth, 1980).

[150] Environment Act 2021, Part 7c. See further the Law Commission, *Conservation Covenants* (Law Commission Report No 349, 2014) https://s3-eu-west-2.amazonaws.com/lawcom-prod-storage-11jsxou24uy7q/uploads/2015/03/lc349_conservation-covenants.pdf.

[151] Barnes, *Property Rights* (n 40) 159.

[152] Yannacone, 'Property and Stewardship: Private Property Plus Public Interest Equals Social Property' (1978) 23 *San Diego Law Review* 71, 74.

[153] Karp, 'A Private Property Duty of Stewardship: Changing Our Land Ethic' (1993) 23 *Environmental Law* 735.

[154] Hunter, 'An Ecological Perspective on Property: A Call for Judicial Protection of the Public's Interest in Environmentally Critical Resources' (1988) 12 *Harvard Environmental Law Review* 311.

[155] Rodgers, 'Nature's Place? Property Rights, Property Rules and Environmental Stewardship' (2009) 68 *CLJ* 550.

[156] Lucy and Mitchell (n 40) esp 584.

[157] See further Barnes, *Property Rights* (n 40) 224–48.

[158] Redgwell, 'Property Law Sources and Analogies in International Law' in McHarg et al (eds), *Property in the Law in Energy and Natural Resources* (Oxford University Press, 2010) 100.

work of Hersch Lauterpacht, in which he advanced the object theory of state territory, which treats the territory of the state akin to the property of the state.[159] This is reflected in the idea of permanent sovereignty over natural resources (PSNR). In the leading account of this concept, Schrijver shows how PSNR moved from being framed initially in terms of nationalism and pragmatic use of resources towards a regime of international cooperation, and then, more recently, into a regime where the focus was on balancing rights and duties in a world where interdependence (both between states and upon resources) is the dominant theme.[160] Whilst not quite advancing a theory of stewardship, where responsibilities take priority over rights, it serves to help locate and articulate the important limits that international law imposes upon the use of things.

At its heart, stewardship is fundamentally an other-regarding set of responsibilities, whether they derive from a fiduciary, managerial or proprietary relationship. There are elements of a fiduciary relationship towards MGR in the BBNJ Agreement. This includes benefit sharing, capacity building for developing states, the promotion of knowledge and technology transfers.[161] However, these are broad objectives and not duties, so they amount to weak other-regarding custodial responsibilities. Stronger other-regarding duties are required to account for the interests of coastal states when MGRs are also located in areas within national jurisdiction.

Other-regarding duties are provided for variously in the BBNJ Agreement, with varying degrees of legal force. For example, Article 9 provides for softer commitments (objectives, not duties) to use the benefits of MGR to build capacity.[162] Article 11(6) asserts:

> Activities with respect to marine genetic resources of areas beyond national jurisdiction *are in the interests of all States and for the benefit of all humanity*, particularly for the benefit of advancing the scientific knowledge of humanity and promoting the conservation and sustainable use of marine biological diversity, taking into particular consideration the interests and needs of developing States. (emphasis added)

This does not establish a duty; rather, it asserts a normative position as if it were a given – which is clearly not the case. The most important set of other-regarding commitments is found in Article 14, which provides that the benefits from MGR activities shall be shared in a fair and equitable manner. It is important to stress that this sets out a framework of considerations and a decision-making process. As such, the effectiveness of other-regarding actions will depend upon how the Agreement is implemented. Monetary benefits from commercialisation of MGR shall be shared fairly and equitably through the

[159] Lauterpacht, in Lauterpacht (ed), *International Law: Being the Collected Papers of Hersch Lauterpacht* (Cambridge University Press, 1970) 367.

[160] Schrijver, *Sovereignty Over Natural Resources: Balancing Rights and Duties* (Cambridge University Press, 1997).

[161] BBNJ Agreement, Art 9.

[162] ibid Art 9(b).

financial mechanism established under Article 52.[163] Non-monetary benefits shall be shared in the form of access to samples, digital sequence information, FAIR (findable, accessible, interoperable, and reusable) scientific data, transfer of technology (according to the terms of Part V), capacity-building support, technical and scientific cooperation, and other forms of benefits as may be determined by the Conference of the Parties – taking account of recommendations of the access and benefit-sharing committee.[164] Whilst technology transfer should account for the capacity and needs of developing states,[165] the provision of technology will depend upon further cooperative measures,[166] and it is still likely to take place on a largely commercial basis. There are some protections for traditional knowledge holders, with a duty to ensure that resources are not accessed without prior and informed consent, and involvement of indigenous peoples and local communities.[167] Given that many resources will be exploited by private persons, states are required to adopt the 'necessary legislative, administrative or policy measures, as appropriate, to ensure the implementation of this Agreement'.[168] The effectiveness of the Agreement will depend heavily on the extent to which such implementing measures affectively shape private rights and responsibilities under domestic law.

Although the text of the Agreement has been finalised, it is important to note that much will depend upon the more specific rules or guidance that will emerge from the institutional procedures established under the Agreement, including the functions of the Conference of the Parties and the clearing-house mechanism.[169] Here, the stewardship function vests in the institutional machinery of the BBNJ instrument, rather than in individual states. These mechanisms may serve to exert a managerial influence on duty holders by subjecting them to interactions that challenge and influence their behaviour towards other-regarding objectives.

It is perhaps the proprietary account of stewardship that is most revealing about the limits of the BBNJ Agreement's commitments to stewardship. Indeed, few stewardship responsibilities can be identified in this mould in the Agreement. Whilst states' other-regarding commitments can be identified in terms of custodial or managerial responsibilities, the text does not directly address states' interests in MGR in proprietary terms. This is unsurprising, given that sovereignty does not extend to ABNJ, and so analogues of ownership, such as permanent sovereignty, do not easily apply to commons spaces.[170]

[163] ibid Art 14(3).
[164] ibid Art 14(2).
[165] ibid Art 41.
[166] ibid Art 43.
[167] ibid Arts 7(j) and (k), 13, 44(1)(b) and Annex II(iii).
[168] ibid Art 53. See also Art 14(11).
[169] On the role of the Conference of the Parties, see BBNJ Agreement, Arts 6, 14(2)(h), 14(5)–(7), 15(2)–(6), 16(1) and (3) and Part VI. On use of the clearing house mechanisms, see Arts 11(3), 12, 13, 15(3)(d), 15(4), 16, 29(5) and (6), 31(1)(a) 32, 33, 34(3), 36(2) 37, 42(4) and 51.
[170] This is specifically excluded under the BBNJ Agreement, Art 11(4).

Also, it would have meant directly resolving the fundamental conflict of views between states favouring either freedom of the high seas or the common heritage that plagued the negotiations. It is notable that both principles that concern the status of the ABNJ feature in the list of general principles in Article 7. The agreement maintains the position under UNCLOS that the Area is not susceptible to sovereign claims. Article 11(4) of the BBNJ Agreement provides that no state may claim or exercise sovereignty or sovereign rights over MGR in ABNJ. Nor shall any such claims be recognised. Furthermore, the collection in situ of MGR shall not constitute the legal basis for any claim to part of the marine environment or its resources. The agreement prohibits the emergence of property rights in ABNJ or its resources.[171] This does not deny control; it merely ensures that ABNJ is subject to collective governance.

It is notable that the final text is quite silent on the question of property rights in general and intellectual property rights in particular.[172] During the negotiations, such provisions were the object of considerable debate. Earlier draft provisions sought to ensure that intellectual property rights were governed in a way that did not undermine the objectives of the Agreement, such as benefit sharing,[173] and that applications for intellectual property rights would not be approved if they did not comply with the Agreement. In part, the disappearance of provisions on property rights, including the provision on technology transfer, reflects the desire of the parties to prevent the BBNJ Agreement from impinging upon the mandates of other international bodies. In part, it shows that states were unable to agree upon the normative priority between questions of private property and wider benefit sharing. This is symptomatic of wider challenges of addressing regime complexity.[174] This deliberate excision of property issues from the text suggests that when potential stewardship commitments reach beyond the state, they may come up against strong resistance from well-established regimes of private property. This is not to suggest that such issues have been resolved; far from it. It is clear that such issues will return to the surface when the Agreement becomes operational, either through the clearing-house mechanism or other cooperative mechanisms. These mechanisms will be important sites for the development of meaningful stewardship obligations, as they apply to modalities of resource access, use and benefit sharing, as well as technology transfer.

[171] BBNJ Agreement, Art 11(5).

[172] See Krabbe, 'A Long Discussion Based on a Limited Perspective: Evaluating the Marine Genetic Resource Discussion and the New Rules Under the Law of the Sea', ch 3 of this book.

[173] Revised draft text of an agreement under the United Nations Convention on the Law of the Sea on the conservation and sustainable use of marine biological diversity of areas beyond national jurisdiction, 18 November 2019, A/CONF.232/2020/3, Art 12(1).

[174] Alter and Raustiala, 'The Rise of International Regime Complexity' (2018) *Annual Review of Law and Social Science* 329.

E. Accountability for Stewardship

The beneficiaries of stewardship may seek to enforce their stewardship interests through legal claims. However, the means of protecting beneficial interests assumes the existence of two things: first, the existence of legal persons able to assert their beneficial interests; and second, the availability of institutions capable of determining such interests, ie courts. Legal accountability for stewardship only works if the beneficiary is a recognised legal person with the standing to pursue legal remedies. Further, such remedies depend upon the existence of some court tribunal or other mechanisms capable of protecting the beneficial interests. However, these circumstances do not prevail in every situation, thereby weakening the accountability of the stewardship duty holder. For example, in the context of environmental stewardship, the environment may be defined as a beneficiary but it may lack legal standing to bring a claim, and other persons may not have an interest or capacity to act on behalf of the environment. This presents a challenge at both the domestic and international levels, where rights of standing are often limited. Particularly at the international level, there may not be courts suitable for resolving claims that stewardship duties are not being met. Furthermore, if the state is the holder of stewardship responsibilities (either individually or collectively), as will be the case for stewardship of international spaces or resources, then questions must be asked about how the state or groups of states can be held to account. At the international level, the absence of strong institutional machinery to support stewardship may weaken the concept to a significant degree. Of course, accountability does not only depend upon one's ability to advance one's interests and rights in court; there may be other processes by which accountability is advanced, such as political dialogue. Development of a wider concept of accountability of actors in international law goes beyond the scope of the present chapter, but a couple of key observations can be made on how accountability relates to stewardship.[175]

Although states may be held to account according to the law of state responsibility, this is an option of infrequent resort. Accountability as used in international law involves justifying one's actions and being held to account for those actions.[176] Accountability thus understood is more usually located within governance arrangements where decision-makers are required to give explanations for action and justify behaviour (giving account).[177] A stronger version of accountability focuses on 'holding to account'. It depends not only upon the existence of some process where the decision-maker is required to give account,

[175] See further Curtin and Nollkaemper, 'Conceptualizing Accountability in International and European Law' (2007) 36 *Netherlands Yearbook of International Law* 3; Boström and Garsten (eds), *Organizing Transnational Accountability* (Edward Elgar Publishing, 2008). On accountability for marine resource regulation, see Rosello, *IUU Fishing as a Flag State Accountability Paradigm* (Brill, 2021).

[176] Mulgan, '"Accountability": An Ever-Expanding Concept?' (2000) 78 *Public Administration* 555.

[177] ibid 555.

but also some process where an assessment or judgement of that account is provided.[178] If stewardship is to be meaningful, then it depends upon this second, stronger version of accountability. Central to this version of accountability is the need for a clear account of the stewardship relationship to be defined in law. This means specifying as clearly and certainly as possible each of the previous elements of stewardship. In every legal system, accountability is framed first and foremost as accountability to the law.[179] This is only effective if the law clearly determines the standards and means of accountability. This means, for example, in the context of the BBNJ Agreement, there must be clearly delimited standards of conduct applicable to states or other actors who assume stewardship responsibilities or are designated as stewards. This, in turn, means ensuring that rules of procedures for the Conference of the Parties, Secretariat, Clearing House, and Scientific and Technical Committee strengthen their responsibilities through procedural safeguards, including transparency, access to information and accountability for decisions. These fora should ensure that stewards of ABNJ or its resources and the beneficiaries of such resources are brought together in a way that enables the actions of the former to be scrutinised and evaluated by the latter. Stewardship depends upon a dynamic between these two sets of actors. This is challenging generally at the level of international law because most international fora focus on interstate dynamics and do not accommodate other actors, or do so only indirectly. In the context of the BBNJ Agreement, this means the creation of procedures that are inclusive of non-state actors. It also means procedures that can represent the interests of beneficiaries and enable them to engage states or others in ways that assess their conduct and which can require them to change their behaviour if such behaviour falls short of established stewardship standards.

In the BBNJ Agreement text, there are two sets of procedures that might enable accountability for the use of MGRs: Article 16, on monitoring, which is central to accountability for the use or stewardship of MGRs; and the Part VI provisions on institutional arrangements.

Article 16 states that monitoring and transparency of MGR activities shall be secured through the clearing-house mechanism, according to procedures adopted by the Conference of the Parties. It then calls upon the Conference of the Parties to 'determine appropriate, guidelines for the implementation of [monitoring provisions]'. The precise extent of information to be provided to the Clearing House is not stated, but it should include a detailed account on how MGR activities are monitored. Although monitoring seems relatively light touch and focused on processes for gathering information, without obvious opportunities for engagement by non-states actors, it is reinforced through other mechanisms. For example, the proposed Scientific and Technical Body is expert

[178] Brunnée, 'International Legal Accountability Through the Lens of the Law of State Responsibility' (2005) 36 *Netherlands Yearbook of International Law* 3.
[179] See, eg Waldron (n 135) 316–17.

driven, with the possibility of representation from Indigenous Peoples and not a wider range of beneficiaries.[180] More significant is the proposed duty upon states parties to submit reports to the access and benefit-sharing committee, who, in turn, report to the Conference of the Parties.[181] This at least may entail some duty to give an account of conduct in ABNJ and so meet the weak version of accountability. Where this becomes more meaningful is in respect of the interface with the monitoring and review requirements in respect of other activities in ABNJ (ie area-based management measures, environmental impact assessment and capacity building).[182] This is important because states will have to rationalise not just their regulation of MGRs, but their wider conduct in ABNJ in such accounts. This seems to be envisaged as part of the clearing-house process,[183] but is reinforce by the general reporting requirements under the Agreement. It will draw into the accounts of resource use wider commitments and interests, and these will need to be reconciled with each other.

Institutional arrangements are set out in Part VI of the Agreement. The Conference of the Parties is intended to be the principal governance mechanism of the BBNJ regime.[184] As such, it will have a broad, although unspecified, responsibility for ensuring that stewardship commitments are met. Much of this responsibility for stewardship will be done indirectly by controlling procedures and guiding conduct within the proposed regime. Thus, it will determine how subsidiary bodies such as the Scientific and Technical Body or the Clearing House operate.[185] It shall monitor the implementation of the regime and has the powers to issue decisions or recommendations, promote cooperation, establish new subsidiary bodies and control budgets.[186] The Conference of the Parties is supported in this by an Implementation and Compliance Committee (ICC).[187] The ICC is a facilitative body, so operates in a non-adversarial and non-punitive way. Its main function is to consider individual and systemic issues of implementation and to make periodic reports and recommendations to the Conference of the Parties. Compliance committees in other environmental agreements indicate the potential for such a body to enhance the accountability of states for delivering upon their commitments.[188]

The wide range of powers bestowed upon the Conference of the Parties may result in strong accountability for activities in ABNJ. Or it may not. Much

[180] BBNJ Agreement, Art 49.
[181] ibid Art 16(2) and (3).
[182] ibid Arts 26, 35–37 and 45.
[183] ibid Art 51(3).
[184] ibid Art 47.
[185] ibid Art 47(4).
[186] ibid Art 47(6).
[187] ibid Art 55.
[188] eg the Aarhus Compliance Committee. See Ryall, 'The Aarhus Convention: Standards for Access to Justice in Environmental Matters' in Turner, Shelton, Razzaque, McIntyre and May (eds), *Environmental Rights: The Development of Standards* (Cambridge University Press, 2019)116; Samvel, 'Non-judicial, Advisory, Yet Impactful? The Aarhus Convention Compliance Committee as a Gateway to Environmental Justice' (2020) 9 *Transnational Environmental Law* 211.

will depend upon how the states make use of such powers and respond to the monitoring and reporting requirements. As with much of the rest of the BBNJ Agreement, the institutional part is a framework. Detailed procedural rules remain to be worked out. Absent strong other-regarding commitments to steward resources, there is a risk that such powers will not be directed to stewardship responsibilities; they will be susceptible to the promotion of more limited self-interests of powerful actors.[189] The fact remains that the Conference of the Parties remains very much focused on the interests of states, so is vulnerable to the charge that it may ignore those without a voice, such as future generations or the environment, but also current generations that lack a strong voice in international fora.

V. APPLYING STEWARDSHIP TO MGRs: SOME FINAL THOUGHTS

More research is required to develop a more complete account of stewardship under international law, but at this stage we can at least see the outline and potential for such a theory of stewardship as a principle or concept of international law. As Riding has argued, it presents a different way of reframing the existing balance of rights and duties in respect of BBNJ.[190] However, if stewardship is to really make a difference, it must amount to more than a restatement of existing duties. This entails a clear understanding of the structure and implications of stewardship. In particular, stewardship needs to represent both a shift in thinking and a change in how other-regarding interests are acted upon by states and other actors.

Stewardship can be delimited according to the object of stewardship, the duty holder, the beneficiary and the nature of the duty. It also entails mechanisms for holding stewards to account. The potential object of stewardship has a material impact upon the construction of the stewardship: thus, the location, size and precision of the object as well as its physical attributes, in part determine the scope of the stewardship duties. This is important for ABNJ in general and MGRs in particular, since it determines both who can and who should act as stewards. Furthermore, the fact that stewardship in the BBNJ Agreement is broadly directed at all of ABNJ suggests that it extends to both wider ocean space and individual resources. If so, then states and other actors need to ensure that the stewardship responsibilities at each level are coherent.

A range of actors can take up stewardship responsibilities, but the extent of their responsibilities will be limited to their authority to act. States may have the widest authority to act as stewards, but there is also scope for stewardship

[189] See, eg Martin, 'Interests, Power, and Multilateralism' (1992) 46 *International Organization* 765; Benvenisti and Downs, 'The Empire's New Clothes: Political Economy and the Fragmentation of International Law' (2007) 60 *Stanford Law Review* 595.

[190] Riding (n 14).

to vest in intergovernmental organizations and other bodies. Given activities in ABNJ will involve private persons, care needs to be taken to ensure such actors also conduct themselves faithfully towards the objectives of the BBNJ regime. At present, the BBNJ Agreement is largely focused on states, and its designation of responsibilities to other actors is rather ill-defined. Accordingly, much will depend on how states engage with these other actors through the BBNJ Agreement or in other fora, and how they implement BBNJ commitments in domestic law.

The beneficiaries of stewardship should include a wide range of legal persons, including present and future generations, as well as the environment. The BBNJ Agreement designates the first two categories as the beneficiaries of stewardship, but is silent on the environment as a beneficiary, at least directly. The challenge with respect to beneficiaries is not so much their designation as establishing mechanisms that allow non-immediate interests (future generations, the environment and, to a lesser extent, non-state actors in the present) to hold stewards to account for their responsibilities. Stewardship is fundamentally an other-regarding set of responsibilities. These responsibilities, at a minimum level, may be inferred from the basic conditions of cooperation and interdependency inherent in the international legal system. According to a custodial or fiduciary account of sovereignty, states can rarely act alone or without consequence for others in a world based upon material and political interdependence. This should drive other-regarding action. Stronger other-regarding responsibilities may be attributed to states and other actors within the managerial structure of treaty regimes or according to proprietary notions of sovereignty. Whilst some management of stewardship action may be possible through the BBNJ process, the specific challenge that MGRs pose to stewardship comes from the existence of strong private property-orientated accounts of intellectual property. These tend to resist the imposition of stewardship responsibilities that direct the use of such rights towards others. This is something that states will have to address when developing the rules of procedures for the BBNJ institutions while implementing the BBNJ Agreement. Finally, stewardship entails strong institutional processes to enable stewards to be held to account. Whilst the BBNJ Agreement indicates strong potential here, there is a risk that this could be hampered by the absence of clearly defined stewardship duties and a potential lack of engagement in such processes by the beneficiaries of stewardship. This is a critical issue if the Agreement is to advance the interests of those without a voice, such as future generations or the environment, or those without a strong voice, such as developing or disadvantaged states. One hopes that some of these issues are developed under the BBNJ Agreement in a way that helps to realise a strong stewardship regime. Otherwise, stewardship will remain an empty form of rhetoric and not a regime that advances the solidarity required for governing a critical common space and its resources.

3

A Long Discussion Based on a Limited Perspective: Evaluating the Marine Genetic Resource Debate and the New Rules under the Law of the Sea

NIELS KRABBE

I. THE MARINE GENETIC RESOURCE DEBATE – A DISCUSSION ON PRE-EXISTING PRINCIPLES

WITH THE HISTORIC decision in New York on 4 March 2023 on a new treaty on biological diversity in marine areas beyond national jurisdiction (BBNJ),[1] the question of the legal status of marine genetic resources in ocean commons was finally settled after more than 15 years of negotiations and an even longer scholarly debate. The interest in deep-sea genetic resources relates to an unlikely coincidence: deep-sea organisms are remarkably exotic from both a biological and a legal perspective. The ecosystems which contain genetic resources with some of the rarest properties in the biosphere are located in an environment which is not only physically but also legally distinct from the rest of the planet. The physical elements of the deep seas confront life with extreme conditions, including immense pressures and complete darkness. To withstand this hostile environment, organisms have had to develop unique biological characteristics by means of evolution. The realisation that the technological application of these bioactive properties could be valuable, particularly in the pharmaceutical sector, ignited a polarised debate in the 1990s on how genetic resources should be considered under the law of the sea. This problem soon attracted political attention and became a central part of the BBNJ negotiations.

[1] Agreement under the United Nations Convention on the Law of the Sea on the Conservation and Sustainable Use of Marine Biological Diversity of Areas beyond National Jurisdiction (adopted 19 June 2023) www.un.org/bbnj/ (BBNJ Agreement).

Whereas the 1982 United Nations Convention on the Law of the Sea[2] (UNCLOS) had confirmed exclusive and sovereign rights for coastal states over natural resources in the continental shelf, it was agreed that the deep seabed would not be subjugated by states. Instead, a considerable part of the convention was devoted to establishing an innovative commons regime for the seabed beyond the shelf (referred to as *the Area* in UNCLOS). The negotiation of these rules had been almost exclusively concerned with minerals. As a result, a comprehensive and conceptually creative legal framework was set up to control how mineral fortunes should be exploited and divided based on commons principles. Rather than accepting the premises of coastal state sovereign rights or open access, which had been the basis for the regimes for coastal state maritime zones and the high seas respectively, the rules for the deep seabed and its resources came to be based on the principle of the common heritage of mankind (CHM).[3] Similar to the freedoms of the high seas, which apply in the overlying water column, CHM precludes exercise of sovereignty or sovereign rights. But instead of providing that its resources a priori belong to no one and may be freely accessed, CHM vests the deep-seabed resources in all of mankind. Private and public appropriation is consequently prohibited.[4] Moreover, the principle entails concerted management based on global institutional mechanisms, equal sharing of benefits, prohibition of military uses and the preservation for future generations.[5] To coordinate the expected deep-sea mining bonanza, the International Seabed Authority was established as a global agency to organise and control activities in the Area, particularly with a view to administering the resources.[6]

In the mid-1990s, however, it became clear that the commercial mining that had been projected to generate huge wealth and had been the motivation for the deep-seabed regime had failed to materialise. Nor did it seem likely that deep-seabed mining would deliver more than negligible economic output for the foreseeable future. Instead of minerals, it became increasingly apparent that genetic resources, which were not considered during the negotiation of the seabed regime nor mentioned in the final convention, likely represented the most lucrative resource of the deep seabed. This *irony* of the deep-seabed regime, as it was described by Lyle Glowka, ignited a lively legal discussion.[7] Whereas it became widely recognised that the negotiation of the deep-seabed regime of UNCLOS appeared to have taken aim at the wrong target, there were different

[2] The United Nations Convention on the Law of the Sea (signed in Montego Bay, Jamaica on 10 December 1982, effective 16 November 1994) 1833 UNTS 397.

[3] UNCLOS, Art 136.

[4] ibid Art 137.

[5] Proelss, *United Nations Convention on the Law of the Sea: A Commentary* (Hart Publishing, 2017) 950.

[6] UNCLOS, Art 157.

[7] Glowka, 'The Deepest of Ironies: Genetic Resources, Marine Scientific Research, and the Area' (1996) 12 *Ocean Yearbook Online* 154.

opinions on the legal implications. Should the regime of the deep seabed (the Area) be considered to extend also to genetic resources, even though it referred to minerals and was negotiated with such resources in mind?

Rather than exploring the practical use of genetic resources and the challenges it entailed for regulation, much of the legal debate thus concerned the extent of the scope of the pre-existing rules. This connected not only to the convention's ambiguous definitions of *resources* (for which it made clear that the principle of CHM applied in the Area); it also reflected different understandings of how the Area regime should be conceptually understood. Was it a geographically defined concept, prescribing rules for everything situated in it, including genetic resources? Or was it only a set of rules to manage minerals, which could hardly be applied to other objects?[8]

Depending on interpretation, genetic resources in the seabed would either fall under the principle of CHM, which would imply that sovereign as well as private appropriation would be precluded (some observers even considered this principle to apply to genetic resources in the water column[9]), or the convention would lack rules prohibiting access and exploitation.[10] The latter position was based on the reference to minerals in central parts of the seabed regime, which was considered to imply a legal vacuum for non-mineral resources. In the water column, genetic resources should, as *living resources*, be considered as falling

[8] Several provisions of UNCLOS have been referred to by the different positions in this debate. Of particular importance is Art 136 UNCLOS, which declares that 'The Area and its resources are the common heritage of mankind', and Art 133, which, under the heading 'Use of terms', declares that 'For the purposes of this Part: (a) "resources" means all solid, liquid or gaseous mineral resources in situ in the Area at or beneath the seabed, including polymetallic nodules; (b) resources, when recovered from the Area, are referred to as "minerals"'. These two provisions have been referenced by supporters of a restrictive interpretation as evidence that the CHM principle merely applies to minerals. Proponents of a more extensive reading of the principle, extending to all resources of the Area or the Area at large, have referred to other provisions indicating that the Area (and thus the scope of the CHM principle), like coastal state maritime zones, should be considered to include everything physically located in it. Accordingly, Art 1 UNCLOS provides that the 'Area' means the seabed and ocean floor and subsoil thereof, beyond the limits of national jurisdiction. Art 134 explicitly states that 'Activities in the Area shall be governed by the provisions of this Part'. Similarly, Art 136 declares that *both* the Area *and* its resources form part of the common heritage of mankind.

[9] See, eg the 'Co-Chair's Summary of Discussions at the Ad Hoc Open-ended Informal Working Group to study Issues Relating to the Conservation and Sustainable Use of Marine Biological Diversity beyond Areas of National Jurisdiction' (25 July 2014) Annex A/69/177, para 47; Tanaka, 'Reflections on the Conservation and Sustainable Use of Genetic Resources in the Deep Seabed Beyond the Limits of National Jurisdiction' (2008) 39 *Ocean Development and International Law* 129; Elferink, 'The Regime of the Area: Delineating the Scope of Application of the Common Heritage Principle and Freedom of the High Seas' (2007) 22 *International Journal of Marine and Coastal Law* 143; Armas-Pfirter, 'How Can Life in the Deep Sea Be Protected?' (2009) 24 *International Journal of Marine and Coastal Law* 281 (although Armas-Pfirter acknowledges that some legal development would need to occur to operationalise the application of common heritage to genetic resources).

[10] A useful overview of the CHM versus freedoms of the high seas positions is found in de La Fayette, 'A New Regime for the Conservation and Sustainable Use of Marine Biodiversity and Genetic Resources Beyond the Limits of National Jurisdiction' (2009) 24 *International Journal of Marine and Coastal Law* 221.

within the high seas rules for the water column, and thus be covered by the open-access principles of the high seas freedoms.[11]

Since the text of the convention and its negotiation documents provided arguments for both interpretative positions of this debate, it was apparent that the legal status of genetic resources could not be resolved by means of judicial reasoning. On the political side, it was clear that many states would find it difficult to accept any interpretation which limited the scope of the principle of CHM, which has been recognised as one of the most important successes for developing states in multilateral negotiations. For these states, insisting on its applicability to genetic resources was not only a matter of principle, but connected to arguments of equity and a perceived fear that the limited number of states with the technological capabilities to access the deep seas would grab its riches. Similar concerns, but in relation to genetic resources within their territories, had guided developing state positions in the negotiations of the Convention on Biological Diversity[12] (CBD), which had confirmed the sovereign rights of states over genetic resources within their territories. The stalemate between different positions on the applicability of pre-existing principles was the rationale for including the legal status of genetic resources as one of the four issues to be examined by the UN Ad Hoc Open-ended Informal Working Group to study issues relating to the conservation and sustainable use of marine biological diversity beyond areas of national jurisdiction (BBNJ), which subsequently would develop into a preparatory committee and eventually lead to an intergovernmental conference negotiation.

However, neither the establishment of the working group nor the start of more formalised negotiations would mark an end to the discussions of the applicability of pre-existing principles. In their interventions throughout the lengthy process, G77 states kept repeating that the CHM principle also applied to genetic resources, or, alternatively, that the principle should be extended to encompass such resources.[13] While other states maintained the position that genetic resources should be considered as open-access resources, most eventually shifted to a more pragmatic approach, supporting the development of a

[11] Leary, *International Law and the Genetic Resources of the Deep Sea* (Nijhoff, 2010); Allen, 'Protecting the Oceanic Gardens of Eden: International Law Issues in Deep-Sea Vent Resource Conservation and Management' (2001) 13 *Georgetown International Environmental Law Review* 563; Glowka (n 7) (although Glowka argues that an international regime would be desirable to ensure fair and equitable utilisation).

[12] The Convention on Biological Diversity, regarding the conservation of biodiversity, the sustainable use of its components and the fair and equitable sharing of the benefits arising thereof (signed at the Earth Summit in Rio de Janeiro, Brazil in 1992, entered into force on 29 December 1993) 1760 UNTS 69 (CBD). It currently has 196 parties.

[13] See, eg 'Summary of the Working Group on Marine Biodiversity Beyond Areas of National Jurisdiction: 13–17 February 2006' (2006) 25 *Earth Negotiations Bulletin*; de La Fayette (n 10) 269; Scovazzi, 'Mining, Protection of the Environment, Scientific Research and Bioprospecting: Some Considerations on the Role of the International Sea-Bed Authority' (2004) 19 *International Journal of Marine and Coastal Law* 383.

new *sui generis* regime for genetic resources beyond national jurisdiction as a middle way between open access and common heritage (while still maintaining that CHM did not apply).[14] Undertakings relating to benefit sharing, capacity building and the transfer of technology were proposed as measures for making developing states accept that the mining regime for the Area would not simply be extended to encompass genetic resources.[15] Yet, it soon appeared that the willingness to accept such a trade-off was limited among developing states. The stalemate between different interpretative positions persisted and forced the final negotiation round to run on, before a compromise was finally reached.

The final BBNJ Agreement enables its Conference of the Parties to decide by qualified majority on mandatory sharing of benefits from the utilisation of genetic resources.[16] In the period leading up to such a decision, developed states undertake to make an annual contribution to a special fund, amounting to 50 per cent of that party's assessed contribution to the budget.[17] As regards the question of the legal status of genetic resources, the final deal does not provide a straight answer. Instead, both 'the principle of the common heritage of humankind which is set out in the Convention' and 'the freedom of marine scientific research, together with other freedoms of the high seas' are cited among its general principles.

II. INTRA-LEGAL AND LAW OF THE SEA PERSPECTIVES

The question of the legal status of genetic resources was thus the most difficult issue of the negotiation, from the start until the end. The focus on the relationship between this pre-existing legal principle and genetic resources can be regarded as the result of isolated political positions and a lack of willingness to compromise on the issue of CHM. However, it can also be explained by the context of the debate.

Throughout the discussions on marine genetic resources at the United Nations, perspectives from fields other than law have been surprisingly absent. Despite ambitious information sessions at the BBNJ working group stage, involving contributions from scientists dealing with different strands of marine genetic research and application, few interventions have concerned

[14] de Lucia, 'The Question of the Common Heritage of Mankind and the Negotiations Towards a Global Treaty on Marine Biodiversity in Areas Beyond National Jurisdiction: No End in Sight?' (2020) 16 *McGill International Journal of Sustainable Development Law and Policy* 138, 151.

[15] Scovazzi, 'Negotiating Conservation and Sustainable Use of Marine Biological Diversity in Areas Beyond National Jurisdiction: Prospects and Challenges' (2015) 24 *Italian Yearbook of International Law* 61; Broggiato et al, '*Mare Geneticum*: Balancing Governance of Marine Genetic Resources in International Waters' (2018) 33 *International Journal of Marine and Coastal Law* 3.

[16] BBNJ Agreement, Art 14.7.

[17] ibid Art 14.6.

practical use, commercial and technological aspects or scientific knowledge.[18] It appears that the essentially intra-legal context has prevented the exploration of how genetic resources and biotechnology call for developing law.[19] The lack of consideration in terms of the difference in how genetic resources are used compared to traditional economic resources is surprising, since it was the perceived values connected to biotechnological use that ignited the genetic resource debate in the 1990s.[20]

The lack of consideration to practical aspects is particularly reflected in the notion that causal links can be established between access to genetic resources and profits based on their use. Article 14.7 of the BBNJ Agreement mandates the conference of parties to introduce mandatory sharing of monetary benefits.[21] Concerns expressed by stakeholders on the practical difficulties in implementing such measures appear to have been little considered.[22] Indeed, many of the interventions in the discussions reflect an understanding that genetic resources are more or less directly marketed as biotechnological products and that genetic resources per se represent a value which can be subject to different types of obligations.[23] Assessing the benefits arising from genetic resources[24] would in

[18] Intersessional workshops aimed at improving understanding of the issues and clarifying key questions as an input to the work of the Working Group in accordance with the terms of reference annexed to General Assembly resolution 67/78 distributed 10 June 2013, UN Doc A/AC.276/6.

[19] Tessnow-Von Wysocki and Vadrot have provided a comprehensive overview and critical analysis of the academic debate: see Tessnow-von Wysocki and Vadrot, 'The Voice of Science on Marine Biodiversity Negotiations: A Systematic Literature Review' (2020) 7 *Frontiers in Marine Science*. David Leary has summarised the discussions on genetic resources in the preparatory committee of the BBNJ process: see Leary, 'Agreeing to Disagree on What We Have or Have Not Agreed On: The Current State of Play of the BBNJ Negotiations on the Status of Marine Genetic Resources in Areas Beyond National Jurisdiction' (2019) 99 *Marine Policy* 21. Even if such perspectives have not been at the centre of debate, ambitious attempts to investigate extra-legal perspectives have been presented, see eg Leary et al, 'Marine Genetic Resources: A Review of Scientific and Commercial Interest' (2009) 33 *Marine Policy* 183; Blasiak et al, 'Corporate Control and Global Governance of Marine Genetic Resources' (2018) 4 *Science Advances* 1; Oldham et al, *Valuing the Deep: Marine Genetic Resources in Areas Beyond National Jurisdiction* (Defra, 2014).

[20] Glowka (n 7).

[21] See also de Lucia (n 14); Leary, 'Agreeing to Disagree' (n 19).

[22] In a study based on semi-structured interviews of 24 people from five different stakeholder groups – the scientific research community, private sector, developing states, developed states and civil society – stakeholders preferred a light-touch governance approach to access, with notification before (and possibly also after) collection of MGR in situ. Mandatory non-monetary benefit sharing at the point of sampling was considered most appropriate, possibly with scope for voluntary monetary benefit sharing at the point of commercialisation. See Collins, Vanagt and Huys, 'Stakeholder Perspectives on Access and Benefit-Sharing for Areas Beyond National Jurisdiction' (2020) 7 *Frontiers in Marine Science*.

[23] In particular, many of the proposals on benefit sharing reflect this understanding. In spite of reminders from some delegations, such as the USA and Japan, that the realisation of monetary benefits from marine genetic resources are unpredictable and require lengthy processes, any developing states appear to consider monetary benefit-sharing schemes to be integral components of benefit-sharing regimes. See Morris-Sharma, 'BBNJ and MGRs: Practical Solutions for Benefit-Sharing' in Heidar (ed), *New Knowledge and Changing Circumstances in the Law of the Sea*, vol 92 (Brill, 2020).

[24] 'Benefits arising from activities with respect to genetic resources' is the terminology used in Art 14 of the BBNJ Agreement.

most cases require a complex analysis of value chains, where marine genetic resources may represent only a minor component. Unlike other marine economic resources, genetic resources are in most cases one of many input goods in biotechnological product development, which is primarily made up of technology and know-how. This intrinsic relation between biological resource and technology appears to have been largely disregarded in discussions.

Not only has the debate on marine genetic resources suffered from the limited role accorded to perspectives from beyond law; the legal arguments as well as the actors involved have also belonged to one specific regime of international law, that of the law of the sea. From the start of the discussion, it has predominantly involved law of the sea scholars. When the issue started to gain political attention and the UN General Assembly decided to convene a working group, it was decided in the yearly so-called omnibus resolution on the oceans and the law of the sea.[25] The law of the sea orientation was further reinforced in 2011 by the agreement on a common position by the EU and the G77/China to work towards the establishment of an intergovernmental negotiating process for a multilateral agreement under UNCLOS based on a 'Package Deal' including marine genetic resources that would 'address the conservation and sustainable use of marine biodiversity in areas beyond national jurisdiction, in particular, together and as a whole'.[26]

By packaging genetic resources with other issue areas, the debate chiefly came to involve ocean lawyers, despite obvious connections to issues beyond the marine domain, such as genetic technology and the central role of intellectual property rights in the biotechnological use of genetic resources. Traditionally, the law of the sea has primarily been concerned with activities carried out in the marine domain. When facing a new type of resource, this inclination to focus on activities in the sea and disregard other aspects was not questioned.[27] Accordingly, the ambition of the BBNJ process was not to encompass the use of genetic resources in a broad sense, but to extend, recycle and to the extent necessary develop the law of the sea. The process mandate thereby made states

[25] United Nations General Assembly Resolution 59/24, Oceans and the law of the sea, A/RES/59/24, 4 February 2005, para 73. The UNGA decision to convene the working group was preceded by a meeting in the Informal Consultative Process on Oceans and the Law of the Sea under the theme 'New sustainable uses of the oceans, including the conservation and management of the biological diversity of the seabed in areas beyond national jurisdiction', see 'Report on the Work of the United Nations Open-ended Informal Consultative Process on Oceans and the Law of the Sea at Its Fifth Meeting', letter dated 29 June 2004 from the Co-chairpersons of the Consultative Process addressed to the President of the General Assembly, A/59/122, 1 July 2004.

[26] The full list of issues in the package, which since 2011 has formed the basis for the negotiations, includes marine genetic resources, including questions on the sharing of benefits; measures such as area-based management tools, including marine protected areas; environmental impact assessments; capacity building; and the transfer of marine technology. See letter dated 15 May 2008 from the Co-chairpersons of the Ad Hoc Open-ended Informal Working Group to study issues relating to the conservation and sustainable use of marine biological diversity beyond areas of national jurisdiction addressed to the President of the General Assembly, UN Doc A/65/68, 2010.

[27] UNGA Resolution 59/24 (n 25) para 73.

as well as observers focus on exploring the extent to which existing rules also apply directly or mutatis mutandis to genetic resources.[28] From the start, this emphasis logically focused the discussion on internal law of the sea arguments and made participators approach this new issue by organising it within familiar structures.[29] The emphasis on the status of legal principles in the genetic resource debate can be understood not merely as the expression of different political interests, but as the result of the influence of semiotics of law or how legal argument rhetorically manages its relationship to external contexts.

III. THE ROLE OF OTHER REGIMES OF INTERNATIONAL LAW

Whereas much effort was spent on exploring connections to different parts of UNCLOS, there was less interest in building on the extensive work and regulation of genetic resources and biotechnology by treaties and institutions beyond the law of the sea. This is particularly apparent in relation to the extensive work and discussions within the World Trade Organization (WTO) on the trade aspects of biotechnology and the patentability of genetic resources. By providing the global rules for patent law, the WTO Agreement on Trade-Related Aspects of Intellectual Property Rights has far-reaching implications for biotechnological use of genetic resources.[30] Although states may declare plants and animals ineligible for patenting, microorganisms may not be excluded.[31] The rule does not provide for any exception in relation to marine genetic resources, and WTO members are thus bound to provide for patentability irrespective of how the rules in the new BBNJ treaty are formulated. Nevertheless, many states were reluctant to discuss intellectual property rights perspectives, considering such elements to fall outside of the remit of the BBNJ negotiations, and the proposed provision on intellectual property rights never made it into the final text.[32] From a practical perspective, it would appear more rational

[28] Up until the UNGA decided in 2011 to convene an intergovernmental conference to develop a legally binding new treaty, it was an open question if a new treaty was necessary or if existing law of the sea rules should be considered to apply also to genetic resources. United Nations General Assembly, International legally binding instrument under the United Nations Convention on the Law of the Sea on the conservation and sustainable use of marine biological diversity of areas beyond national jurisdiction A/72/249, 19 January 2018.

[29] Analysis of the impact of international legal discourse is often associated with critical legal studies, in particular with David Kennedy, who declared: 'I was curious to know whether one might explain the international legal order from the inside – as the fulfilment of public international law's self-image or as the consequence of its rhetorical framework rather than as a product of history, ideology and politics'. Kennedy, *International Legal Structures* (Nomos, 1987) 287.

[30] Agreement on Trade-Related Aspects of Intellectual Property Rights, 15 April 1994 (TRIPS); Marrakesh Agreement Establishing the World Trade Organization, Annex 1C, 1869 UNTS 299.

[31] See TRIPS, Art 27.

[32] The division between states on intellectual property rights during the negotiation is reflected in the 2020 draft text of the proposed Art 12, see article-by-article compilation of textual proposals for consideration at the fourth session dated 15 April 2020. See also Leary, 'Agreeing to Disagree' (n 19) and the discussion on intellectual property rights in World Maritime University, *Workshop and Side*

to consider such aspects, or to at least explore the connections to intellectual property rights. After all, patents represent a central output and indeed are the commercial motivation behind the interest in genetic resources. It appears particularly difficult to discuss benefit sharing from the use of genetic resources without considering the connections between genetic resources, patents and biotechnological products.

The precedence of and connections to the CBD and the Nagoya Protocol,[33] which provides detailed rules on access and benefit sharing of genetic resources within national jurisdictions, were considered to a higher degree than intellectual property rights. During the BBNJ process, states generally strived for terminological congruency with these treaties. The rules on access, benefit sharing and the clearing-house mechanism of the BBNJ Agreement, eg for monitoring access to and use of genetic resources, is modelled on the Nagoya Protocol.[34] Similarly, when rules on digital sequence information were finally introduced into the Agreement text during the last negotiation round, delegates were careful to avoid duplication in relation to the CBD rules.

But there were also limitations in the ability of modelling the rules in the BBNJ Agreement on the CBD and the Nagoya Protocol. The pre-existing rules on genetic resources were chiefly concerned with reaffirming the sovereign rights of states to genetic resources within their national jurisdiction. They provide little guidance on areas beyond national jurisdiction, which were excluded from the scope of the rules.[35] At the heart of the approach to access and benefit sharing under the Nagoya Protocol lie the requirements to obtain prior informed consent of the state that is the country of origin of the resource, and to share in a fair and equitable way the benefits arising from the utilisation of genetic resources, including subsequent applications and commercialisation.[36] This builds on a relationship between two states. The country where the genetic resource is being utilised must ensure that prior informed consent and mutually agreed terms have been established with the providing state.[37] This implies a contractual arrangement between two states, which cannot be emulated in areas beyond national jurisdiction, where there is no state providing the genetic resource.

Events Report: Biodiversity Beyond National Jurisdiction: Towards the Development of a Balanced, Effective and Universal International Agreement (2020).

[33] Nagoya Protocol on Access to Genetic Resources and the Fair and Equitable Sharing of Benefits Arising from their Utilization to the Convention on Biological Diversity, 3009 UNTS, 29 October 2010 (Nagoya Protocol).

[34] Marciniak, 'The Legal Status of Marine Genetic Resources in the Context of BBNJ Negotiations: Diverse Legal Regimes and Related Problems' in Heidar (n 23); Leary, 'Agreeing to Disagree' (n 19).

[35] See CBD, Arts 2, 4, 22.

[36] The country of origin is the country supplying genetic resources collected from in situ sources, see CBD, Art 2. In a marine context, the country of origin would be the coastal state. See further CBD, Arts 5.1, 6.1.

[37] CBD, Art 15; Salpin, 'The Law of the Sea: A Before and an After Nagoya?' in Morgera, Buck and Tsioumani (eds), *The 2010 Nagoya Protocol on Access and Benefit-Sharing in Perspective* (Brill, 2013).

To compensate for this lack of providing state, Article 12 of the BBNJ Agreement includes an obligation to provide for a long list of different types of information to the clearing-house mechanism both before and after the collection of genetic resources in areas beyond national jurisdiction. It is clear that the introduction of these requirements places an additional burden on researchers, who have hitherto been unrestricted by virtue of the freedom to conduct marine scientific research. It also raises practical difficulties. The new rules require the geotagging of samples, but the provenance of existing genetic resources in biobanks, collections and data is often difficult to ascertain. Yet the agreement applies also to resources collected before its entry into force unless states make explicit exceptions under Article 10.

Establishing the global institutional structure for controlling the use of genetic resources and curating collections of research findings also involves considerable bureaucracy and costs. The considerably more flexible model of the Nagoya Protocol has already been criticised for providing disincentives for biotechnological development.[38] Within national jurisdiction, as regulated by the Nagoya Protocol, conditions for accessing genetic resources reflect state sovereign rights to natural resources. In areas beyond national jurisdiction, where states lack sovereign rights, the motivation for imposing control elements rather connects to a fear that only those with advanced technology would harvest the resources of ocean commons, in line with the logic of CHM and the seabed regime.

IV. THE DIFFICULTY OF RECYCLING APPROACHES FOR TRADITIONAL MARINE RESOURCES

The recycling of pre-existing principles of the law of the sea would have been less problematic if genetic resources had been more like the resources for which these rules were created. The traditional approach of the law of the sea is to consider economic resources as generic commodities. Regularly, the same substance that has been extracted in bulk as raw material is subsequently consumed. Quality is regularly constant irrespective of where the resource has been extracted. Demand for traditional marine resources is therefore predominantly quantitative in nature.[39] Where extraction interests differ across occurrences of marine resources, these differences relate foremost to the costs associated with exploitation or logistics.[40] As a consequence of these elements, in combination with the supply constraint represented by limited

[38] See, eg Watanabe, 'The Nagoya Protocol: big Steps, New Problems' (2017) 67 *Bioscience*.

[39] Hallwood, *Economics of the Oceans: Rights, Rents and Resources* (Routledge, 2014); Posner and Sykes, 'Economic Foundations of the Law of the Sea' (2010) 104 *American Journal of International Law* 569.

[40] Most evidently, this is the case with offshore oil extraction.

natural supply, the law of the sea has mainly been concerned with establishing principles for allocating rights to physical access to marine resources between states.

The law of the sea thus provides for exclusive rights for coastal states to economic resources within its maritime zones. In the deep seabed of the Area and the high seas, CHM and high seas freedoms apply respectively.[41] For certain resources, such as straddling and highly migratory fish stocks, several states are considered to have legitimate interests, and UNCLOS thus provides for interested states to cooperate in dividing and allocating rights of exploitation.[42]

These conventional approaches to regulating access to marine resources are unfit to use as role models for regulating genetic resources in areas beyond national jurisdiction because human interest in genetic resources is fundamentally different from the interest in the fish, minerals, hydrocarbons and other economic resources considered during the development of UNCLOS. In general, quantitative aspects are largely irrelevant in the biotechnological use of genetic resources. Rather than collection in bulk, both commercial and scientific interests relate to qualitative elements, namely the function and genetic composition of bioactive properties in organisms. Almost all of the carefully selected genetic resource compounds which have been sampled in the marine environment are discarded during initial screening for useful properties. Other steps in biotechnological development, such as laboratory isolation and testing, take years and are highly selective.[43] It is often difficult to distinguish and assess to what extent biotechnological products are based on a natural genetic resource.[44] In bio-based pharmaceutical development generally, the role of natural genetic components varies considerably across cases.[45] Furthermore, natural compounds are commonly technologically modified, thus blurring the line between synthetic research and bioprospecting.[46] These elements make traditional law of the sea approaches difficult to apply.

In fisheries management, the principles of optimum utilisation, maximum sustainable yield, total allowable catch and quota systems have been developed to promote optimum utilisation, and to divide and allocate exclusive rights

[41] It should be noted that the high seas freedom of fisheries does not imply a lack of regulations, but merely the lack of sovereign or exclusive rights for individual states. For instance, UNCLOS provides that states should cooperate for the conservation and management of living resources in the high seas (Art 118). The mandate and regulations of regional fisheries management organisations in many cases also extend to high seas areas, see Agreement for the Implementation of the Provisions of the United Nations Convention on the Law of the Sea of 10 December 1982 relating to the Conservation and Management of Straddling Fish Stocks and Highly Migratory Fish Stocks, 4 August 1995, 2167 UNTS 3 (UN Fish Stocks Agreement) (United Nations 1997).

[42] See UNCLOS, Arts 63–64.

[43] Arnaud-Haond, 'Mind the Gap Between Biological Samples and Marine Genetic Resources in Areas Beyond National Jurisdiction: Lessons From Land' in Heidar (n 23).

[44] Oldham et al (n 19).

[45] Arnaud-Haond (n 43).

[46] Martins et al, 'Marketed Marine Natural Products in the Pharmaceutical and Cosmeceutical Industries: Tips for Success' (2014) 12 *Marine Drugs* 1066.

for harvested stocks.[47] These concepts, which form the basis for regulating access to living resources within national jurisdiction as well as in the high seas, would be difficult to extend to genetic resources, and not just because the demand for genetic resources is limited, unregular and unpredictable. Whereas it is already challenging to assess the status of a limited number of commercially exploited fish stocks, it would be virtually impossible to establish the same scientific basis for the myriad of species with potentially interesting genetic resources. Indeed, the lack of scientific knowledge of these organisms is often the reason for the interest. Limited previous human involvement and the small samples taken in deep-sea biodiversity hotspots, however, do not preclude detrimental environmental impacts. For endemic species, the impact of even a small sampling may be as detrimental as large-scale harvesting of more numerous species.[48] Fisheries management approaches to access regulation would be ill-suited to assessing or preventing such risks.

The disputed CHM principle and the deep-seabed regime would also be difficult to extend to genetic resources. Similar to systems for offshore hydrocarbon prospecting within national jurisdictions, the regime of the Area builds on the granting of exclusive exploration and exploitation licences for specific areas by a central authority. Some states have long proposed that the International Seabed Authority should have the same central role for genetic resources as it has for minerals.[49] This, however, would be difficult, not only because it is designed to coordinate mineral mining, but also because the rules would be difficult to apply to the sampling of living organisms. Geographically defined licence systems would also be impractical for genetic resources, where several different sampling expeditions targeting different sites or species could conduct sampling in the same area without interfering with one another.

Moreover, the distinction in the law of the sea between the water column and the seabed gives rise to additional complications. Although resources beyond national jurisdiction in both these marine dimensions fall under commons principles and preclude special rights for individual states, the legal principles of the seabed regime of the Area and the high seas rules for the water column are radically different. Contrary to the prohibition of appropriating resources in the Area, living resources can be freely exploited under the high seas freedoms provided that certain obligations are fulfilled, including the general principles of fisheries management, which apply mutatis mutandis to the high seas.[50]

[47] See in particular UNCLOS, Arts 61–62.

[48] Leary, 'Agreeing to Disagree' (n 10).

[49] Scovazzi, 'The Assumption That the United Nations Convention on the Law of the Sea Is the Legal Framework for All Activities Taking Place in the Sea' in Arico (ed), *Ocean Sustainability in the 21st Century* (Cambridge University Press, 2015) 241.

[50] The more detailed rules in the UN Fish Stocks Agreement thus apply also to the high seas, and the mandate of regional fisheries management organisations in many cases extend also to such areas.

The organisms that have attracted interest for their genetic resources are particularly difficult to place in this dichotomy of the seabed and the water column, since their behaviour transcends this distinction. Many are sessile or sedentary in one phase of their life cycle but mobile or pelagic in other phases.[51] It has thus been stressed that for any set of rules to be effective, it is necessary to include and apply the same set of rules to all genetic resources beyond national jurisdiction, irrespective of whether they are located on the seabed or in the water column.[52] Accordingly, Article 3 of the BBNJ Agreement makes no distinction between the Area and the high seas, but simply refers to areas beyond national jurisdiction as its scope of application. While this is rational from a practical perspective, it has some important implications: since the CHM principle has a central role in the new agreement, the scope of this seabed principle is effectively expanded to also encompass the water column.[53]

V. THE FOCUS ON PHYSICAL EXTRACTION

The predominant law of the sea perspective in the discussions on genetic resources thus effectively made pre-existing law of the sea principles the central reference point in the discussions and came to extend their scope of application. It also oriented the debate on the type of activities most familiar to the law of the sea: the physical extraction of natural resources in the marine domain. The law of the sea is traditionally little concerned with the use of marine resources once they are removed from the sea. The emphasis of the convention is on establishing the extent of exclusive and sovereign rights of states to extract resources in different marine areas as well as the conditions for such access, rather than how resources are used once they have been caught, mined or harvested.[54]

Accordingly, rather than fully considering how genetic resources are used, it was presumed that restricting and conditioning physical access in the natural environment is an effective way of regulating the use of genetic resources.[55] Although it was recognised early in the process that genetic resources could be accessed by means other than physical sampling, proposals in the

[51] Ramirez-Llodra et al, 'Deep, Diverse and Definitely Different: Unique Attributes of the World's Largest Ecosystem' (2010) 7 *Biogeosciences* 2851; Koslow, *The Silent Deep: The Diversity, Ecology and Conservation of the Deep Sea* (UNSW Press, 2007) 288.

[52] Mossop, 'Marine Genetic Resources and the Need for an Integrated Approach to the Seabed and the Water Column' in De Paiva Toledo and Tassin (eds), *Guide to the Navigation of Marine Biodiversity Beyond National Jurisdiction*, vol 8 (Editora D'Plácido, 2018) 554.

[53] In Art 7, 'the principle of the common heritage of humankind which is set out in the Convention' is cited as a principle to guide the parties in achieving the objectives of the agreement.

[54] Morgera and Kulovesi, *Research Handbook on International Law and Natural Resources* (Edward Elgar Publishing, 2016).

[55] De Santo et al, 'Stuck in the Middle With You (and Not Much Time Left): The Third Intergovernmental Conference on Biodiversity Beyond National Jurisdiction' (2020) 117 *Marine Policy*.

BBNJ negotiations have exclusively concerned physical in situ collection. Accordingly, Article 12 of the Agreement provides for different conditions on notification, permits and licences, including requirements for indicating geographical origin.

Regulating access to genetic resources in a manner similar to other marine resources, however, has some considerable shortcomings. In fisheries, whaling, drilling and mining, the process of turning the raw material of the marine resource into product essentially consists of refinement. Most of the final products also regularly consist of the physical marine resource itself, in terms of both value and physical representation. Since use of the product requires consumption of the marine resource itself, a continuous input flow of newly extracted marine resource is required. Much of the investment required for economic use of the resources also relates to the equipment and human resources associated with the extraction. Economic values can be increased by harvesting larger volumes. Indeed, for generic commodities, the value is more or less constant, depending on market fluctuations. It is thus not surprising that regulation of marine resources has focused on states' rights to and conditions for access. In the absence of such rules, there is not only a risk for competition and conflict between states; the resources may also become exhausted. Rules for access are thus of central relevance for enabling sustainable economic activity and preventing conflict.[56]

The human interest in genetic resources is fundamentally different by being exclusively qualitative in nature. Quantity is largely irrelevant. Where the function of a genetic resource retrieved in a natural sample may be of value to biotechnological development, such value cannot be multiplied by collecting more samples of the same type. Indeed, for biotechnological purposes, it is regularly sufficient to catch one individual organism containing a genetic resource to enable the sequencing of its genome and explore its properties. Once this process has been completed, there is in principle no need to sample the same species again.[57]

In bio-based pharmaceutical development, bioactive functions of organism samples are identified in laboratories by distinguishing relevant molecules or genetic sequences. Different procedures relating to refining or engineering of the relevant property may also involve considerable alteration, rendering it difficult to draw a sharp line between bio-based and purely artificial products.[58] The actual physical pharmaceutical product, once it has been developed after lengthy and costly procedures, including clinical trials, only in exceptional cases

[56] Allocation of exclusive rights to certain states, however, can also be regarded as enclosure or grabbing of global commons. See Ranganathan, 'Ocean Floor Grab: International Law and the Making of an Extractive Imaginary' (2019) 30 *European Journal of International Law* 573.

[57] Arico and Salpin, *Bioprospecting of Genetic Resources in the Deep Seabed: Scientific, Legal and Policy Aspects*, vol 20 (Institute of Advance Studies, 2005).

[58] Leary et al (n 19).

includes physical components from nature. In most cases, the bioactive property retrieved from nature merely functions as a model or source of inspiration.[59] Whereas the information from a genetic resource may be reproduced in an endless number of objects, the physical representation of the genetic resource in the final product is regularly non-existent.

The minimal need for physical natural material coupled with the limited part of the development operation conducted in the marine environment has important consequences for regulation. Firstly, the likelihood for physical resource-related constraints is small. Where there is competition, constraints are more likely to be represented by patent rights than a shortage of physical resource. The environmental risks associated with deep-sea sampling are also different from those associated with the extraction of other marine resources. The impact on individual species and ecosystems of genetic resource sampling has been deemed to be limited. The high prevalence of rare and sought-after properties in sensitive and endemic ecosystems may yet call for careful considerations of potential adverse impacts.[60] It has been considered that the types of potential impacts involved in sampling are better addressed by precautionary assessments than by systems of quotas, concessions or exclusive rights used in fisheries, mining or hydrocarbon exploitation.[61] This is not only because such access-based approaches have been unsuccessful in preventing the depletion of other natural resources.[62] They are also ill-suited to serve as the basis for regulating a resource where human interest is qualitative in nature, as opposed to traditional marine resources.

It was not until the last round of the BBNJ negotiations that delegates started exploring how the proposed obligations would apply to genetic resources originating in areas beyond national jurisdiction but accessed by means other than natural sampling. In the final days, agreement was reached on including digital sequence information (DSI) within the scope of the agreement. However, as a result of the limited time available for considering the difference between access to physical genetic resources and DSI, important differences were not fully considered. This includes the difficulty of upholding legal obligations for states in relation to DSI data, which regularly transcend borders and jurisdictions. The possibility of accessing genetic resources by means of DSI also

[59] Fattorusso, Gerwick and Taglialatela-Scafati, *Handbook of Marine Natural Products* (Springer, 2012).

[60] Warner, *Protecting the Oceans Beyond National Jurisdiction: Strengthening the International Law Framework* (Martinus Nijhoff, 2009); Leary, *International Law* (n 11).

[61] Hunt and Vincent, 'Scale and Sustainability of Marine Bioprospecting for Pharmaceuticals' (2006) 35 *Ambio* 57; Broggiato, 'Exploration and Exploitation of Marine Genetic Resources in Areas Beyond National Jurisdiction and Environmental Impact Assessment' (2013) 4 *European Journal of Risk Regulation* 247.

[62] Finley, *All the Fish in the Sea: Maximum Sustainable Yield and the Failure of Fisheries Management* (University of Chicago Press, 2011).

makes it even more difficult to assess the connection between genetic resource and commercial product, and what role the genetic resource has played in the final product among other input goods, including different operations throughout its development cycle.

VI. BIOBANKS, DATABASES AND DECREASED DEMAND FOR IN SITU ACCESS

The use of marine genetic resources does not require repeated extraction or large quantities, and the demand for physical resource is thus limited. But does it even require limited natural sampling? The increased coupling of two factors may render in situ access altogether unnecessary. Firstly, current trends and developments in biotechnology are greatly facilitating access to genetic resources that have already been brought ashore. Secondly, the lines between scientific research and commercial development are becoming increasingly blurred.

Whereas the retrieval of genetic samples from deep-sea habitats involves high costs and requires advanced technology, it is considerably cheaper to access genetic resources in biobanks, databases and other collections. Partly as the result of investments to promote biotechnological development, collections of marine genetic resources have increased in recent years and become more accessible. Conditions for using genetic information in such repositories as the basis for product development are in most cases limited. Information is often exchanged on an open-access basis.[63] As a result, costly marine expeditions are becoming necessary only in exceptional cases.

Even if such facilitated access has accelerated, basing biotechnological development on genetic resources in collections is not new. The rapid development of genetic technology in the 1990s not only led to a search for bioactive properties in the wild. In parallel, library collections set up during centuries of botanical and zoological research started to be used for genetic exploration. The emphasis in legal discussions on collection in the wild largely overlooked this development. Ascertaining the legal status of genetic resources in collections is often difficult. Sovereign claims could be made both by the state owning or hosting the collection and by the state where the genetic material originates. The aim of preventing such conflicts was a central motivation for the negotiation of the Nagoya Protocol. The Protocol established rules for safeguarding the sovereign rights and ensuring fair compensation for the state of origin of genetic resources. However, it provided little guidance for cases in which information on the origin is uncertain or where the resource may have originated

[63] OECD, *Marine Biotechnology Definitions, Infrastructures and Directions for Innovation* (OECD Science, Technology and Innovation Policy Papers, 2017); Oldham et al (n 19).

beyond national jurisdiction.[64] Even where there are geographical indications as to the origin of genetic resources, such information is often unspecific. This is particularly problematic for marine genetic resources, where references to a sea area could entail maritime areas of several different states, as well as areas beyond national jurisdiction. The migration and distribution of marine species also render it difficult to distinguish jurisdictional origin based on known occurrence of species.[65] Although the BBNJ Agreement provides for the geotagging of samples, according to Article 10, states parties are able to exempt resources collected before the BBNJ Agreement enters into force. By accessing genetic information in collections where the hosting state has made such an exemption, there are thus extensive possibilities for circumventing burdensome obligations under the Agreement, such as that of the fair and equitable sharing of benefits provided by Article 14. The possibilities of accessing genetic information within the jurisdiction of non-parties will represent an even greater challenge to the system set up by the Agreement.

The possibility of basing biotechnological development on genetic resource information without having to conduct physical sampling thus effectively provides a loophole which risks rendering the operative obligations of the BBNJ Agreement less relevant. Given these factors, it appears unfortunate that so little effort in the genetic resource discussion has been made to explore the implications of the facilitated access to genetic resources already brought ashore.

VII. ADDRESSING THE SHORTCOMINGS OF THE NEW RULES

The law of the sea context of the negotiation of new rules on marine genetic resources in areas beyond national jurisdiction made the discussion focus on principal legal arguments and physical access to resources. The practical elements of biotechnological development and application drew less interest. The relevance of other modes of access were not considered until the end of the negotiation, when DSI was finally included in the scope of the treaty. But many legal implications of the ability to access genetic resources in a multitude of ways, without accessing physical samples in the marine environment, remain to be considered. The practical role of genetic resources in biotechnological development raises substantial issues for the new rules. Most evidently, this includes the difficulty of distinguishing the degree to which the benefits of biotechnological products depend on the use of genetic resources. The role of laboratory processes, the combination of different components

[64] Buck and Hamilton, 'The Nagoya Protocol on Access to Genetic Resources and the Fair and Equitable Sharing of Benefits Arising From Their Utilization to the Convention on Biological Diversity' (2011) 20 *RECIEL* 47; Morgera et al (n 37).

[65] Oldham et al (n 19).

and the increasing blurring of bio-based and synthetic development are likely to render such assessments difficult. This will make it hard to implement central elements of the BBNJ Agreement, such as assessing the extent to which monetary benefits are derived from the utilisation of genetic resources, as is called for by Article 14.5. In the period leading up to the entry into force of the Agreement, states and observers involved must better consider how genetic resources are used in biotechnological development and address the challenges of practically applying the new rules.

4

Protecting the Environment in Areas Beyond National Jurisdiction Through International Trade Law: Challenges and Reflections

ALEKE STÖFEN-O'BRIEN

I. INTRODUCTION

AREAS BEYOND NATIONAL jurisdiction (ABNJ) are increasingly a central focus of the international community as current efforts are underway to negotiate an international legally binding agreement for the biodiversity of ABNJ.[1] This chapter does not focus on the status of the negotiations, but rather explores a topic which has not been dealt with at depth in the literature, namely the interrelationship between trade law, the law of the sea and international environmental law at the nexus of ABNJ. The chapter explores how these regimes may work together to develop suitable measures for the protection and conservation of the marine environment as a whole and in particular focusing on ABNJ. One of the most challenging tasks of the international community is to balance the interests of use of the marine resources against their conservation and preservation. The conflict of interest is most evident in relation to the high seas, where no state exercises territorial jurisdiction or exclusive rights and therefore the law as such is less well equipped to handle these kinds of issues. The law of the sea provides obligations for states in the high seas, among others relating to the protection of the marine environment. But compared to other maritime areas, states can carry out activities there with relatively few restrictions, in line with the freedom of the high seas. The economic interest and the ecological dilemma of ABNJ can be best illustrated by the essay 'The Tragedy of the Commons', published by the American

[1] Freestone, 'The UN Process to Develop an International Legally Binding Instrument Under the 1982 Law of the Sea Convention: Issues and Challenges' in Freestone (ed), *Conserving Biodiversity in Areas Beyond National Jurisdiction* (Brill Nijhoff, 2019) 3–5.

economist and microbiologist Garret Hardin in 1968.[2] Drawing on the example of an openly accessible pasture, Hardin develops thought experiments, which he also applies to the high seas, and arrives at an understanding that it is not possible to efficiently use freely accessible yet limited resources.[3] Increasingly, the international community has initiated steps to protect and conserve these ABNJ. However, this chapter argues that such efforts must not remain within a specific silo but must consider the plethora of fora which may contribute to the preservation of the marine environment. This includes, among others, the nexus of the protection of the marine environment (in ABNJ) and trade law. Admittedly, this nexus is a very broad topic and may be substantially developed and analysed from different angles. However, this approach has scarcely been addressed in the literature, except for specific sectoral questions on fisheries, marine genetic resources and intellectual property.[4] This chapter provides an overview of the main questions and outlines the complexity of regulating this nexus. In doing so, it focuses on two issues: natural living resources and pollution. While it can be argued that certain aspects have been advanced in some regimes, mainly that of natural living resources under the World Trade Organization (WTO) regime, other aspects have not (yet) been considered,[5] although current work at the WTO might suggest that some contextual factors have changed.[6]

The UN 2030 Sustainable Development Agenda (Agenda 2030) exercises something of a guiding function in relation to the (marine) environment and trade nexus in global policy. The role of trade has been identified in the framework of Agenda 2030 as a cost-effective and efficient 'means of implementation' for the entire Agenda.[7] This paradigm therefore can be seen as forming an umbrella framework which encompasses other UN Sustainable Development Goals (SDGs). Applied to the two issues addressed in this chapter, two SDGs are particularly important: SDG 12, on sustainable production and consumption,

[2] Hardin, 'The Tragedy of the Commons' (1968) 162 *Science* 1243. In his thoughts, Hardin draws on the work of William Forster Lloyd on population growth in 'Two Lectures on the Checks to Population' (1833).

[3] Hardin (n 2) 1243. Hardin summarises: 'Ruin is the destination toward which all men rush, each pursuing his own best interest in a society that believes in the freedom of the commons. Freedom in a commons brings ruin to all.'

[4] Chiarolla, 'Intellectual Property Rights and Benefit Sharing From Marine Genetic Resources in Areas Beyond National Jurisdiction: Current Discussions and Regulatory Options' (2014) 4(3) *Queen Mary Journal of Intellectual Property* 171; Gorina-Ysern, 'Marine Scientific Research Activities as the Legal Basis for Intellectual Property Claims?' (1998) 22 *Marine Policy* 337, 357; Anders, 'Principles for Fisheries Management in Areas Beyond National Jurisdiction: The Essential Role of Incentive-Based Approaches' [2018] *SSRN Electronic Journal*.

[5] By way of example, the OECD focuses on four central areas: trade, climate change and renewable energy; trade and biodiversity; trade and resource efficient circular economy; and digitalisation, trade and the environment.

[6] By way of example, see the newly adopted WTO Agreement on Fisheries Subsidies in 2022, www.wto.org/english/tratop_e/rulesneg_e/fish_e/fish_e.htm.

[7] UN-DESA, 'Sustainable Development Goal 17' (United Nations, 2021) https://sdgs.un.org/goals/goal17.

and SDG 14, on life below water. Sustainable production and consumption is at the core of Agenda 2030. SDG 12 focuses explicitly on the need for a transition to more sustainable consumption and production patterns, and reflects a long history of diplomatic efforts to achieve this since the 1992 Rio Summit. Furthermore, SDG 14.6 is applicable to the subject matter of this chapter as it addresses harmful fisheries subsidies, for which trade law plays a particularly important role in the law of the sea and trade nexus.

II. TRADE AND IMPACTS ON THE MARINE ENVIRONMENT IN ABNJ

There is no generally accepted definition of the term 'marine environment' under the law of the sea. During the negotiations to develop the UN Convention on the Law of the Sea (UNCLOS),[8] states discussed the issue[9] but did not adopt a definition. In the end, the negotiators agreed that the marine environment should be considered to include marine life.[10] Read in conjunction with Part XII of UNCLOS, however, it becomes evident that 'marine environment' according to UNCLOS entails more than marine life.[11] Article 192 UNCLOS sets out the general obligation 'to protect and preserve the marine environment' instead of focusing on specific aspects of the ecosystem or specific risk assessments in the regime. Therefore, UNCLOS assumes a very broad understanding of what constitutes the marine environment.

Moreover, in this discussion, the concepts of blue economy and sustainable ocean economy are particularly relevant. Whereas there are several conceptual ambiguities around these concepts,[12] which are at times used as buzzwords, the Organisation for Economic Co-operation and Development (OECD) defines the ocean economy 'as the sum of the economic activities of ocean-based industries, together with the assets, goods and services provided by marine ecosystems,

[8] United Nations Convention on the Law of the Sea, Montego Bay, 10 December 1982, 1833 UNTS 3.

[9] See the Maltese proposition in Malta: draft articles for the preservation of the marine environment (including pollution), UN Doc A/AC.138/SC.III/L.33, 16 March 1972, ILM 12 (1973) 583. It outlines that 'the marine environment comprises the surface of the sea, the air space above, the water column and the sea-bed beyond the high-tide mark including the biosystem therein or dependent thereon'.

[10] Reports to the plenary by the Chairman of the Third Committee, Results of the negotiations, on Part XII, UN Doc A/CONF.62/RCNG/1, extract from the Official Records of the United Nations Conference on the Law of the Sea, vol X (1978) 13, 96 (97).

[11] See UNCLOS, Art 194(5), 'fragile ecosystems'.

[12] 'Blue economy' is not used equally across different jurisdictions. By way of example, the United Nations Economic Commission for Africa's definition of blue economy includes oceans as well as lakes, rivers and other bodies of water. See https://archive.uneca.org/publications/blue-economy. For an in-depth analysis, see Voyer et al, 'Shades of Blue: What Do Competing Interpretations of the Blue Economy Mean for Oceans Governance?' (2018) 20 *Journal of Environmental Policy and Planning* 595. The analysis developed four lenses that were applied to the interpretation of the blue economy: (i) Oceans as Capital; (ii) Ocean as Livelihoods; (iii) Oceans as Good Business; and (iv) Ocean as Driver of Innovation.

and recognizes the interdependency of those two pillars'.[13] Understanding and framing trade and blue economy aspects of the management of the marine environment in ABNJ may also be stifled by the limited consideration given to the environment and trade nexus at the interface of ABNJ in relevant assessments, such as the Second World Ocean Assessment.[14]

A. A Hesitant Attempt to Understand Impacts of Trade on the Marine Environment of ABNJ

Different approaches for measuring and assessing the direct and indirect environmental effects of trade may be applied. Particularly with regard to pollution, be it chemical or plastic pollution, the measurement of direct or indirect impacts particularly in ABNJ is very challenging as the impacts may not yet be known or quantified for ABNJ. The impact of trade on the marine environment can be preliminarily divided into three non-exhaustive categories: (i) pollution effects; (ii) resource effects; and (iii) biodiversity effects.[15] Whereas these three approaches appear seemingly oversimplified, they may structure and provide an indication as to how trade and challenges of marine environmental protection of ABNJ may be approached. Pollution effects cover the increase or decrease in the impacts of pollution in environmental media during the life cycle of products or services.[16] These pollution effects may emanate from direct impacts from shipping, illegal, unreported and unregulated fishing (IUU fishing),[17] overfishing,[18] deep-seabed mining and dumping, etc. Resource effects refer in particular to the increased use of natural resources in the life cycle of products or services, such as raw materials, living natural resources, biodiversity and marine genetic resources.[19] Biodiversity effects are those which

[13] OECD, *The Ocean Economy in 2030* (OECD Publishing, 2016).

[14] United Nations, *World Ocean Assessment II* (United Nations, 2021) esp 441–65, www.un.org/regularprocess/sites/www.un.org.regularprocess/files/2011859-e-woa-ii-vol-ii.pdf-.

[15] This distinction is derived from Altmann, *Ansatzpunkte für eine stärkere Berücksichtigung von Umweltaspekten in regionalen und interregionalen Freihandelsabkommen* (UBA Berichte 10, 2002) 42ff; Zengerling, *Stärkung von Klimaschutz und Entwicklung durch internationales Handelsrecht* (WBGU, 2020).

[16] Zengerling (n 15) 6.

[17] Illegal, unreported and unregulated (IUU) fishing is defined broadly to include fishing and fishing-related activities that violate national, regional and international laws in relation to fisheries utilisation, conservation and reporting; Food and Agricultural Organization (FAO) International Plan of Action to Prevent, Deter and Eliminate Illegal, Unreported and Unregulated Fishing (IPOA-IUU), adopted 23 June 2001, para 3.

[18] Sumaila et al, 'WTO Must Ban Harmful Fisheries Subsidies' (2021) 374(6567) *Science* 544.

[19] Zengerling (n 15) 6; Warner, 'Oceans of Opportunity and Challenge: Towards a Stronger Governance Framework for Conservation and Sustainable Use of Biodiversity in Marine Areas Beyond National Jurisdiction' (2018) 3 *Asia-Pacific Journal of Ocean Law and Policy* 157; Royal Society, 'Future Ocean Resources: Metal-Rich Minerals and Genetics – Evidence Back' (2017) https://royalsociety.org/~/media/policy/projects/future-oceans-resources/future-of-oceans-evidence-pack.pdf; Glowka, 'The Deepest of Ironies: Genetic Resources, Marine Scientific Research, and the

may impact biodiversity in the high seas, including highly migratory species. The UN Convention on Biological Diversity (CBD)[20] defines biological diversity as 'the variability among living organisms from all sources including, inter alia, … marine and other aquatic ecosystems and the ecological complexes of which they are part; this includes diversity within species, between species and of ecosystems'.[21]

In a study on the environmental effects of the North American Free Trade Agreement, Grossmann and Krueger identified three mechanisms through which trade agreements indirectly affect the environment.[22] The environmental impacts of trade may be structured according to the effects of scale, composition and technique.[23] According to the 'scale effect', trade liberalisation may lead to an increase in trade flows, and without appropriate protective measures this is accompanied by rising transport emissions, higher resource exploitation and pollution. A correlation exists between increasing trade and rising greenhouse gas emissions.[24] The 'composition effect' describes how trade agreements may lead to sectoral specialisation whereby countries specialise in activities in which they have a competitive advantage.[25] Whether such specialisation affects the environment in a negative or positive way depends on the (marine) environmental activities and industries, and their corresponding impacts on the structure of the national economy.[26] An increase in environmentally friendly products and services in the economy in question may be considered as positive. The relationships between these factors have been explored in the sustainability impact assessments that the EU has conducted for regional free trade agreements.[27] These studies also include forecasting corresponding composition effects.

Finally, the 'technique effect' states that trade agreements are associated with technology transfer.[28] The type of technology supported may also impact

Area' (1996) 12.1 *Ocean Yearbookook Online* 154; Correa, 'Access to and Benefit Sharing of Marine Genetic Resources Beyond National Jurisdiction: Developing a New Legally Binding Instrument' (South Centre, 2017).

[20] Convention on Biological Diversity, Rio de Janeiro, 5 June 1992, 1760 UNTS 79 (CBD).

[21] ibid Art 2.

[22] Grossman and Krueger, 'Environmental Impacts of a North American Free Trade Agreement' (National Bureau of Economic Research, 1991) NBER Working Papers 3914, 3ff.

[23] ibid 3ff; Zengerling (n 15) 7.

[24] World Resources Institute/Climate Watch, 'Historical GHG Emissions', www.climatewatchdata.org/ghg-emissions.

[25] Cole and Rayner, 'The Uruguay Round and Air Pollution: Estimating the Composition, Scale and Technique Effects of Trade Liberalization' (2000) 9 *Journal of International Trade & Economic Development* 339, 354.

[26] Zengerling (n 15) 2.

[27] ibid 2; European Commission, 'Sustainability Impact Assessment', https://ec.europa.eu/trade/policy/policy-making/analysis/policy-evaluation/sustainability-impact-assessments/. The impacts on the high seas from shipping and pollution have also been included in some of the SIA issued by the European Commission.

[28] Zengerling (n 15) 2; Fischer-Kowalski et al, *Decoupling Natural Resource Use and Environmental Impacts from Economic Growth* (UNEP/International Resource Panel, 2011) 67ff, http://wedocs.

(marine) environmental protection and conservation.[29] This may be particularly important for pollution in the marine environment from noise, light and/or chemicals, among other things.

The challenge with regard to ABNJ and the determination of composition effects, technique effects and scale effects is that there is very little knowledge available on the extraterritorial impacts of trade activities in ABNJ.

The United Nations Conference on Trade and Development (UNCTAD)'s report on Advancing the Potential of Sustainable Ocean-Based Economies: Trade Trends, Market Drivers and Market Assessment[30] develops a Sustainable Oceans Economic Classification (SOEC), which 'provides a comprehensive mapping of all industries which are part of the marine environment'.[31] In doing so, the SOEC only focuses on industries which are considered to be a lower risk to the marine environment and thereby excludes any industries with a high risk of environmental harm.[32] Coincidentally, the SOEC thereby potentially excludes any activities taking place in ABNJ insofar as

> industries with high risk of environmental harm, not included in the classification, can be grouped as follows: offshore oil and gas; deep and ultra-deep water oil and gas; marine and seabed mining; and support activities for oil and gas operations.[33]

Shipping in the high seas is only mentioned in passing in the context of pollution as a market driver in the report. This is only one example of many in which trade or blue economy aspects of ABNJ are excluded from analysis or classification.[34] Admittedly, one has to identify the location where the impacts of trade activities may apply and whether this is included in any measures. First, there are certain activities which are taking place in ABNJ which can be associated with a country. This relates, among others, to the jurisdiction over entities engaged in trade-related activities and pollution, in which flag state jurisdiction may be linked to the (detrimental) environmental impact.

On the other hand, so-called relocation problems may undermine environmental protection.[35] A distinction can be made here between two overlapping perspectives: (i) the relocation of production and thus of environmental impacts; and (ii) the spatial separation of consumption and production and the

unep.org/bitstream/handle/20.500.11822/9816/Decoupling_FReport_EN.pdf?sequence=1&isAllowed=y.

[29] Zengerling (n 15) 2.

[30] UNCTAD, 'Advancing the Potential of Sustainable Ocean-Based Economies: Trade Trends, Market Drivers and Market Assessment' (2021) UNCTAD/DITC/TED/INF/2021/2.

[31] ibid 1.

[32] ibid 6.

[33] UNCTAD, 'WTO Negotiations on Environmental Goods and Services: A Potential Contribution to the Millennium Development Goals' (2009) UNCTAD/DITC/TED/2008/4.

[34] See the assessment of areas beyond national jurisdiction of the Second World Ocean Assessment which did not indicate any trade-related information: UN, Regular Process, Second World Ocean Assessment.

[35] Frankel, 'Environmental Effects of International Trade' (2009) Expert Report No 31 to Sweden's Globalisation Council.

related impacts embodied in trade.[36] Concerns are being raised that companies can circumvent stricter national environmental regulations through relocation to less regulated third countries. This may also evoke the potential role of regional or national policies relating to environmental impacts of trade policies, such as subsidies.[37] Harmful fisheries subsidies, by way of example, are considered as 'government payments that incentivize overcapacity and lead to over-fishing', yet they continue 'to be implemented and used to support national fishing fleets'.[38] This reconfirms that these subsidies may be seen as a global challenge rather than a national issue. For activities in ABNJ, the issue of the free-rider problem in such a collective arrangement in particular needs to be addressed, and it is argued that the law of the sea regime may be particularly relevant for setting standards in this context. This will be developed further in section V.

B. UNCLOS and Trade Measures Linked to Activities in ABNJ

Historically, the various international legal regimes, such as international trade law, international environmental law and human rights law, developed in isolation from each other. A legal instrument that integrates the different rationalities and interests of the sub-areas of law and ensures an appropriate balance, as is the task of national constitutions, is lacking at the level of international law. UNCLOS has developed a complex set of rights and obligations for member states. It follows a framework character which allows for an evolutionary interpretation of its rules and obligations over time.[39] Overall, the scope of UNCLOS was aimed to be as comprehensive as possible and universal in its participation.[40]

ABNJ include the high seas (Part VII of UNCLOS) as well the Area (Part XI).[41] According to Part VII, states enjoy the freedom of the high seas, as stipulated in Article 87. Accordingly, states may pursue a range of activities, some of which are also relevant to trade aspects, such as freedom of navigation, freedom to lay cables and pipelines, freedom of fishing and freedom of scientific research. These rights

[36] Peters and Hertwich, 'Structural Analysis of International Trade: Environmental Impacts of Norway' (2006) 18(2) *Economic Systems Research*.

[37] Sumaila et al (n 18).

[38] Sumaila et al, 'Updated Estimates and Analysis of Global Fisheries Subsidies' (2019) 109 *Marine Policy* 103695.

[39] Evans, 'The Law of the Sea' in Evans (ed), *International Law*, 4th edn (Oxford University Press, 2014) 651, 653.

[40] Boyle, 'Further Development of the 1982 Convention on the Law of the Sea: Mechanisms for Change' in Freestone, Barnes and Ong (eds), *The Law of the Sea: Progress and Prospects* (Oxford University Press, 2006) 40.

[41] This chapter will not dive any further into the development of the different jurisdictional zones established by UNCLOS. Instead, some of the most central provisions as they relate to trade and corresponding obligations are presented.

'shall be exercised by all States with due regard for the interests of other States in their exercise of these freedom of the high seas', as well as with due to regard to other rights under UNCLOS with respect to the Area.[42] According to Article 89, no state may 'appropriate' any part of the high seas. On the high seas, the flag state has a particular duty to exercise its jurisdiction and control over ships flying its flag.[43] While the flag state exercises jurisdiction over the ship, the latter does not constitute a 'floating territory'.[44] Flag sovereignty is an independent form of exercising state sovereignty, which is neither a subcategory of personal sovereignty nor a component of the flag state's territorial sovereignty. States are also able to enforce obligations relating to the high seas in their own ports through the port state regime established by UNCLOS, under which port states may assume a regulatory and enforcement role for foreign-flagged vessels for effects beyond the port or even in ABNJ.[45] Among others, this could include, by way of example, providing access to foreign vessels in their own port based on their conduct in the high seas, therefore potentially impacting trade flows.[46]

With regard to biodiversity and conservation of living resources, according to Article 116 UNCLOS, states have the right to fish in the high seas subject to treaty obligations and rights and duties as well as interests of the coastal state. This right is not without limitations, as is evidenced by other UNCLOS obligations, guidance for states and cases.[47] Centrally, Article 117 outlines that states are under the duty to adopt measures for the conservation of the living resources of the high seas. Notably, Article 119 provides that, in determining conservation measures for the living resources in high seas, states shall take account of 'generally recommended international minimum standards, whether sub regional, regional or global'. The reliance on external rules is in line with the framework character, however, and has been subject to extensive legal scholarship, wherein 'generally recommended' is different from 'generally accepted', as is used in Article 211(2) UNCLOS. Therefore, Article 119

[42] UNCLOS, Art 87(2).

[43] ibid Art 94.

[44] Colombos, *The International Law of the Sea* (Longmans, Green & Co, 1967) 6. Similar, Lagoni, 'Merchant Ships' (Oxford Public International Law, 2011) http://opil.ouplaw.com/view/10.1093/law:epil/9780199231690/law-9780199231690-e1197.

[45] For discussions on the challenges associated with port state control, see Kopela, 'Port-State Jurisdiction, Extraterritoriality, and the Protection of Global Commons' (2016) 47 *Ocean Development and International Law* 89; Ryngaert and Ringbom, 'Introduction: Port State Jurisdiction: Challenges and Potential' (2016) 31 *International Journal of Marine and Coastal Law* 379.

[46] This may be applicable in the case that no positive right of access is stipulated by another treaty, such as the 1923 Convention and Statute on the International Regime of Maritime Ports, Geneva, 9 December 1923, 58 League of Nations Treaty Series 285. The Panel and Appellate Body of the WTO was called on two cases in which unilaterally imposed rules that have the effect of denying access to ports were seen as being in contradiction with WTO law. However, both cases were settled before a decision was reached. For a further overview, see www.wto.org/english/tratop_e/dispu_e/dispu_subjects_index_e.htm.

[47] See the FAO, *Code of Conduct for Responsible Fisheries* (1995); FAO, *International Guidelines for the Management of Deep-Sea Fisheries in the High Seas* (2009). See also WTO, 'Chile Measures Affecting the Transit and Importance of Swordfish' (WT/DS193/3).

'still leaves open the possibility for States to derogate from such standards where they are not bound by positive treaty obligations'.[48] Also, the obligation to conserve and manage marine mammals of Article 65 UNCLOS also applies to the high seas.[49]

In case of incompatibility of (unilateral) national measures based on activities in ABNJ with trade law, reliance on standard-setting processes through competent international organisations or conferences may ameliorate the situation.

Under UNCLOS, states may take measures which are not regulated in UNCLOS, such as trade-related measures, if these are recognised in other areas of international law.[50]

C. Trade within the Agreement on Biodiversity Beyond National Jurisdiction

The international community has been discussing the necessity and importance of preserving the biodiversity of ABNJ. In 2015, the United Nations General Assembly adopted a decision to commence negotiations on an international legally binding instrument under UNCLOS addressing the conservation and sustainable use of marine biological diversity of ABNJ (the BBNJ Agreement[51]). The established preparatory committee's (PrepCom) aim is to develop a series of recommendations for the United Nations General Assembly on specific elements of such a Draft BBNJ Agreement. The terms of reference of this PrepCom were fairly narrow in that the conservation and sustainable use of marine biological diversity of ABNJ, marine genetic resources, area-based management tools, environmental impact assessments, capacity building and transfer of marine technology were to be addressed. As noted above, aspects of trade are cross-thematic, and may span and be relevant for several aspects of these elements. Most notably, this may relate to marine scientific research and marine genetic resources. However, the outlined text and discussions of the Intergovernmental Conference (IC) on Marine Biodiversity of Areas Beyond National Jurisdiction suggest that the discussions have to a certain degree been conducted in isolation from institutions and aspects pertaining to non-law of the sea dimensions of marine resources, including trade. In 2019, the President of the IC published the revised draft text of an agreement under UNCLOS on the conservation and sustainable use of marine biological diversity of ABNJ

[48] Rayfuse, 'Art 119 UNCLOS' in Proelss (ed), *The United Nations Convention on the Law of the Sea: A Commentary* (Beck/Hart Publishing, 2017).

[49] UNCLOS, Art 120 in conjunction with Art 65.

[50] See UNCLOS, Art 311 on the relation to other conventions and international agreements as well as Preamble, para 8.

[51] Agreement under the United Nations Convention on the Law of the Sea on the Conservation and Sustainable Use of Marine Biological Diversity of Areas beyond National Jurisdiction (adopted 19 June 2023) www.un.org/bbnj/.

(2019 Draft BBNJ Agreement).[52] The 2019 Draft BBNJ Agreement indeed made reference to trade in Article 12 on intellectual property, as well as within the context of the polluter pays principle.[53]

According to the Draft BBNJ Agreement published in 2022 (2022 Draft BBNJ Agreement),

> the objective of this Agreement is to ensure the conservation and sustainable use of marine biological diversity of areas beyond national jurisdiction, for the present and in the long term, through effective implementation of the relevant provisions of the Convention and further international cooperation and coordination.[54]

Most notably with regard to issues relating to regime interactions, Article 4 of the 2022 Draft BBNJ Agreement states that:

> 3. This Agreement shall be interpreted and applied in a manner that [respects the competences of and] does not undermine [the effectiveness of] relevant legal instruments and frameworks and relevant global, regional, subregional and sectoral bodies and that promotes coherence and coordination with those instruments, frameworks and bodies.[55]

The only section in which the draft text makes reference to trade is Article 12 in the context of intellectual property rights; the reference to trade in the context of the polluter pays principle was deleted during negotiations.

Textual proposals submitted at an early stage in the negotiations by delegations in 2020[56] reflected the diverging opinion of delegates towards the inclusion of intellectual property rights, patents and trade. This became even more evident by the textual submissions by delegations for consideration in the fifth session of the IC on an international legally binding instrument on BBNJ in 2022.[57] The two applicable submissions with regard to trade were

[52] Intergovernmental Conference on Marine Biodiversity of Areas Beyond National Jurisdiction, Draft text of an agreement under the United Nations Convention on the Law of the Sea on the conservation and sustainable use of marine biological diversity of areas beyond national jurisdiction, A/CONF.232/2019/6, 17 May 2019.

[53] President's aid to discussions for IGC 1 A/CONF.232/2018/3 and Aid to Negotiations for IGC 2 A/CONF. 232/2019/1.

[54] 2022 Draft BBNJ Agreement, Art 2. See also Intergovernmental conference on an international legally binding instrument under the United Nations Convention on the Law of the Sea on the conservation and sustainable use of marine biological diversity of areas beyond national jurisdiction, fifth session, New York (15–26 August 2022); Further revised draft text of an agreement under the United Nations Convention on the Law of the Sea on the conservation and sustainable use of marine biological diversity of areas beyond national jurisdiction, Note by the President, A/CONF.232/2022/5.

[55] The brackets are included so as to reflect any disagreement.

[56] Law of the Sea on the conservation and sustainable use of marine biological diversity of areas beyond national jurisdiction (the Conference) in response to the invitation by the President of the Conference in her Note of 18 November 2019, A/CONF.232/2020/3.

[57] Intergovernmental conference on an international legally binding instrument under the United Nations Convention on the Law of the Sea on the conservation and sustainable use of marine biological diversity of areas beyond national jurisdiction, fifth session, New York (15–26 August 2022),

in relation to intellectual property rights and the potential reference to the inclusion of the WTO, by way of example.[58]

Whereas no further detailed discussion about this particular question in the context of the IC is envisaged in this chapter, it is important to note 'the extent to which the international legally binding instrument can and should impose obligations on states to do this to ensure that benefit sharing can come about'.[59] This may also relate to future challenges in the regime interactions between UNCLOS and WTO law.

III. MARINE ENVIRONMENT AND ABNJ CONSIDERATIONS IN MULTILATERAL ENVIRONMENTAL AGREEMENTS AND AT THE TRADE NEXUS

Beyond UNCLOS, there are also several instruments which deal in a more or less sectoral manner with aspects of trade as they relate to the two identified themes above. Admittedly, for some activities and industries in the high seas, it is very difficult to delineate between different activities. By way of example, fisheries may impact natural living resources directly, eg in the form of so-called IUU fisheries, but also as a source of marine pollution. It may be remarked that all of these instruments are applicable to activities taking place in the high seas as well as, as the case may be, through the regulation of activities under the jurisdiction of a state which may impact the marine environment of the ABNJ through transboundary movements.

With regard to pollution, the International Maritime Organization (IMO) is the responsible organisation relating to shipping and dumping, and also certain activities within the fisheries sector. Other instruments cover aspects relating to (i) discharges and emission standards, (ii) construction, equipment and design, (iii) liability and compensation, (iv) preparedness standards and (v) navigation standards. Each flag state is responsible for ensuring that the provisions of the instruments it has ratified are adhered to by the vessels flying its flag, also on the high seas.

Marine living resources are governed mainly by the FAO and regional fisheries management organisations (RFMOs), which have adopted specific sectoral

textual proposals submitted by delegations by 25 July 2022, for consideration at the fifth session of the Intergovernmental conference on an international legally binding instrument under the United Nations Convention on the Law of the Sea on the conservation and sustainable use of marine biological diversity of areas beyond national jurisdiction (the Conference) in response to the invitation by the President of the Conference in her Note of 1 June 2022 (A/CONF.232/2022/5) article-by-article compilation, A/CONF.232/2022/INF.5.

[58] ibid; see the submission from the Republic of Türkiye and the International Union for the Conservation of Nature.

[59] Jaspars and Brown, 'Benefit Sharing: Combining Intellectual Property, Trade Secrets, Science and an Ecosystem Focused Approach' (University of Aberdeen School of Law, 2020) Working Paper Series No 001/20, www.abdn.ac.uk/law/research/working-papers-696.php.

instruments relating to different subject matters. This is complemented by certain multilateral environmental agreements (MEAs) which are aligned along the trade and environment nexus. Among these are the Washington Convention on International Trade in Endangered Species of Wild Fauna and Flora (CITES)[60] and the CBD. CITES aims to protect endangered species of wild animals and plants from overexploitation. Today, CITES grants varying degrees of protection to more than 37,000 animal and plant species, regardless of whether the trade concerns live specimens, their parts or products made from them.[61] The CBD aims to conserve biological diversity and ensure the sustainable use of its components, together with the fair and equitable sharing of the benefits arising out of the utilisation of genetic resources, including by appropriate access to genetic resources and by appropriate transfer of relevant technologies, taking into account all rights over those resources and to technologies, and by appropriate funding.[62] The text of the CBD also outlines that states have a

> sovereign right to exploit their own resources pursuant to their own environmental policies, and the responsibility to ensure that activities within their jurisdiction or control do not cause damage to the environment of other States or of areas beyond the limits of national jurisdiction.[63]

However, the CBD does not apply to marine genetic resources in ABNJ and UNCLOS does not mention marine genetic resources.[64] Under the CBD, the issue of marine genetic resources has been discussed.[65] There are also suggestions that under the CBD regime, key information is not being disclosed due to confidentiality claims and that therefore the intended aim of the benefit sharing may be difficult to achieve.[66] The 2022 Kunming–Montreal Global Biodiversity Framework (GBF) under the CBD also includes trade in its targets – specifically target 5, which outlines that contracting parties are to

> ensure that the use, harvesting and trade of wild species is sustainable, safe and legal, preventing overexploitation, minimizing impacts on non-target species and ecosystems, and reducing the risk of pathogen spill-over, applying the ecosystem approach,

[60] Convention on International Trade in Endangered Species of Flora and Fauna, Washington DC, 3 March 1973, 973 UNTS 243.

[61] CITES, 'What Does It Address?' https://cites.org/eng/disc/what.php.

[62] CBD, Art 1.

[63] ibid Art 3.

[64] de La Fayette, 'A New Regime for the Conservation and Sustainable Use of Marine Biodiversity and Genetic Resources Beyond the Limits of National Jurisdiction' (2009) 24 *International Journal of Marine and Coastal Law* 221.

[65] Ma, 'An Economic and Legal Analysis of Trade Measures Against Illegal, Unreported and Unregulated Fishing' (2020) 117 *Marine Policy* 103980.

[66] Muller, *Genetic Resources as Natural Information: Implications for the Convention on Biological Diversity and Nagoya Protocol* (Earthscan/Routledge, 2015) 39, 41, 67.

> while respecting and protecting customary sustainable use by indigenous peoples and local communities'.[67]

In order to achieve the targets, the GBF outlines tools for implementation. By way of example, target 14 GBF outlines the aim to 'ensure the full integration of biodiversity and its multiple values into policies, regulations, planning and development processes … within and across all levels of government and across all sectors'.[68] Further, target 18 GBF aims to eliminate and phase out incentives, including subsidies that are harmful to biodiversity.[69] All of these different instruments establish standards, some of which may be used in the trade–environment nexus.[70]

The relationship between MEAs and the WTO has been subject to extensive legal analysis and scholarship.[71] There are well over 250 MEAs, addressing issues such as biodiversity protection, protection of the atmosphere, the marine environment and the regulation of waste, as well as procedural aspects such as environmental impact assessment and access to information.[72] These MEAs develop evidence-based information as well as trade restrictions measures around three themes: (i) to provide means of monitoring uncontrolled trade; (ii) to ensure compliance with MEA requirements; and (iii) to ensure the enforcement of MEAs, by prohibiting trade with non-complying parties or non-parties.[73]

The WTO's Committee on Trade and the Environment (CTE) has developed a matrix on trade-related measures pursuant to selected MEAs.[74] Table 4.1 presents an overview of the different instruments which may set standards and provide further substantiation of the trade and environment nexus, differentiated between pollution and marine living resources. While it is not possible to cover all of these extensively in the context of this chapter, the breadth of instruments already shows the complexity and at certain times the depth of possible standards and aspects to be considered in future analyses.

[67] CBD 15th Meeting of the Conference of the Parties, Kunming–Montreal Global Biodiversity Framework (GBF), 19 December 2022, www.cbd.int/article/cop15-final-text-kunming-montreal-gbf-221222.

[68] ibid (emphasis added).

[69] ibid.

[70] United Nations Environment Programme, *Environment and Trade: A Handbook* (2000) 41ff.

[71] Eckersley, 'The Big Chill: The WTO and Multilateral Environmental Agreements' (2004) 4(2) *Global Environmental Polititics* 24, 50; Brack and Gray, 'Multilateral Environmental Agreements and the WTO' (IISD, 2003); European Parliament, *Trade and Biodiversity* (June 2020) PE 603.494.

[72] Brack and Gray (n 71).

[73] Charnovitz, 'Multilateral Environmental Agreements and Trade Rules' (1996) 26(4) *Environmental Policy and Law*.

[74] WTO/CTE, 'A Matrix on Trade-Related Measures Pursuant to Selected MEAs' (19 March 2021) WT/CTE/W/160/Rev.9 TN/TE/S/5/Rev.7.

Table 4.1 Non-exhaustive overview of instruments pertaining to marine resources and pollution and their potential impacts on trade

	Instruments	**Trade Aspects**
Pollution	London Dumping Convention London Dumping Protocol MARPOL Convention Anti-Fouling Convention Ballast Water Management Convention STCW COLREG OPCR HNS Protocol Bunker Oil Convention	Supply chain Subsidies Sustainability impact assessments Pollution standards
Marine living resources (including biodiversity)	Fisheries RFMOS Straddling Fish Stock Agreement Convention on Biological Diversity Nagoya Protocol CITES	Import control Subsidies Prohibition of market access Access and benefit sharing Digital sequence information Bans or restrictions Intellectual property (patents, copyrights and trademarks) Repositories of information[a] Disclosure of origin Trade secrets

Based on the table by C Deere Birkbeck, 'Greening International Trade: Pathways Forward' (Global Governance Centre and the Forum on Trade, Environment & the SDGs, 2021) 26.

[a]For an introduction to database rights, see Brown et al, *Contemporary Intellectual Property: Law and Policy*, 5th edn (Oxford University Press, 2019) 31, 203, 219, 231.

IV. (MARINE) ENVIRONMENTAL CONSIDERATIONS WITHIN TRADE LAW

Beyond the discussion on the inclusion of trade or intellectual property in the new BBNJ Agreement, the question arises: what concrete contribution to solving such global environmental problems can the regulatory framework of the world trade order make in its current form? What possibilities does the WTO framework give its member states to unilaterally incentivise the internalisation of transboundary negative externalities in the country of origin in order to counteract an actual or presumed endangerment or destruction of world public goods, rather than doing so on the basis of a relevant international environmental protection agreement?

The link between trade law and ocean conservation is rooted in the predecessor of the WTO, the General Agreement on Tariffs and Trade (GATT), which stipulated exceptions to international free trade principles for the benefit of environmental protection.[75] The WTO system, which came into being with the establishment of the WTO in 1995, comprises the WTO and a number of agreements, of which the GATT 1994, GATS (General Agreement on Trade in Services), TRIPS (Trade-related Intellectual Property Rights) and DSU (Dispute Settlement Understanding) are but a few.[76] The current WTO system has also addressed the nexus through its dispute settlement mechanism as well as an institutionalised committee.[77] However, the rules of international law governing world trade go beyond the agreements concluded within the framework of the WTO, since numerous trade issues are legally regulated in free trade agreements, in regional bilateral agreements or through regional integration regimes.[78]

The protection of the marine environment through international trade law can be examined through several lenses. The member states of the WTO are also committed to the principle of sustainable development. In its non-legally binding preamble, the Marrakesh Agreement, through which the WTO was set up, holds that

> relations in the field of trade and economic endeavour should be conducted with a view to raising standards of living, ensuring full employment and a large and steadily growing volume of real income and effective demand, and expanding the production of and trade in goods and services, while allowing for the optimal use of the world's resources in accordance with the objective of sustainable development, seeking both to protect and preserve the environment and to enhance the means for doing so in a manner consistent with their respective needs and concerns at different levels of economic development.

[75] The predecessor to the GATT, the Havana Charter, related to 'measures taken in pursuance of any inter-governmental agreement which relates solely to the conservation of fisheries resources, migratory birds or wild animals'. See also the Convention for the Regulation of the Meshes of Fishing Nets and Size Limits of Fish, London, 5 April 1946.

[76] For an overview of trade and environment considerations during the pre-WTO period, see Garg, *Environmental Issues in the Multilateral Trading System: Past, Present and Possible Future* (CUTS International, 2021). Most notably, the GATT Secretariat prepared a report on industrial pollution control and trade (Note by the GATT Secretariat, Industrial Pollution Control and International Trade, L/3538, 9 June 1971, www.wto.org/gatt_docs/English/SULPDF/90840247.pdf), and a Group on Environmental Measures and International Trade (EMIT) was established in 1972. Further key milestones were the 1973–79 Tokyo Rounds of Negotiations, the Brundtland Report and the 1992 UNCED Rio Conference.

[77] Balogh and Mizik, 'Trade–Climate Nexus: A Systematic Review of the Literature' (2021) 9 *Economies* 99.

[78] Morin, Dür and Lechner, 'Mapping the Trade and Environment Nexus: Insights From a New Data Set' (2018) 18 *Global Environmental Politics* 122, 139. A free trade agreement is an agreement between two or more countries aimed at reducing barriers for import and export of goods and services among them. One example is the United States–Mexico–Canada Agreement (USMCA).

However, the integration of ecological and social interests into a regime that was originally programmed to operate according to economic terms (economic liberalism) poses a major challenge.[79] In the substantive regulatory structure of WTO law, environmental protection appears primarily in the form of exceptions to the general free trade principles. The central conflict rule is Article XX GATT, which regulates various exceptions to the above-mentioned principles of the WTO. The exceptions relevant to environmental protection are:

> [N]othing in this Agreement shall be construed to prevent the adoption or enforcement by any contracting party of measures:
>
> (b) necessary to protect human, animal or plant life or health;
>
> …
>
> (g) relating to the conservation of exhaustible natural resources if such measures are made effective in conjunction with restrictions on domestic production or consumption. (emphasis added)

If national or sub-national environmental, animal welfare or climate protection regulations are initially incompatible with WTO law, they may be justified by way of exception if all the factual requirements of Article XX GATT are fulfilled. In various decisions, the Appellate Body of the WTO Dispute Settlement Mechanism has construed in rulings the above-mentioned requirements of Article XX GATT. Prominent examples are the Tuna–Dolphin and Shrimp–Turtle cases from the field of environmental harm or animal welfare.[80] Environmentally motivated trade-restrictive measures are therefore in principle admissible under the WTO legal order. However, one of the controversial questions within the framework of Article XX GATT is the application of national trade-restrictive measures to protect extraterritorial legal interests.

First, it must be examined whether Article XX GATT in principle allows for extraterritorial application of trade-restrictive measures. The sovereign equality of UN members as enshrined in Article 2(1) of the UN Charter also includes the prohibition of intervention in the internal affairs of states. This delimits the spheres of competence of states vis-à-vis other states on the one hand and vis-à-vis international law on the other. The territorial sovereignty of states is

[79] Pitschas, 'Sustainable Development and the Multilateral Trading System – Options and Limits to Strengthening Sustainable Development Under the WTO' [2018] *GIZ* 93.

[80] For an overview on disputes, see www.wto.org/english/tratop_e/dispu_e/dispu_subjects_index_e.htm. In an attempt to understand how many marine-related cases have been brought in front of the DSU, an index is used which is differentiated by the subject matter of the WTO disputes. A precise understanding is difficult to achieve since there are often manifold ways to classify the subject of a given dispute. It is also difficult to conclude from the information if any of the cases also relate to considerations which may touch on areas beyond national jurisdictions. Several of the cases also relate to broader maritime activities and industries, such as subsidies for shipbuilding and ports of entry, though they do not directly address marine environmental concerns. At the time of writing, there were: nine cases relating to shrimps, six cases relating to salmon, three cases relating to scallops, three cases relating to seals and one each relating from fish fillets, herring, pangasius, sardines, swordfish and tuna.

protected under international law.[81] In the case of cross-border effects of state action, there is a difference between the sovereignty interest of the acting state and the integrity of the affected state which must be approached by an evaluative weighing. The prerequisite, however, is that the interests of two states are actually affected and that there must be a connecting factor between the object and the regulation of the regulating state. In international law, several concepts exist to depict this, such as a genuine link or sufficient nexus.[82] Environmental impacts often have a transboundary effect. In this case, a connection to the impact on a neighbouring state is given.[83] Both the polluting state and the affected state will exercise their right to determine their own environmental standards from their state sovereignty. This ultimately brings to bear the principles of limited territorial sovereignty and limited territorial integrity.[84] In the case of affected global commons such as ABNJ, such a connecting factor is also sufficiently given.

In Tuna I, the Panel concluded that Articles XX(b) and XX(g) GATT only provide for measures to protect goods within the jurisdiction of the importer country.[85] It was argued that extra-jurisdictional application would jeopardise the purpose of the GATT and should therefore be rejected.[86]

In Tuna II, the Panel distinguished between extraterritoriality and extra-jurisdictionality.[87] According to the Panel's interpretation, Article XX GATT does not impose territorial limitation with respect to the protected good.[88] Article XX(b) GATT[89] does not exclude the application of measures to protect

[81] See principle 21 of the Stockholm Declaration: 'States have in accordance with the Charter of the United Nations and the principles of international law, the sovereign right to exploit their own resources pursuant to their own environmental policies, and the responsibility to ensure that activities within their jurisdiction or control do not cause damage to the environment of other States or of areas beyond the limits of national jurisdiction.'

[82] See, among others, Song, 'Liberal or Constrained? Judicial Incorporations of Other Rules of International Law in UNCLOS and the Application of the Genuine Link Test' (2020) 13 *Journal of East Asia and International Law* 161; Faber, 'Stretching the Margins: The Geographic Nexus in Environmental Law' (1995) 48 *Stanford Law Review* 1247.

[83] See, eg in the *Trail Smelter* case: 'Under the principles of international law … no state has the right to use or permit the use of territory in such a manner as to cause injury by fumes in or to the territory of another of the properties or persons therein, when the case is of serious consequence and the injury is established by clear and convincing evidence'. *United States v Canada*, 3 Reports of International Arbitral Awards 1907 (1941).

[84] Blay, 'Territorial Integrity and Political Independence' in *Max Planck Encyclopedia of Public International Law*.

[85] GATT, United States – Restrictions on Import of Tuna (Tuna I), Report of the Panel of 3 September 1991 (not adopted) DS21/R – 39S/155, paras 5.26 and 5.31.

[86] GATT, Tuna I (n 85) paras 5.27 and 5.32.

[87] Cheyne, 'Environmental Unilateralism and the WTO/GATT System' (1995) 24 *Georgia Journal of International and Comparative Law* 433, 452–53; Ahn, 'Environmental Disputes in the GATT/WTO: Before and After Shrimp–Turtle Case' (1999) 20 *Michigan Journal of International Law* 819, 831. GATT, United States – Restrictions on Imports of Tuna (Tuna II), Report of the Panel of 16 June 1994 (not adopted) DS29/R, paras 5.20 and 5.31.

[88] GATT, Tuna II (n 87) paras 5.20 and 5.31.

[89] Contrary to GATT, Art XX(f), Art XX(b) does not contain the limitation 'national'.

extraterritorially located goods.[90] In this respect, the Panel concluded that, in contrast to Tuna I, an extraterritorial application of state measures under Article XX GATT was in principle possible.[91] However, the Panel noted that a state may only regulate within the remit of its jurisdiction and therefore for its own nationals or for ships flying its flag.[92]

The Panel justified this on the basis of the active personality principle.[93] The Panel outlined that Article XX GATT cannot be interpreted as permitting states to intervene in the policies of other states which are within their jurisdiction.[94] However, it may be argued that the admissibility of extraterritorial measures may – de facto – influence policies of other states.

The Appellate Body would have had an opportunity in Shrimp–Turtle to explicitly address whether Article XX GATT imposes a limitation on jurisdiction. It determined a 'sufficient nexus' between the US measure and the protected turtles as a migratory species which also occurs in US waters.[95] The Appellate Body also implicitly recognised the possibility of influencing policies in other states.[96] Therefore, the Appellate Body in Shrimp–Turtle did not explicitly rule out the extraterritorial application of trade-restrictive measures.[97] Generally, the admissibility of extraterritorial application of national trade-restrictive measures within the framework of Article XX GATT is widely recognised today. The compatibility of such measures with the GATT must be considered in weighing the interests of the state affected by the measure and the balancing of these interests by means of proportionality.

In the WTO, the CTE[98] was set up in 1994 through the Marrakesh Ministerial Decision on Trade and Environment. The CTE is mandated to identify the relationship between trade measures and environmental measures in order to promote sustainable development and to develop recommendations on whether any modifications of the provisions of the multilateral trading system are required, compatible with the open, equitable and non-discriminatory nature of the system. Increasingly, environmental aspects are pervading through WTO technical discussions. One of the central aspects is the WTO as the responsible organisation in addressing SDG 14.6, whose stipulated aim is to, 'by 2020, prohibit certain forms of fisheries subsidies which contribute to overcapacity

[90] GATT, Tuna II (n 87) para 5.16; Diem, *Freihandel und Umweltschutz in GATT und WTO* (Nomos, 1996) 115ff.

[91] Mavroidis, 'Trade and the Environment After the Shrimps–Turtles Litigation' (2000) 1 *Journal of World Trade* 34, 73.

[92] GATT, Tuna II (n 87) paras 5.17 and 5.33.

[93] Cheyne (n 87) 455.

[94] GATT, Tuna II (n 87) para 5.26.

[95] WTO, United States – Import Prohibition of Certain Shrimp and Shrimp Products (Shrimp–Turtle), Report of the Appellate Body of 12 October 1998, WT/DS58/AB/R, para 133.

[96] Ahn (n 87) 848.

[97] Shrimp–Turtle (n 95) para 164.

[98] WTO, Decision on Trade and Environment, 1994, www.wto.org/english/docs_e/legal_e/56-dtenv_e.htm.

and overfishing, eliminate subsidies that contribute to illegal, unreported and unregulated (IUU) fishing and refrain from introducing new such subsidies'. Indeed, after years of negotiations, the WTO Agreement on Fisheries Subsidies was adopted in 2022.[99] Whereas ABNJ are not specifically mentioned in the provisions, the Agreement makes reference to flag state and port state responsibilities and jurisdictions, which both have effect in relation to the conservation of biodiversity in ABNJ.[100]

V. EMERGING DISCUSSIONS AT THE WTO ON TRADE AND PLASTIC POLLUTION

At the WTO, several processes may be relevant which may also hold importance for the protection of ABNJ. In 2020, the WTO Informal Dialogue on Plastic Pollution and Environmentally Sustainable Plastic Trade was established during the Twelfth Ministerial Conference (MC12) to develop a new informal process on 'how the WTO could contribute to domestic, regional and global efforts to reduce plastics pollution and transition to more circular and environmentally sustainable plastics trade'.[101] The work has continued and has focused on synergies with the ongoing negotiations towards an International Legally Binding Agreement on Plastic Pollution, including Marine Litter[102] as well as sustainable alternatives and substitutes for plastics in the trade context.[103] A Ministerial Statement on plastic pollution and environmentally sustainable plastic trade was issued in November 2021.[104] The signatories of the Statement outlined their intention to identify ways to improve the understanding of global trade in plastics, including flows of plastics embedded in internationally traded goods or associated with them (such as plastic packaging), and to enhance transparency regarding trade policies relevant to reducing plastic pollution and more environmentally sustainable plastics trade. Furthermore, the states envisage enhanced cooperation with other international organisations and the identification of effective trade policies or measures to support the implementation of actions under other

[99] WTO Ministerial Conference, Twelfth Session, 12–15 June 2022, Agreement on Fisheries Subsidies, https://docs.wto.org/dol2fe/Pages/SS/directdoc.aspx?filename=q:/WT/MIN22/33.pdf&Open=True.

[100] ibid Art 3.

[101] WTO, Informal Dialogue on Plastic Pollution and Environmentally Sustainable Trade, November 2021, www.wto.org/english/tratop_e/envir_e/member_event_no_2_wto_informal_dialogue_on_plastics_pollution_and_environmentally_sustainable_plastics_trade.pdf.

[102] United Nations Environment Programme, www.unep.org/about-un-environment/inc-plastic-pollution, last.

[103] WTO, Informal Dialogue on Plastic Pollution and Environmentally Sustainable Plastics Trade (IDP), 7 December 2022, www.wto.org/english/news_e/news22_e/ppesp_07dec22_e.htm.

[104] WTO IDP, MC12 Ministerial Statement on Plastic Pollution and Environmentally Sustainable Plastics Trade, WT/MIN(21)/8, 22 November 2021.

international processes and efforts and to strengthen cooperation and policy coherence within the rules and mechanisms of the WTO.

In November 2021, a structured discussion on trade and environmental sustainability at the WTO was launched. The discussion aims to allow interested WTO members, as well as non-WTO experts (eg academics, non-governmental organisations, international organisations and the private sector), to explore the nexus between trade and environmental sustainability.[105]

VI. REFLECTIONS

Addressing the marine environmental and trade law nexus is a complex issue. This relates to limited knowledge and data on the impacts of trade on the marine environment of ABNJ as well as to the fragmentation between different regimes. The phenomenon of fragmentation may be addressed by regime interaction. It cannot be reduced to a treaty conflict as in itself the obligations under UNCLOS relating to the high seas are not in conflict with WTO law. Rather, the instruments were developed in different sectoral 'silos' of public international law and may have some divergent interests and focal areas. In light of the different legal bases for development and adoption of these instruments, one can argue that the regime interaction relates to interaction of goals as well as the consequential interactions between institutions.

What can be implemented in the short to medium term is improved cooperation between the environment, the law of the sea and trade regimes. In this respect, no new bodies would have to or should be established, but the exchange and collaboration of existing bodies should be intensified. The aim of the intensified cooperation may be to develop concrete measures to establish suitable monitoring and assessment measures to understand and classify trade-related impacts on the marine environment, including ABNJ. Such collaboration can also support the achievement of the UN Sustainable Development Agenda, MEAs and the potential new treaty on plastic pollution in the marine environment and/or the BBNJ Agreement. Similarly, the role of developing countries, least developed countries and the Small Island Developing States must be considered as an important issue in terms of developing significant regulatory and policy measures at the trade, law of the sea and marine environmental nexus.

Standard setting in both the law of the sea and trade law may be an important step forward in strengthening the nexus. According to Article 2.5 of the Technical Barriers to Trade (TBT) Agreement, the compliance of a technical regulation with an international standard may support arguments that such a standard may not be considered as an obstacle to international trade. UNCLOS similarly provides rules of reference. However, both UNCLOS

[105] WTO, Communication on Trade and Environmental Sustainability, WT/CTE/W/249, 17 November 2021.

and the TBT Agreement, by way of example, do not stipulate which international organisations may have the mandates to promulgate such standards. The Division for Ocean Affairs and Law of the Sea of the Offices of Legal Affairs has, however, developed a non-exhaustive matrix[106] for identifying obligations of states under UNCLOS that also covers international standards beyond UNCLOS.[107] The matrix makes reference to different relevant standards stipulated by UNCLOS, including protection and conservation of the marine environment[108] and marine scientific research.[109] Whereas this approach may be possible, Du and Deng argue that the approach taken within WTO to interpreting international standards within the meaning of Article 2.5 TBT Agreement is beset by inconsistencies and therefore leads to uncertainties. The authors make reference to the EC – Sardines case and US – Tuna II.[110] This may evoke the possibility to further develop guidance and clarity on the interpretation of standards within the meaning of Article 2.5 of the TBT Agreement.

VII. CONCLUSION

Whereas overall the nexus of trade, law of the sea and marine environment appears to have gained attention in different fora which traditionally were not focused on the integration of these fields, the paradigm is that of focusing on key issues, mostly relating to trade and climate change and trade and fisheries, among others, thereby leaving other areas out of focus, such as marine genetic resources, biodiversity and pollution effects. The inclusion of pollution and the protection of living resources in ABNJ in the trade and environment nexus is only considered and applied in a very limited manner. The complexity of regime interaction and the effectiveness of the WTO system to address these kinds of questions may currently pose a challenge.[111] Notwithstanding this, there are clear indications that certain items, mainly relating to fisheries subsidies and pollution, are advancing at the WTO. In general, the topic of environment, law of the sea and trade at the interface of ABNJ is very complex, and needs to be unravelled and unpacked in greater detail through further scholarship and research.

[106] UN Doc A/RES/49/28, 78th Plenary Meeting, 6 December 1994.

[107] UN/Office of Legal Affairs, *The Law of the Sea: Obligations of States Parties under the United Nations Convention on the Law of the Sea and Complementary Instruments* (2004) 42ff.

[108] ibid 50ff.

[109] ibid 61.

[110] Du and Deng, 'International Standards as Global Public Goods in the World Trading System' (2016) 43(2) *Legal Issues of Economic Integration* 113, 132.

[111] For a recent account on this topic issued by the European Commission, see European Commission, 'Reforming the WTO: Towards a Sustainable and Effective Multilateral Trading System' (2021) https://trade.ec.europa.eu/doclib/docs/2021/april/tradoc_159544.1329_EN_02.pdf.

5

Digital Sequence Information: Possible Implications for the Law on Access to Genetic Resources and Benefit Sharing from their Utilisation, with Special Emphasis on Marine Genetic Resources in Areas Beyond National Jurisdiction

CHRISTIAN PRIP

I. INTRODUCTION

GENETIC RESOURCES – defined as biological materials of actual or potential value containing functional units of heredity[1] – are essential for much of the world's economic activity. This includes the improvement of agricultural crops and the development of traditional medicines on which most of the world's population still depend. The uses of genetic resources from plants, animals, microorganisms and invertebrates range from basic research to the development of products in sectors such as the pharmaceutical industry, agriculture, aquaculture, horticulture, cosmetics and biotechnology. The combined annual global markets for the products derived from genetic resources have been estimated to be between 500 and 800 billion USD.[2]

Increasingly, the search for new and useful genetic resources is conducted in the maritime realm, including the deep sea beyond national jurisdiction. Since 1999, the number of patents originating from marine genetic resources (MGR) has increased by an average of 12 per cent each year. Today, there are

[1] CBD definition of genetic resources.

[2] Ten Kate and Laird, *The Commercial Use of Biodiversity: Access to Genetic Resources and Benefit-Sharing* (Earthscan, 1999).

over 18,000 products with their origins in marine organisms belonging to 4800 named species.[3]

The actual and potential benefits from genetic resources – and the fact that the South is generally richer in biodiversity and genetic resources than the North, where much of the scientific and technological capacity to utilise genetic resources is found – has made access to genetic resources and benefit sharing from their use a complex and controversial topic in international law. This includes the now concluded negotiations under the United Nations Convention on the Law of the Sea (UNCLOS) on an implementing agreement on the conservation and sustainable use of the marine biological diversity of areas beyond national jurisdiction (BBNJ), which were also mandated to cover this topic.[4]

Complexity and controversy have deepened as new technological developments significantly reduce the demand for physical genetic material. Such material can now be digitally sequenced, and data exchanged rapidly between researchers, institutions, countries and databases. The amount of digital sequence information (DSI) in publicly available databases is increasing exponentially, as is the exchange and use of such data.

This chapter examines the discussions in international forums on the legal aspects of DSI, emphasising how the emergence of DSI has affected a new BBNJ instrument under UNCLOS.

II. THE INTERNATIONAL LEGAL FRAMEWORK FOR ACCESS TO GENETIC RESOURCES AND BENEFIT-SHARING FROM ITS USE

Many developing countries saw the Convention on Biological Diversity (CBD), which entered into force in 1993, as an opportunity to share in the benefits derived from 'their' genetic resources and to rectify what was seen as an unjust situation dating back to colonial times, when the colonial powers reaped huge profits by exploiting natural resources without sharing the benefits. The CBD and its principle of access to genetic resources and benefit sharing from their use (ABS) has since had considerable implications for international law in such diverse areas as agriculture, intellectual property rights, health and human rights.[5]

[3] Krabbe, *Bioprospecting and Deep-Sea Genetic Resources in a Fragmenting International Law* (University of Gothenburg School of Business, Economics and Law, 2021).

[4] Intergovernmental Conference on an international legally binding instrument under the United Nations Convention on the Law of the Sea on the conservation and sustainable use of marine biological diversity of areas beyond national jurisdiction, General Assembly Resolution 72/249.

[5] Glowka and Normand, 'The Nagoya Protocol on Access and Benefit-sharing: Innovations in International Environmental Law' in Morgera, Buck and Tsioumani (eds), *The 2010 Nagoya Protocol on Access and Benefit Sharing in Perspective: Implications for International Law and Implementation Challenges* (Martinus Nijhoff, 2013) 21–51.

The CBD has three objectives: the conservation of biodiversity; the sustainable use of the components of biodiversity; and the fair and equitable sharing of the benefits arising from the utilisation of genetic resources. Based on the principle of national sovereignty and equity, the CBD establishes that benefits from using genetic resources shall be shared fairly and equitably with the provider of the resources, in return for providing access. Such access granted under the CBD is subject to prior informed consent (PIC) by the providing country, on mutually agreed terms with the user.[6]

ABS was a controversial issue during the negotiations and remained so after the entry into force of the CBD. Discussions on implementing ABS provisions focused on how to operationalise access, with scant attention being paid to the question of how to ensure benefit sharing and compliance with provider country access legislation. Developing countries reported cases of alleged 'biopiracy', typically concerning inventions based on genetic resources and associated traditional knowledge that were patented without the PIC of the providing country and/or the community that held the knowledge. This fuelled mistrust between developed and developing countries.[7] The former were concerned about early instances of domestic access legislation in developing countries, which they deemed overly bureaucratic, with a protectionist approach aimed at preventing biopiracy rather than incentivising bioprospecting.[8] The latter held that developed countries, as hosts to most of the users of genetic resources, were obliged to take measures to prevent misappropriation and to ensure that benefits were actually shared.

Developing countries argued for a protocol to complement the CBD, with clear legal obligations for 'user countries' to support compliance with provider countries' access regulations. The developed countries resisted for many years, but in 2002 the World Summit on Sustainable Development in Johannesburg adopted a recommendation to 'negotiate within the framework of the CBD an international regime to promote and safeguard the fair and equitable sharing of benefits arising out of the utilization of genetic resources'.[9]

The Johannesburg recommendation led to a long and complicated negotiating process within the CBD, which was only completed at the Tenth Meeting of the Conference of the Parties to the CBD (COP 10) in Nagoya 2010. Here, parties adopted the Nagoya Protocol (NP)[10] as part of a 'Nagoya Package', which also included the CBD Strategic Plan 2011–2020, the 'Aichi Targets'[11] and

[6] CBD, Art 15.

[7] Oberthür and Rosendal, *Global Governance of Genetic Resources: Access and Benefit Sharing After the Nagoya Protocol* (Routledge, 2014).

[8] Smagadi, 'National Measures on Access to Genetic Resources and Benefit Sharing: The Case of the Philippines' (2005) 1(1) *Law, Environment and Development Journal* 50.

[9] Johannesburg Plan of Implementation, para 44(o).

[10] UNEP/CBD/COP/DEC/X/1.

[11] UNEP/CBD/COP/DEC/X/2.

a global strategy for resource mobilisation for biodiversity.[12] The package aims to balance the interests of developing and developed countries, with developing countries demanding the NP and the resource mobilisation strategy and developed countries demanding the Aichi Targets. The NP entered into force in 2014; to date, it has been ratified by 130 parties.

The NP further elaborates on the CBD provisions on ABS, representing a delicate compromise between developed and developing country preferences. The NP obliges parties with users of genetic measures under their jurisdiction to take various measures to prevent misappropriation and violation of access regulation in provider countries.[13] Moreover, parties shall take measures aimed at ensuring that traditional knowledge associated with genetic resources and held by indigenous and local communities is accessed with their approval.[14]

The NP allows for sector-specific ABS regimes, provided that such regimes are consistent with and do not run counter to the objectives of the NP and the CBD.[15] When a specialised ABS instrument is in place, that instrument is to prevail over the NP.[16]

This left no doubt about the legal status of the FAO International Treaty on Plant Genetic Resources for Food and Agriculture (ITPGRFA), which came into force in 2004 and has now been ratified by 147 countries.[17] The ITPGRFA had been developed because of the CBD and mirrored the latter's objectives: conservation, sustainable use, and fair and equitable sharing of benefits derived from the use of plant genetic resources. The ITPGRFA, however, created an approach to access and benefit sharing that differs from that of the CBD by establishing a multilateral system of access and benefit sharing (MLS).[18] Within this system, the parties are to provide facilitated access to each other's genetic resources covered by the system for research breeding, conservation and training. The multilateral system includes 35 food crops and 29 forage crops, listed in Annex 1 to the Treaty.

The background for the ITPGRFA system with facilitated access and a multilateral instead of bilateral approach can be found in the crucial role of plant genetic resources in providing food for a growing world population. Benefit sharing was decoupled from the provider and the resources accessed because of the incremental improvement and multiple sources that characterise seeds and plant breeding. However, incremental improvement, multiple sources and interdependence all indicate that there is no one, single end product linked to the accession, and that identifying a 'source country' can be difficult: a provider may

[12] UNEP/CBD/COP/DEC/X/3.
[13] NP, Arts 15, 17 and 18.
[14] ibid Art 16.
[15] ibid Art 4.2.
[16] ibid Art 4.4.
[17] FAO International Treaty on Plant Genetic Resources for Food and Agriculture (ITPGRFA).
[18] ibid Part IV.

become a user, and vice versa. Thus, a need was seen for a regime to promote the exchange of crops and their genes with as few restrictions as possible.

Another sector-specific ABS instrument is the WHO Pandemic Influenza Preparedness (PIP) Framework adopted in 2011. Its objectives are to improve and strengthen the sharing of influenza viruses with human pandemic potential; and to increase the access of developing countries to vaccines and other pandemic-related supplies.[19]

Although the ITPGRFA and the PIP Framework are specialised instruments that create a multilateral system to facilitate access to genetic resources, they also, like the CBD/NP framework, provide for individual transaction-based agreements on physical genetic resources between the resource holder and the party seeking access. The difference is that such agreements are individually negotiated under the CBD and the NP, whereas a standard material transfer agreement (SMTA) is involved under the ITPGRFA and PIP Framework.

A. Genetic Resources and Intellectual Property Rights

The reinforcement of national sovereignty to genetic resources as a backbone of the CBD ABS regime was largely intended to counterbalance the rapid evolution in modern biotechnology and the increased opportunities for obtaining intellectual property rights on seeds and other living material at a time when the question of access to genetic resources had shifted towards a 'common heritage of mankind' approach with open access. In general, the developing countries were sceptical, viewing intellectual property rights (IPRs) as enabling industry in developed countries to monopolise 'their' genetic resources without compensation, while also imposing a high price for 'reintroduction' of the patented products based on these resources.

The development of IPRs was enshrined in the Agreement on Trade-Related Aspects of Intellectual Property Rights (TRIPS), one of the pillars of the World Trade Organization, which was negotiated in parallel to the CBD negotiations but with no formal interconnections. TRIPS requires its member states to make patents available for inventions in any kind of technology – including technology on living organisms, cells and genes. From this general point of departure, TRIPS allows states certain exemptions: they may exclude from patentability 'plants and animals other than micro-organisms, and essentially biological processes for the production of plants or animals other than non-biological and microbiological processes'. However, members 'shall provide for the protection of plant varieties either by patents or by an effective *sui generis* system or by any combination thereof'.[20]

[19] WHO Pandemic Influenza Preparedness (PIP) Framework. The PIP Framework is not legally binding.

[20] TRIPS, Art 27.3(b). Concerning plant genetic resources for food and agriculture, many countries have opted for a *sui generis* system in the form of Plant Breeders' Rights under the Convention

Developing countries on the TRIPS Council have attempted to promote mutual supportiveness between the two regimes by introducing the obligation to disclose in patent applications the source and/or country of origin of biological resources and of associated traditional knowledge, and the country of legal acquisition of such resources if those resources and/or traditional knowledge are contained in an invention for which the applicant is seeking a patent. The intention is to make transparent and subject to public scrutiny whether ABS obligations have been met, and to facilitate identification of potential cases of misappropriation when a patent application is made. Despite increasing support from developed countries, others – the USA, in particular – have prevented the adoption of this proposal in the TRIPS Council.[21]

B. Implementation and Perceptions of the ABS Regime

The level of national implementation of the CBD provisions on ABS has generally been low. The NP was intended to provide greater legal clarity and new momentum, but the its national implementation has also been progressing at a slow pace. Beyond reporting that legal and institutional measures were still at an early stage of development, a 2018 assessment and review was unable to provide any conclusive data on the amount of monetary or non-monetary benefits triggered as a result of ABS transactions regulated by the NP.[22]

A Compliance Committee has been established to oversee implementation of the NP.[23] A report to this Committee from April 2020 shows that 95 country parties (77 per cent of the total) have now established ABS measures of varying types and degrees of specificity and comprehensiveness. (In fact, many of these were adopted prior to the adoption of the NP.) Currently, 59 countries are revising existing ABS measures or developing new ones to implement the NP.[24]

While laws and institutions are prerequisites for the system to work, their existence does not necessarily guarantee substantive progress. Studies have found that the benefits envisioned by the CBD and the NP have remained largely unfulfilled for states as well as indigenous peoples and local communities – also in states with well-developed ABS measures in place.[25]

and the Union for the Protection of Plant Varieties (UPOV). This form of IPR provides breeders with exclusive rights to the propagating material (such as seeds) of new plant varieties.

[21] See BIORES, 'Disclosure of Origin Again on the TRIPS Council Agenda, reporting from a TRIPS Council meeting in 2007. Lack of adoption by the TRIPS Council has not prevented several countries from introducing disclosure requirements in their national legislation. These countries include Belgium, Bolivia, Brazil, China, Colombia, Costa Rica, Denmark, Ecuador, Egypt, India, Norway, Peru, the Philippines, South Africa and Switzerland. However, the provisions differ as to their binding nature, scope, and consequences in case of non-compliance.

[22] CBD/NP/MOP/DEC/3/1.

[23] UNEP/CBD/NP/COP-MOP/DEC/1/4.

[24] CBD/NP/CC/3/3.

[25] Muller, *Access to Genetic Resources and Benefit Sharing 25 Years On: Progress and Challenges* (International Centre for Trade and Sustainable Development, 2018).

Quantifying non-monetary benefits may be difficult, but it is generally agreed that monetary benefit sharing thus far has been insignificant in an otherwise multibillion dollar market. The benefits for the conservation of biodiversity seem even less apparent.[26] It should be noted, however, that processes of research, development and commercialisation in terms of genetic resources do take time.

A common view among scientists is that the ABS regime still creates obstacles to research, since national legal frameworks often make no distinction between access to genetic resources for research and for commercial use. From the commercial side, it is often claimed that many companies have reduced or abandoned their interest in natural products because of legal uncertainties and other hurdles in accessing genetic resources.[27] On the other hand, countries of origin have been reluctant to work with multinational companies, because of suspicions of 'biopiracy'. To some extent, then, the two parties to an ABS contract, who need to make the system work, have backed out. One possible result of this could be countries of origin failing to gain their share of possible benefits from their biodiversity, while a rich source of chemical diversity present in species from around the world is being neglected.[28]

Questions have been raised as to whether the legal ABS framework is compatible with the bioprospecting 'value chain' from collection in nature to a manufactured product. This chain involves many steps and intermediaries, and thereby also many providers and users.[29] Indeed, some studies have claimed that the system works against the intention of greater equality between North and South.[30] Overall, the initial enthusiasm for the ABS regime in the 1990s has been replaced by growing concerns about the lack of implementation and how implementation is conducted.

III. THE EMERGENCE OF DSI AND IMPLICATIONS FOR THE ABS LEGAL FRAMEWORK

Further ammunition to the view that developments have overtaken the current ABS regime of the CBD and the NP in providing fair and equitable benefit sharing has come with the rapid technological development of *digital sequence information.* Although its precise meaning and scope remain disputed, the term refers to advances in bioinformatics, an interdisciplinary

[26] ibid.

[27] Amirkia and Heinrich, 'Natural Products and Drug Discovery: A Survey of Stakeholders in Industry and Academia' (2015) 6 *Frontiers in Pharmacology*.

[28] Heinrich et al, 'Access and Benefit Sharing Under the Nagoya Protocol – Quo Vadis? Six Latin American Case Studies Assessing Opportunities and Risk' (2020) 11 *Frontiers in Pharmacology*.

[29] Prip and Rosendal, 'Access to Genetic Resources and Benefit-Sharing From Their Use (ABS) – State of Implementation and Research Gaps' (2015) FNI Report 5/2015.

[30] Deplazes-Zemp et al, 'The Nagoya Protocol Could Backfire on the Global South' (2018) 2 *Nature Ecology & Evolution* 917.

field of knowledge that develops and uses methods and software tools to extract knowledge from biological material. This development has reached the point where once a genome has been deposited, its genes can be compared against hundreds of other genes for similarities and differences, helping to clarify its function and importance. Building on decades of scientific research, DSI is useful mainly in connection with the assembled data, rather than single DNA sequences. DSI has a wide range of applications, including gene editing and synthetic biology.[31]

The ABS presumes that providers and users negotiate agreements and exchange physical material with clear provenance, ownership and value – and further, that this material can be tracked through the research process. However, technological developments have significantly reduced the demand for physical genetic material: now it can be digitally sequenced relatively cheaply, with rapid exchange of data between researchers, institutions, countries and databases.[32] Funders and publishers of scientific research demand that data be disclosed and made openly available. Indeed, the amount of DSI in publicly available databases is increasing exponentially, together with the exchange and use of such data.

The use of DSI takes place without applying the concept of benefit sharing under the ABS mechanism, since it is extremely difficult to identify the original source of the sequences or to pinpoint the 'benefits' arising from its use. Now that 'information' can be extracted, disembodied or dematerialised from genetic resources, questions arise regarding the relevance of biological material in relation to ABS and as the vehicle for that disembodied information.[33]

This situation has brought ABS into the spotlight again, with sharply divided views between North and South on how to deal with DSI. A core area of disagreement concerns whether the use of DSI should be seen as 'utilisation' of genetic resources and thereby covered by the NP – or merely as descriptive information and thus beyond regulatory scope.[34]

Many developing countries have feared that the free access to and exchange of DSI will undermine the third objective of the CBD, and thereby also their incentives to protect biodiversity. They have argued for DSI to be squarely part of the ABS regime, and with obligations on sequences mirroring those for genetic resources collected in the field. They hold that, as sequence information at some point originated from a physical source, this is a subsequent use derived from access: therefore, the use of sequence information entails utilisation of

[31] CBD/DSI/AHTEG/2020/1/3, Digital sequence information on genetic resources: concept, scope and current use.

[32] Laird et al, 'Rethink the Expansion of Access and Benefit Sharing' (2020) 367(6483) *Science* 1200.

[33] Muller (n 25).

[34] Morgera, Switzer and Geelhoed for the European Commission, 'Possible Ways to Address Digital Sequence Information – Legal and Policy Aspects' (Strathclyde Centre for Environmental Law and Governance, 2020).

genetic resources and is subject to the obligations for fair and equitable benefit sharing.[35]

By contrast, many developed countries have argued that DSI is merely descriptive information and thus beyond the regulatory scope. In their view, free accessibility is essential in all areas of the life sciences, including biodiversity research, food security and human health. Setting barriers to the already well-established free access and exchange would undermine research and industrial development, to the detriment of both developed and developing nations.[36]

The DSI topic had a significant impact on the negotiation process and the outcome of the overall post-2020 Global Biodiversity Framework (GBF), with goals and targets adopted at CBD COP 15 in December 2022. Developing countries had set resolving the question of benefit sharing from the use of DSI as a key condition for their support to the overall GBF. During the preparatory process prior to COP 15, extended by two years due to COVID-19, webinars and other online forums on DSI organised by the CBD and others proliferated to foster a common understanding.[37] The focus of the discussions shifted from legal disputes as to whether DSI is covered by the CBD/NP legal framework to pragmatic explorations of ways to create a system to cover how and which benefits to share from the expanding use of DSI. Options on how to address DSI included exchange of DSI through standard agreements and non-transaction/contract-based approaches, whether through a subscription/fee system or technical and scientific cooperation.[38]

In the end, it was agreed that the benefits from the use of DSI on genetic resources should be shared fairly and equitably, and not on a transaction/bilateral base, recognising 'that tracking and tracing of all digital sequence information on genetic resources is not practical'. To this end, it was decided to establish a multilateral mechanism for benefit sharing from the use of DSI, including a global fund as well as a time-bound process to further develop and operationalise the mechanism. This work is to be finalised at COP 16 in 2024.[39]

DSI has also had a significant influence on developments (or the lack thereof) in the ITPGRFA. The Eighth Meeting of the Treaty Governing Body in 2019 was expected to adopt a significant revision of the MLS of the Treaty with two key components: an expansion of the list of crops included in the MLS and the introduction of a subscription system for access to MLS crops. However, negotiations on the MLS collapsed, with the emerging use of DSI being the

[35] Hammond and Lim, 'Discussions on Sequence Information Unravel at Biodiversity Meeting' (Third World Network, 2018).

[36] Lawson and Rourke, 'Digital Sequence Information as a Marine Genetic Resource Under the Proposed UNCLOS Legally Binding Instrument' (2020) 122 *Marine Policy* 103878.

[37] CBD webinar series on digital sequence information on genetic resources.

[38] CBD webinar 3: Policy Options for Access and Benefit Sharing and Digital Sequence.

[39] CBD/COP/DEC/15/9, Digital sequence information on genetic resources.

critical element.[40] It is likely that the agreement reached under the CBD will have a positive influence on the ongoing process of revising the MLS.

IV. TOWARDS AND IMPLEMENTING AGREEMENT UNDER UNCLOS, ON BIODIVERSITY IN AREAS BEYOND NATIONAL JURISDICTION

Since 2008, a process has been underway under various mandates towards an international legally binding instrument under UNCLOS on the conservation and sustainable use of marine biodiversity of areas beyond national jurisdiction (the BBNJ Agreement). In 2017, an Intergovernmental Conference (IGC) was established to elaborate the text of such an instrument.[41] Negotiations of an agreed text were concluded by the IGC on 4 March 2023.[42]

Marine genetic resources found in marine areas beyond national jurisdiction (ABNJ) are outside the scope of the CBD and the NP. The legal framework regulating activities in ABNJ is UNCLOS, which entered into force in 1994. Such marine areas cover nearly half of the Earth's surface and two-thirds of all marine areas.

The exploration and exploitation of MGR is of increasing interest to the pharmaceutical, food and other industries. Marine molecules have been used to develop now commercialised pharmaceutical drugs, including anti-cancer medication, as well as for treatments for HIV or Alzheimer's patients.[43] Research has shown that 10 developed countries account for 90 per cent of patents related to MGR.[44]

Despite extreme conditions of cold, complete darkness and high pressure, the deep seabed is host to varied forms of life associated with such features as hydrothermal vents, cold-water seeps, seamounts and deep-water coral reefs. These habitats support forms of life with unique genetic characteristics and are therefore of great interest for marine bioprospecting. As yet, only a few states and private entities have access to the financial means and technologies needed to reach the deep seabed and gather samples of organisms found there, and to study and isolate in laboratories the genetic material deriving from such organisms.

The results of this research could lead to the development of commercially valuable products.[45] Unsurprisingly, developing countries have strongly

[40] Earth Negotiating Bulletin, Summary of the Eighth Session of the Governing Body of the International Treaty on Plant Genetic Resources for Food and Agriculture, 11–16 November 2019.

[41] UNGA Resolution 72/249.

[42] Draft agreement under the United Nations Convention on the Law of the Sea on the Conservation and Sustainable Use of Marine Biological Diversity of Areas beyond National Jurisdiction.

[43] Leary et al, 'Marine Genetic Resources: A Review of Scientific and Commercial Interest' (2009) 33 *Marine Policy* 183.

[44] Arnaud-Haond, Arrieta and Duarte, 'Marine Biodiversity and Gene Patents' (2011) 331(6024) *Science* 1521.

[45] Scovazzi, 'The Rights to Genetic Resources Beyond National Jurisdiction: Challenges for the Ongoing Negotiations at the United Nations' in Banet (ed), *The Law of the Seabed* (Brill, 2020).

advocated for the BBNJ Agreement to include a regime for fair and equitable sharing of any benefit from the use of genetic resources in ABNJ, compatible with and complementary to the regime under the CBD and the NP.

The mandate for negotiating the BBNJ instrument, which was finally agreed in March 2023, was a package addressing

> the conservation and sustainable use of marine biological diversity of areas beyond national jurisdiction, in particular, together and as a whole, MGR, including questions on the sharing of benefits, measures such as area-based management tools, including marine protected areas, environmental impact assessments and capacity building and the transfer of marine technology.[46]

The legal status of MGR in ABNJ is, by definition, different from that of genetic resources within national jurisdiction to which the existing ABS regime applies. With no sovereign rights recognised in ABNJ, there is no legally recognised 'provider' entitled to PIC and a share of the benefits arising from genetic resource use under bilateral arrangements.

The path towards a new legal instrument was long and bumpy, and the issue of sharing of benefits from the use of MGR was the most complicated negotiation issue to resolve.[47] As has often been the case in negotiations under the CBD, it was a polarising topic, the outcome of which could have impacts on the outcome of negotiations on other topics, including provisions on conservation and sustainable use. At the end of the negotiations, unlocking the parts of the instrument related to this issue was the key to reaching an agreement.

Along the negotiation process, discussions on modalities for access and benefit sharing gradually moved away from a CBD-framed transaction approach and towards a multilateral benefit-sharing system based on activities of collection, research and development more appropriate to the unique nature and legal status of MGR in ABNJ. This was in line with the recent scholarly deliberations referred to above focusing on the need for a benefit-sharing system that is not dependent on a transactional approach but that can still create incentives for governments and stakeholders to be transparent about the collection and use of genetic resources of ABNJ, and to share benefits from their use.

A multilateral benefit-sharing approach is also more conducive to encompassing benefit sharing in relation to the increasing intangible aspects of genetic resources, such as DSI. As is the case with the other international forums addressing access to genetic resources and benefit sharing, such as the CBD and the ITPGRFA, the question on whether and how to address DSI was also a controversial issue here. One reason may have been the potential 'spill over' of a

[46] UNGA Resolution 72/249.

[47] Earth Negotiation Bulletin, Summary Report of the Resumed 5th Session of the Intergovernmental Conference (IGC) on BBNJ, 20 February–4 March 2023.

decision into the other forums.[48] The final negotiations of the BBNJ instrument were expected to be finalised at IGC5 in September 2022, but in the absence of an agreement, the meeting was suspended and reconvened at the end of February–early March 2023. In the meantime, COP15 of the CBD had adopted the Global Biodiversity Framework, including a decision to establish a multilateral mechanism for benefit sharing from the use of DSI. It is very likely that this decision provided the BBNJ negotiators with a concept that helped them to reach agreement both on how to address DSI and on the broader multilateral mechanism established on MGR.

Under the provisions on access and benefit sharing, MGR and DSI are treated on an equal footing. In its preamble, the BBNJ Agreement

> acknowledge[s] that the generation of, access to, and utilization of digital sequencing information (DSI) on MGRs of ABNJ, together with the fair and equitable sharing of benefits arising from its utilization, contribute to research and innovation and to the general objective of this Agreement.

A key question to be resolved in the final hours was which of the two overarching UNCLOS principles should apply. Those principles are as follows.

Common heritage of humankind. This principle, generally supported by developing countries and applying to minerals of the deep seabed, implies that resources cannot be accessed exclusively by any state, but only for the benefit of humankind under some sort of international arrangement or regime.[49]

Freedom of the high seas. This principle implies freedom of access to, and unrestricted exploitation of, MGR and was generally supported by developed countries.[50]

The final compromise was to include both principles under the article on general principles and approaches.[51]

Another major point of divergence was whether the benefits to be shared should include monetary benefits or only non-monetary ones such as sharing of research data, scientific cooperation, capacity building and technology transfer. Here, developed countries in the end accepted that monetary benefits from the utilisation of MGR and DSI on MGR of ABNJ, including commercialisation, should be shared fairly and equitably, through the financial mechanism established by the instrument. Developed countries are to make annual contributions to be determined by the first BBNJ Conference of Parties to the BBNJ Agreement along with the modalities

[48] Scholtz et al, 'A New Dawn for Global Benefit-Sharing: Capitalizing on the Global Biodiversity Framework for Marine Genetic Resources from Areas Beyond National Jurisdiction' (IUCN, 2023).

[49] UNCLOS, Part XI.

[50] Scovazzi (n 45).

[51] Agreement under the United Nations Convention on the Law of the Sea on the Conservation and Sustainable Use of Marine Biological Diversity of Areas Beyond National Jurisdiction (adopted 19 June 2023) Art 7, www.un.org/bbnj/ (BBNJ Agreement).

for the sharing of monetary benefits from the utilisation of MGRs and DSI on MGR.[52]

Non-monetary benefits to be shared include access to samples and sample collection; access to DSI; open access to FAIR (findable, accessible, interoperable and reusable) scientific data; and transfer of marine technology.[53]

V. CONCLUDING REMARKS

DSI also applies to marine bioprospecting. So far, DSI from MGR in ABNJ amounts to only 1 per cent of the total global DSI dataset.[54] However, with the increasing demand for MGR and their information for research and industry, and the rapid development of DSI technology, this amount is likely to increase, and with it the need for an international regime for fair and equitable sharing of benefits from the use of both MGR as such and their DSI.

The current transaction-based ABS regime under the CBD, which governs access to genetic resources within national jurisdictions, has proven ill-suited for promoting the fair and equitable sharing of benefits, with the dematerialisation of genetic resources through DSI as an exacerbating factor. This applies even more so to MGR and their DSI from ABNJ. The challenge has therefore been to reconstruct the ABS system into one in which benefits are triggered not only by the act of access or utilisation, and where DSI is subject to benefit-sharing requirements.[55] This has been a contentious matter under both the CBD and the BBNJ negotiations.

With the adoption of the Global Biodiversity Framework and the decision on DSI, the CBD COP15 broke a deadlock by acknowledging that fair and equitable sharing of benefits from the use of DSI was needed and by agreeing to establish a multilateral mechanism, including a global fund for that purpose.

This helped the BBNJ Intergovernmental Committee – which for a long time was reluctant to be a first mover on this issue – to also break its deadlock and agree on a multilateral mechanism with MGR and DSI treated on an equal footing and covering both monetary and non-monetary benefits. Under both instruments, it is presupposed that benefit sharing will flow back to conservation and sustainable use, and that the rights of indigenous peoples and local communities, including with respect to the traditional knowledge associated with the genetic resources they hold, shall be taken into account.

[52] ibid Art 14.
[53] ibid Art 14.
[54] Scholtz (n 48).
[55] Lawson and Rourke (n 36).

While the mechanisms under both instruments appear compatible regarding DSI, their modalities for benefit sharing (for monetary benefits under the BBNJ instrument) need to be spelled out by the respective COPs. It will be important that the two instruments interact to harmonise the rules of use of DSI from terrestrial resources and MGR as much as possible and provide simplicity and legal certainty for the use of the whole DSI global dataset.[56]

[56] Scholtz (n 48).

6

Coordinating UNCLOS Regimes: An Analysis of the Interface of the Competencies of the ISA and IMO with Respect to Activities in the Area

ALDO CHIRCOP, ALFONSO ASCENCIO-HERRERA AND FREDRIK HAAG

I. INTRODUCTION

THE UNITED NATIONS Convention on the Law of the Sea, 1982 (UNCLOS) established the international seabed area (the Area) beyond the limits of national jurisdiction and its non-living resources as the common heritage of mankind and the International Seabed Authority (ISA, the Authority) as the sole regulator of exploration and exploitation of those resources.[1] While at this time only seabed exploration activities are underway, exploitation may commence in the years to come. Locations of interest are remote areas in the Atlantic, Indian and Pacific oceans. Activities in the Area and supporting shipping will be inextricably interlinked because the remoteness of the areas will require ships as platforms for mineral recovery and transportation of extracted minerals to markets.

Accordingly, the mandates of the ISA and the International Maritime Organization (IMO) will interface and require coordination. How they interface with respect to activities in the Area was not analysed in detail until a recent study conducted by the ISA and IMO, on which this chapter is based.[2] While

This chapter was originally submitted for publication on 13 May 2021.

[1] United Nations Convention on the Law of the Sea (adopted 10 December 1982, entered into force 16 November 1994) 1833 UNTS 3 (UNCLOS) Arts 1(1)(1), 136 and 156(1)–(2).

[2] International Seabed Authority and International Maritime Organization, 'Competencies of the International Seabed Authority and the International Maritime Organization in the Context of Activities in the Area' (International Seabed Authority 2019) ISA Technical Study No 25.

the ISA is the competent international organisation for activities in the Area, the IMO is the competent international organisation for international shipping and navigation under UNCLOS, as well as for the prevention of pollution from dumping of wastes and other matter at sea. The ISA's roles and tasks are expressly named by UNCLOS in numerous provisions,[3] whereas the IMO's role is usually inferred by reason of the subject matter of the provisions concerned. The topics of interface include maritime safety (human safety and navigation safety), marine environmental protection (operational vessel-source pollution, anti-fouling systems, ballast waters, dumping or disposal of wastes), seafarer training, accommodation of activities in the Area, and responsibility and liability regimes. The two organisations have already anticipated the need for cooperation: they have a framework agreement to facilitate exchange of information on best practices and are exploring issues related to their respective competencies to facilitate development and implementation of the regulatory framework of activities in the Area.[4]

This chapter discusses how the two organisations' competencies interface to provide insights into how separate legal regimes converge to enable the regulation of activities in the Area. In addition to UNCLOS, the discussion draws on the Agreement relating to the Implementation of Part XI of UNCLOS (Implementation Agreement),[5] ISA Exploration Regulations and the Draft Exploitation Regulations under negotiation in the ISA Council, and pertinent IMO conventions and subsidiary instruments. This discussion is undertaken against the backdrop of the Seabed Disputes Chamber's Advisory Opinion on Responsibilities and Obligations of States with respect to Activities in the Area, 2011.[6] The bulk of the chapter focuses on where and how the mandates interface in the respective regulatory efforts and identifies gaps and issues on which further research is needed. The chapter concludes with reflections on cooperation between the ISA and IMO.

II. MANDATES OF THE ISA AND IMO

A. The ISA

The Authority formally came into being on 16 November 1994, the date of the entry into force of UNCLOS. UNCLOS Part XI sets up the ISA as 'the

[3] ISA roles are also inferred in other provisions, eg UNCLOS, Arts 197 and 235(3).

[4] Agreement of Cooperation between the International Maritime Organization (IMO) and the International Seabed Authority (ISA) (signed 23 February and 1 March 2016) www.isa.org.jm/files/documents/EN/Regs/IMO.pdf (IMO-ISA Agreement).

[5] General Assembly resolution 48/263 and the Agreement relating to the implementation of Part XI of the United Nations Convention on the Law of the Sea of 10 December 1982 (adopted 28 July 1994, entered into force 16 November 1994) 1836 UNTS 3 (Implementation Agreement).

[6] Responsibilities and Obligations of States with respect to Activities in the Area (Advisory Opinion) [2011] ITLOS Reports 10 (1 February 2011) para 57.

organization' through which states parties shall 'organize and control activities in the Area'[7] on behalf of mankind in accordance with Part XI and the Implementation Agreement.[8] While the Authority's powers and functions are limited to those expressly conferred, UNCLOS and the Implementation Agreement also provide for incidental powers as necessary.[9] The ISA organises, carries out and controls activities in the Area, and has the power to take measures to ensure compliance, including inspection of installations.[10] It is empowered to adopt and uniformly apply rules, regulations and procedures,[11] including

> to secure effective protection of the marine environment from harmful effects directly resulting from activities in the Area or from shipboard processing immediately above a mine site of minerals derived from that mine site, taking into account the extent to which such harmful effects may directly result from drilling, dredging, coring and excavation and from disposal, dumping and discharge into the marine environment of sediment, wastes or other effluents.[12]

The ISA also has responsibilities with respect to the protection of the marine environment,[13] protection of human life[14] and accommodation of activities.[15] It has the power to adopt rules, regulations and procedures on the protection of the marine environment from any harmful effects that may arise from activities in the Area and to facilitate interstate cooperation concerning liability.[16]

The ISA performs this mandate through the Assembly, as the supreme organ consisting of the entire membership; the Council, as the executive organ; the Secretariat; and the Enterprise (currently not operational), as the organ through which in the future the Authority will undertake activities in the Area directly. The Legal and Technical Commission (LTC)[17] and the Finance Committee[18] are subsidiary organs under the Council and the Assembly, respectively. The Assembly adopts general policies on the Authority's competencies and approves the Council's recommendations of rules, regulations and procedures on prospecting, exploration and exploitation in the Area.[19] The Council is empowered to establish specific policies on any question or matter within the ISA's competence.[20] It supervises and coordinates the implementation of Part XI on

[7] UNCLOS, Art 157(1); Implementation Agreement, annex s 1(1).
[8] UNCLOS, Arts 137(2), 153(1) and 157(1); Implementation Agreement, Art 2(1).
[9] UNCLOS, Art 157(2); Implementation Agreement, annex s 1, para 1.
[10] UNCLOS, Art 153(1).
[11] ibid Art 160 and annex III, Art 17(2)(1).
[12] ibid annex III, Art 17(2)(f).
[13] ibid Art 145.
[14] ibid Art 146.
[15] ibid Art 147(2).
[16] ibid Art 235(3).
[17] ibid Art 165.
[18] Implementation Agreement, annex, s 9.
[19] UNCLOS, Arts 160(1)–(2)(f).
[20] ibid Art 162(1).

all questions and matters within the ISA's competence,[21] approves plans of work for exploration and exploitation,[22] and controls activities in the Area.[23] The LTC formulates and submits to the Council the rules, regulations and procedures after consideration of all relevant factors, including assessments of environmental implications, and maintains them under review.[24] The Finance Committee may make recommendations on proposed financial rules, regulations and procedures on matters under its competence.[25] The regime for activities in the Area has policies for resource development, orderly, safe and rational resource management, and the efficient conduct of activities to avoid unnecessary waste.[26]

The entities that may undertake exploration and exploitation activities include states parties; state enterprises; persons possessing the nationality of states parties who are sponsored by those states parties and meet eligibility requirements; and the future enterprise.[27] Minerals recovered from the Area may only be alienated in accordance with the rules, regulations and procedures of the ISA.[28] Activities in the Area are required to be carried out in accordance with a plan of work reviewed by the LTC and approved by the Council. Upon its approval, the plan of work shall be in the form of a contract.[29]

The pertinent subsidiary instruments adopted by the ISA concern regulations for prospecting and exploration of polymetallic nodules,[30] polymetallic sulphides[31] and cobalt-rich crusts.[32] The ISA has also deliberated on draft regulations for exploitation which are at an advanced stage of development.[33]

B. The IMO

Established in 1948 as a specialised agency of the United Nations, the IMO has a broad mandate to facilitate cooperation in maritime regulation and adoption

[21] ibid Art 162(2)(a).
[22] Implementation Agreement, annex, s 3(11)(a) read together with s 1(6)–(11) in accordance with UNCLOS, annex III, Art 6.
[23] UNCLOS, Art 162(2)(l).
[24] ibid Art 165(2).
[25] Implementation Agreement, annex, s 9(7)(a) and (f).
[26] UNCLOS, Art 150(a)–(b).
[27] ibid Art 153(2).
[28] ibid Art 137(2).
[29] ibid Art 153(3) and annex III, Art 3(5).
[30] Regulations on Prospecting and Exploration for Polymetallic Nodules in the Area (adopted 13 July 2000 and updated and adopted 25 July 2013) www.isa.org.jm/files/documents/EN/Regs/PN-en.pdf (Nodules Regulations).
[31] Regulations on Prospecting and Exploration for Polymetallic Sulphides in the Area (adopted 7 May 2010) www.isa.org.jm/files/documents/EN/Regs/PolymetallicSulphides.pdf (Sulphides Regulations).
[32] Regulations on Prospecting and Exploration for Cobalt-rich Ferromanganese Crusts in the Area (adopted 27 July 2012) https://isa.org.jm/files/files/documents/isba-18a-11_0.pdf (Cobalt Regulations).
[33] Draft Regulations on Exploitation of Mineral Resources in the Area, Prepared by the Legal and Technical Commission, ISBA/25/C/WP.1 (22 March 2019) https://isa.org.jm/files/files/documents/isba_25_c_wp1-e_0.pdf (Draft Exploitation Regulations).

of the highest practicable standards for safety, navigation efficiency and vessel-source pollution prevention.[34] It is empowered to develop legal instruments for adoption by states,[35] and to consider and make recommendations to other intergovernmental organisations.[36] Its portfolio includes over 50 international conventions,[37] the most relevant of which for this chapter concern the IMO's own constitutive convention,[38] maritime safety and security conventions (LLC, COLREGS, SOLAS, SAR, SUA Convention and Protocol),[39] pollution prevention conventions (London Convention and Protocol, MARPOL, AFS, BWMC, Hong Kong Convention),[40] a seafarer training convention (STCW),[41] civil liability and compensation conventions (LLMC, CLC, IOPC, HNS, Bunker Convention),[42]

[34] Convention on the International Maritime Organization (adopted 6 March 1948, entered into force 17 March 1958) 289 UNTS 3 as amended (IMO Convention) Art 1(a).

[35] ibid Art 2(b).

[36] ibid Art 2(a).

[37] IMO, 'Comprehensive Information on the Status of Multilateral Conventions and Instruments in Respect of Which the International Maritime Organization or Its Secretary-General Performs Depositary or Other Functions' (2 March 2021) wwwcdn.imo.org/localresources/en/About/Conventions/StatusOfConventions/Status%20-%202021.pdf.

[38] IMO Convention.

[39] International Convention on Load Lines (adopted 5 April 1966, entered into force 21 July 1968) 640 UNTS 133 (LLC); Convention on the International Regulations for Preventing Collisions at Sea (adopted 20 October 1972, entered into force 15 July 1977) 1050 UNTS 16 (COLREGS); International Convention for the Safety of Life at Sea (adopted 1 November 1974, entered into force 25 May 1980) 1184 UNTS 2 (SOLAS); International Convention on Maritime Search and Rescue (adopted 27 April 1979, entered into force 22 June 1985) 1405 UNTS 97 (SAR Convention); Convention for the Suppression of Unlawful Acts Against the Safety of Maritime Navigation (adopted 10 March 1988, entered into force 1 March 1992) 1678 UNTS 201 as amended by Protocol for the Suppression of Unlawful Acts Against the Safety of Fixed Platforms Located on the Continental Shelf (adopted 10 March 1988, entered into force 1 March 1992) 1678 UNTS 201 (SUA Convention); Protocol of 2005 to the Convention for the Suppression of Unlawful Acts Against the Safety of Maritime Navigation (adopted 14 October 2005, entered into force 28 July 2010) IMO Doc LEG/CONF 15/21 (1 November 2005) as amended by Protocol for the Suppression of Unlawful Acts Against the Safety of Fixed Platforms Located on the Continental Shelf (adopted 14 October 2005, entered into force 28 July 2010) IMO Doc LEG/CONF 15/22 (1 November 2005) (SUA Protocol).

[40] Convention on the Prevention of Marine Pollution by Dumping of Wastes and Other Matter (adopted 29 December 1972, entered into force 30 August 1975) 1046 UNTS 120 (London Convention); Protocol to the Convention on the Prevention of Marine Pollution by Dumping Wastes and Other Matter (adopted 7 November 1996, entered into force 24 March 2006) (1997) 36 ILM 1 (London Protocol); International Convention for the Prevention of Pollution from Ships (adopted 2 November 1973) 1340 UNTS 184 as amended by the Protocol of 1978 relating to the International Convention for the Prevention of Pollution from Ships of 1973 (adopted 17 February 1978, entered into force 2 October 1983) 1340 UNTS 61, and Protocol of 1997 to amend the International Convention for the Prevention of Pollution from Ships, 1973, as modified by the Protocol of 1978 (adopted 26 September 1997, entered into force 19 May 2005) Can TS 2010 No 14 (MARPOL); International Convention on the Control of Harmful Anti-fouling Systems (adopted 5 October 2001, entered into force 17 September 2008) Can TS 2010 No 15 (AFS Convention); International Convention for the Control and Management of Ships' Ballast Water and Sediments (adopted 13 February 2004, entered into force 8 September 2017) IMO Doc BWM/CONF/36 (16 February 2004) (BWMC); Hong Kong International Convention for the Safe and Environmentally Sound Recycling of Ships (adopted 15 May 2009, not yet in force) IMO Doc SR/CONF/45 (19 May 2009) (Hong Kong Convention).

[41] International Convention on Standards of Training, Certification and Watchkeeping for Seafarers (adopted 7 July 1978, entered into force 28 April 1984) 1361 UNTS 2 (STCW Convention).

[42] Convention on Limitation of Liability for Maritime Claims (adopted 19 November 1976, entered into force 1 December 1986) 1456 UNTS 221 as amended by Protocol of 1996 to Amend the

and subsidiary codes and guidelines. The maritime safety and environmental conventions enable the IMO, through its Maritime Safety Committee (MSC) and Marine Environmental Protection Committee (MEPC), to maintain oversight of those instruments and provide for their amendment and the adoption of subsidiary instruments, such as mandatory and voluntary codes, guidelines and resolutions. These instruments provide substantive content to the jurisdictional schemes and prescriptions for cooperation on international navigation and shipping in UNCLOS, as well as helping to maintain public order on the high seas.

The IMO's regulatory role is implicit in rules of reference in UNCLOS provisions. With respect to high seas areas, the role is particularly visible in Part VII on setting the international standards and rules for flag state obligations. Flag states enjoy exclusive jurisdiction and control over their ships on the high seas in administrative, technical and social matters, which amount to a due diligence obligation.[43] This obligation includes: 'manning of ships, labour conditions and the training of crews, taking into account the applicable international instruments';[44] ensuring safety at sea by taking measures so that the 'master, officers and, to the extent appropriate, the crew are fully conversant with and required to observe the applicable international regulations concerning the safety of life at sea, the prevention of collisions, the prevention, reduction and control of marine pollution, and the maintenance of communications by radio';[45] and taking measures on the above matters and on ship construction, equipment and seaworthiness, ship surveys, onboard charts, nautical publications and equipment, qualified masters and officers, and sufficient crew. The measures must conform to generally accepted international regulations, procedures and practices.[46]

Convention on Limitation of Liability for Maritime Claims, 1976 (adopted 2 May 1996, entered into force 13 May 2004) Can TS 2008 No 18 (LLMC); International Convention on Civil Liability for Oil Pollution Damage (adopted 29 November 1969, entered into force 19 June 1975) 973 UNTS 3, as amended by Protocol to Amend the International Convention on Civil Liability for Oil Pollution Damage, 1969 (adopted 27 November 1992, entered into force 30 May 1996) 1956 UNTS 255 (CLC); International Convention on the Establishment of an International Fund for Compensation for Oil Pollution Damage (adopted 18 December 1971, entered into force 16 October 1978) 1110 UNTS 57, as amended by the Protocol of 1992 to Amend the International Convention on the Establishment of an International Fund for Compensation for Oil Pollution Damage, 1971 (adopted 27 November 1992, entered into force 30 May 1996) 1953 UNTS 330 (IOPC Funds Convention); Protocol of 2003 to the International Convention on the Establishment of an International Fund for Compensation for Oil Pollution Damage, 1992 (adopted 16 May 2003, entered into force 3 March 2005) Can TS 2010 No 4 (IOPC Supplementary Fund); International Convention on Liability and Compensation for Damage in Connection with the Carriage of Hazardous and Noxious Substances by Sea (adopted 2 May 1996, not in force) 35 ILM 1406 as amended by Protocol of 2010 to Amend the International Convention on Liability and Compensation for Damage in connection with the Carriage of Hazardous and Noxious Substances by Sea, 1996 (adopted on 30 April 2010, not in force) IMO Doc LEG/CONF.17/10 (4 May 2010) (HNS Convention & Protocol); International Convention on Civil Liability for Bunker Oil Pollution Damage (adopted 23 March 2001, entered into force 21 November 2008) Can TS 2010 No 3 (Bunker Convention).

[43] UNCLOS, Art 94(1).

[44] ibid Art 94(3).

[45] ibid Art 94(4).

[46] ibid Art 94(5).

States parties have a duty to act through the IMO to establish international rules and standards, and to promote the adoption of routing systems designed to minimise accidents which might cause pollution.[47] Flag states are expected to legislate standards for their ships that 'have the same effect as that of generally accepted international rules and standards established through the competent international organization or general diplomatic conference'.[48] They are also required to regulate atmospheric pollution from their ships, wherever they are, 'taking into account internationally agreed rules, standards and recommended practices and procedures'.[49] Indeed, all states 'acting especially through competent international organizations or diplomatic conference' are to endeavour to adopt global rules, standards and recommended practices and procedures for such pollution. Similarly, with respect to dumping as defined in UNCLOS,[50] Article 210(4) allocates roles to competent international organisations, including the IMO. The exercise of prescriptive jurisdiction by states 'shall be no less effective in preventing, reducing and controlling such pollution than the global rules and standards'.[51] Accordingly, the IMO has competence to adopt international, rules, regulations and standards for vessel-source pollution irrespective of the marine area to inform the exercise of prescriptive jurisdiction by states.

Similarly, the exercise of enforcement jurisdiction over ships is informed by IMO rules and standards. States have an obligation to legislate to enable enforcement by implementing 'applicable international rules and standards established through competent international organizations or diplomatic conference' with respect to pollution from or through the atmosphere.[52] The principal IMO instrument nourishing this provision is MARPOL Annex VI, which plays a vital role in regulating a range of harmful emissions from ships. With respect to dumping, Article 216 includes an obligation for flag states to enforce, inter alia, 'applicable international rules and standards established through competent international organizations or diplomatic conference for the prevention, reduction and control of pollution of the marine environment'.[53] This obligation also applies to any other state (eg the sponsoring state and other states receiving minerals from the Area) 'with regard to acts of loading of wastes or other matter occurring within its territory or at its off-shore terminals'.[54]

The London Convention and London Protocol establish regulatory regimes for dumping at sea and serve to nourish UNCLOS, Articles 210 and 216. The London Protocol designates the IMO as 'the' competent organisation, and provides it with a dedicated mandate and several responsibilities.[55] The London

[47] ibid Art 211(1).
[48] ibid Art 211(2).
[49] ibid Art 212(1).
[50] ibid Art 1(5).
[51] ibid Art 210(6).
[52] ibid Art 222.
[53] ibid Art 216(1).
[54] ibid Art 216(1)(c).
[55] London Protocol, Arts 1(2) and 19.

Convention defines dumping consistently with UNCLOS but, together with the London Protocol, excludes 'disposal of wastes or other matter directly arising from, or related to the exploration, exploitation and associated off-shore processing of sea-bed mineral resources'.[56]

III. INTERFACE BETWEEN ACTIVITIES IN THE AREA AND SHIPPING REGULATION

A. The Meaning of 'Activities in the Area'

The Seabed Disputes Chamber provided helpful guidance in shaping our understanding of the meaning and scope of 'activities in the Area' governed by Part XI of UNCLOS. UNCLOS defines the term generically as 'all activities of exploration for, and exploitation of, the resources of the Area'.[57] 'Exploration' and 'exploitation' are not defined, but 'resources' means 'all solid, liquid or gaseous mineral resources *in situ* in the Area at or beneath the seabed, including polymetallic nodules',[58] and 'when recovered from the Area [they] are referred to as "minerals"'.[59]

In considering Article 145 on the protection of the marine environment, the Chamber observed that 'activities in the Area' included 'drilling, dredging, excavation, disposal of waste, construction and operation or maintenance of installations, pipelines and other devices related to such activities, and in respect of which the Authority is empowered to adopt rules, regulations and procedures'.[60] The ISA has regulatory power on the harmful effects produced from mining operations (drilling, dredging, coring excavation) and the disposal of ensuing wastes in the marine environment.[61] Land-based processing and transportation of minerals on the high seas are not included as activities in the Area. However, 'shipboard processing immediately above a mine site of minerals derived from that mine site' is considered as part of activities in the Area.[62]

The notion of 'exploration' in the Nodules Regulations and Sulphides Regulations is broader than 'activities in the Area'.[63] The exploration regulations include 'testing of processing facilities and transportation systems and in that of exploitation, the construction and operation of processing and transportation

[56] London Convention, Art III(1)(c); London Protocol, Art 1(4)(4).
[57] UNCLOS, Art 1(1)(3).
[58] ibid Art 133(a). The ITLOS commented on these definitions. Advisory Opinion (n 6) para 82.
[59] UNCLOS, Art 133(b).
[60] Advisory Opinion (n 6) paras 84–87.
[61] ibid para 86; UNCLOS, annex III, Art 17(2)(f).
[62] Advisory Opinion (n 6) para 88, referring to UNCLOS, annex III, Art 17(2)(f).
[63] Nodules Regulations, reg 1(3)(b) and (a); Sulphides Regulations, reg 1(3)(b) and (a).

systems'.[64] In giving primacy to the narrower provisions of UNCLOS over the broader provisions of the regulations,[65] the Chamber determined that (i) exploration and exploitation include the recovery of minerals from the seabed and lifting them to the surface,[66] (ii) activities separating water from minerals, separation of minerals and disposal at sea are included in activities of the Area, whereas land-based processing is excluded,[67] and (iii) transportation in situ (connected with extraction and lifting) between installations and vessels on the high seas above the Area is included in activities in the Area. Transportation ex situ to unloading points on land is excluded to avoid conflict with the high seas regime.[68] Finally, although prospecting is not included in the notion of 'activities in the Area', 'considering that prospecting is often treated as the preliminary phase of exploration in mining practice and legislation, the Chamber considers it appropriate to observe that some aspects of the present Advisory Opinion may also apply to prospecting'.[69] The Chamber appears to have read down the scope of the exploration regulations, and in doing so pointed to aspects of the interface between the respective competencies of the ISA and IMO.

In summary, 'activities in the Area' generally refer to exploration and exploitation of mineral resources on the seabed and subsoil of the Area, and more specifically comprehend:

- drilling, dredging, coring, excavation and lifting minerals to the surface;
- separating water from minerals on board immediately above a mine site;
- disposal, dumping and discharge into the marine environment of sediment, wastes or other effluents;
- in situ transportation, such as between an installation and a vessel; and
- construction and operation or maintenance of installations, pipelines and other devices related to such activities.

B. Shipping Activities Related to Mining

The consequence of using ships and installations to support activities in the Area is that the UNCLOS regimes for activities in the Area and navigation and shipping interact. Additionally, activities in the Area interface with the regime for dumping at sea.

[64] Advisory Opinion (n 6) paras 91–92.
[65] ibid para 93.
[66] ibid para 94.
[67] ibid para 95.
[68] ibid para 96.
[69] ibid para 98.

Vessels engaged in activities in the Area may be registered in the sponsoring state or by another state, ie a flag state. If the vessels are engaged on international voyages – that is, the port of departure and port of arrival are not ports in the same state – a variety of international maritime rules and standards will apply to those ships. Vessels will also be used on cabotage service, ie using ports of departure and return in the same state. Although a range of rules and standards apply to these vessels, the sponsoring state as the cabotage jurisdiction would likely need to consider the extension of the full range of rules and standards applicable to international shipping to maximise maritime safety and pollution prevention.

The applicable regulations concern maritime safety, environmental protection, labour standards, seafarer training and maritime security. There will likely be new classes of ships, but the range of vessels subject to current maritime regulation include bulk carriers, special purpose ships,[70] offshore supply vessels (OSVs) and offshore installations (eg drillships, semi-submersibles, platforms, mobile offshore drilling units – MODUs).[71] Not all aspects and activities of MODUs are necessarily subject to IMO regulation. For example, whereas construction of MODUs is governed by an IMO standard, the drilling activity itself is not. Similarly, whereas the seafaring crew of a drillship are subject to STCW requirements, the drilling crew are not. However, it is arguable that the International Labour Organization (ILO)'s Maritime Labour Convention, 2006 (MLC) would apply to the crew of a drillship.[72] There will also be other technologies not captured by current regulation, such as seabed excavators, collectors and pipelines. Submersibles are covered in some respects (eg for pollution prevention in MARPOL), but not in the COLREGS.

The 'interface' between legal regimes arises where there is actual or potential interaction of activities and competencies of the ISA and IMO. Identification of an interface is not per se indicative of lead or supportive roles. There are numerous provisions in UNCLOS where multiple organisations are competent with respect to the same provision because each of those organisations may have something to contribute due to their mandates and expertise.[73] Assessment of the interface requires textual interpretation in the overall context of the regimes for seabed mining and navigation and shipping.

[70] Code of Safety for Special Purpose Ships adopted by Resolution MSC.266(84) on 13 May 2008 (SPS Code) reg 3.

[71] Code for the Construction and Equipment of Mobile Offshore Drilling Units adopted by Resolution Res.A.1023(26) on 2 December 2009 (MODU Code) reg 1.3.

[72] Seafarer is defined as 'any person who is employed or engaged or works in any capacity on board a ship to which this Convention applies'. Maritime Labour Convention (adopted 23 February 2006, entered into force 20 August 2013) Can TS 2013 No 16 (MLC) Art II(1)(f).

[73] '"Competent or Relevant International Organizations" under the United Nations Convention on the Law of the Sea', *Law of the Sea Bulletin* No 31, 79–95, www.un.org/depts/los/doalos_publications/LOSBulletins/bulletinpdf/bulletinE31.pdf.

IV. INTERFACE OF ISA AND IMO COMPETENCIES

A. Maritime Safety

(i) Promotion of Human Safety in the Area

Article 46 UNCLOS empowers the Authority to 'adopt appropriate rules, regulations and procedures to supplement existing international law as embodied in relevant treaties' as necessary to ensure effective protection of human life with respect to activities in the Area. The ISA is to regulate for the protection of human life on safety aspects concerning exploration and exploitation in a manner to complement international regulations already adopted by other organisations, namely the IMO on maritime safety and seafarer training and the ILO concerning occupational health and safety on board. The MLC definition of seafarer, namely 'any person who is employed or engaged or works in any capacity on board a ship to which this Convention applies', potentially encompasses workers involved in activities in the Area.[74]

The LTC assesses the plan of work for its content for effective protection of human health and safety.[75] The standard clauses for exploration contain rules of reference to international safety, labour and health standards, together with rules that may be adopted by the ISA.[76]

The Draft Exploitation Regulations set out protection of human life as a regulatory principle,[77] provide for the adoption of 'A Health and Safety Plan and Maritime Security Plan'[78] and detailed regulations on 'Safety, labour and health standards'.[79] Both the Exploration Regulations and the Draft Exploitation Regulations under development appear to rely on IMO and ILO rules and standards.

The IMO maritime safety conventions will apply to ships and installations engaged in activities in the Area. The Draft Exploitation Regulations require contractor compliance with such rules,[80] while flag states are bound to apply IMO and other international standards to their ships. They also require contractors to comply with flag state or sponsoring state regulations as applicable.[81] In general, SOLAS and LLC apply to ships on international voyages when the ports of departure and arrival are in different states.[82] Ships departing and returning

[74] MLC, Art II(4).
[75] Nodules Regulations, reg 21(4); Sulphides Regulations, reg 23(4); Cobalt Regulations, reg 23(4).
[76] eg Sulphides Regulations, reg 15.
[77] Draft Exploitation Regulations, draft reg 2(d).
[78] ibid draft reg 7(3)(f).
[79] ibid draft reg 30.
[80] ibid draft reg 30.
[81] ibid draft reg 30(3).
[82] eg SOLAS, chap 1, reg 1(a); LLC, annex A, Art 2(4).

to the same port constitute cabotage and are not captured by SOLAS and LLC, unless the sponsoring state extends the application of international regulations to cabotage.

SOLAS is the most important maritime safety convention setting out minimum technical standards. Most of its regulations, mandatory codes, recommendations and guidelines are relevant for ships operating in the Area. Examples of the principal SOLAS chapters containing likely relevant regulations include: ship surveys and inspections;[83] ship construction;[84] fire protection;[85] life-saving appliances and arrangements;[86] radiocommunications;[87] safety of navigation;[88] carriage of cargoes;[89] carriage of dangerous goods;[90] safe operation of ships;[91] recognised organisations acting on behalf of the flag state;[92] large bulk carriers;[93] and the mandatory IMO Member State Audit Scheme.[94] Each SOLAS chapter identifies the ships it applies to. The flag state may provide limited exemptions from certain rules.[95]

The LLC is relevant for all ships operating on international voyages in relation to activities in the Area, including vessels that may be loading and transporting minerals. Annex I provides rules for determining the freeboard for safe loading, taking into consideration subdivisions in the hull structure and maintaining stability in damage conditions.[96] The rules include seasonal load lines to factor the different navigation conditions of various geographical regions. This means that activities in the Area in various marine regions will have different load lines under Annex II of LLC.

UNCLOS, Article 147(2)(a) provides that 'installations shall be erected, emplaced and removed solely in accordance with this Part and subject to the

[83] SOLAS, chap 1, reg 1(a).

[84] ibid chap II-1, reg 1. See International Goal-Based Ship Construction Standards for Bulk Carriers and Oil Tankers adopted by Resolution MSC.287(87) on 20 May 2010.

[85] SOLAS, chap II-2, reg 1.1.

[86] ibid chap III, reg 1. See International Life-Saving Appliance (LSA) Code adopted by Resolution MSC.48(66) on 4 June 1996.

[87] SOLAS, chap IV, reg 1. See International Code of Signals, adopted by Assembly Resolution A.IV/Res.80 adopted on 27 September 1965. SOLAS, ch IV is also linked to the International Telecommunication Union (ITU)'s Radio Regulations www.itu.int/pub/R-REG-RR-2016.

[88] SOLAS, chap V, reg 1.

[89] ibid chap VI, reg 1. See International Maritime Solid Bulk Cargoes Code (IMSBC Code) adopted by Resolution MSC.268(85) on 4 December 2008.

[90] SOLAS, chap VII, reg 1. The principal code providing detailed regulation for safe packing, marking, handling and carriage is the mandatory IMDG Code. Other codes apply depending on the cargo carried.

[91] ibid chap IX, reg 2. See International Management Code for the Safe Operation of Ships and for Pollution Prevention adopted by Resolution A.741(18) on 17 November 1993 (ISM Code).

[92] SOLAS, chap XI-1, reg 1.

[93] ibid chap XII, reg 2.

[94] ibid chap XIII, reg 2.

[95] ibid chap 1, reg 4.

[96] See International Code on Intact Stability adopted by Resolution MSC.267(85) on 4 December 2008.

rules, regulations and procedures of the Authority'. The provision does not expressly extend the Authority's mandate to regulate construction and equipment standards. The IMO MODU Code has recommendations on design, construction standards and safety measures to protect personnel on board and the environment.[97] Similarly, the SPS Code provides recommendations for design criteria, construction standards and safety measures for such vessels,[98] but does not apply to MODUs.[99] The Code of Safe Practice for the Carriage of Cargoes and Persons by Offshore Supply Vessels sets out a standard for operators and contractors, applying to vessels 'used for the transportation of stores, materials, equipment or personnel to, from and between offshore installations'.[100]

(ii) Navigation Safety

Navigation safety is addressed by SOLAS, Chapter V and COLREGS, each containing regulations relevant for activities in the Area. SOLAS, Chapter V includes undertakings by states,[101] ships' routing, reporting, safe manning and equipment,[102] and rules for safe navigation.[103] Regulation 10 contains recommendations for the use of ship routing systems by all ships which may be voluntary or mandatory.[104] Routing is particularly valuable to help organise maritime traffic and is an effective tool of marine spatial planning. States submit proposals for routing and reporting measures to the IMO for adoption. Once adopted, states have an obligation to adhere to IMO-designated routing and reporting measures, and their enforcement has to comply with international law, including UNCLOS. The master is required to comply with reporting requirements. Ship reporting could be a useful information management and dissemination tool in relation to activities in the Area.

The COLREGS apply to all vessels navigating on the surface of the high seas and connected navigable waters.[105] They provide the rules of the road, which are central to good seamanship and collision avoidance. Vessels enjoying stand-on vessel rights include a 'vessel restricted in her ability to manoeuvre', defined

[97] MODU Code, preamble.
[98] SPS Code, chap 1, reg 1.1.
[99] ibid reg 1.2.2.
[100] Code of Safe Practice for the Carriage of Cargoes and Persons by Offshore Supply Vessels adopted by Resolution A.863(20) on 27 November 1997, reg 1.1.3.
[101] SOLAS, chap V, regs 5 (meteorological services) and 7 (SAR services).
[102] SOLAS, regs 12 (shipborne navigational equipment), 14 (crewing), 16 (equipment maintenance), 18 (equipment approval, surveys, performance standards), 19 (equipment carriage requirements), 19-1 (long-range identification and tracking of ships) and 20 (voyage data recorder).
[103] SOLAS, regs 21 (signalling and SAR), 22 (navigation bridge visibility), 24 (control systems), 25 (steering gear operation), 27 (nautical information), 28 (recording/reporting), 29 (life-saving signals), 31–32 (danger messages), 33 (distress situations), 34 (safe navigation) and 34-1 (master's discretion).
[104] SOLAS, chap V, reg 10, under whose authority the following were adopted: General Provisions on Ships' Routeing adopted by Resolution A.572(14) on 20 November 1985, as amended.
[105] COLREGS, rule 1(a).

to mean 'a vessel which from the nature of her work is restricted in her ability to manoeuvre as required by these Rules and therefore is unable to keep out of the way of another vessel'.[106] Although the COLREGS do not expressly privilege mining activities, functions performed by vessels conducting activities in the Area, such as dredging, surveying, underwater operations and towage operations, are expressly included.[107]

B. Maritime Security

In addition to ensuring the ship is a safe working space and is navigated with due regard to the safety of other ships, ships may be exposed to security concerns such as armed robbery, piracy and terrorist activity. Ships may carry weapons and may themselves be weaponised. The 1988 SUA Convention and SUA Protocol were specifically designed to address unlawful threats to the safety of navigation of ships and fixed platforms on the continental shelf and, among other things, placed a duty on flag states to legislate a range of offences. The SUA Convention defined 'ship' broadly to include 'a vessel of any type whatsoever not permanently attached to the sea-bed, including dynamically supported craft, submersibles, or any other floating craft'.[108] The 1988 Protocol extended protection to fixed platforms, defined to mean 'an artificial island, installation or structure permanently attached to the sea-bed for the purpose of exploration or exploitation of resources or for other economic purposes'.[109] The range of threats addressed include seizure or control of a ship or fixed platform by force or intimidation, acts of violence on board that endanger safety and destruction of the ship or platform.[110] For ships, the SUA Convention applies 'if the ship is navigating or is scheduled to navigate into, through or from waters beyond the outer limit of the territorial sea of a single State, or the lateral limits of its territorial sea with adjacent States'.[111] The SUA Protocol applies to fixed platforms on the continental shelf. In 2005, the two instruments were amended to broaden their application to a wider range of threats, including the transportation of weapons of mass destruction (biological, chemical, nuclear).[112]

The security of vessels, installations and structures engaged in or supporting activities in the Area could be a concern. These operations will take place in remote areas, far from immediate protection or assistance from policing authorities. UNCLOS does not expressly use the term 'security' in setting out the ISA's

[106] ibid rule 3(g).
[107] ibid rule 3(g).
[108] SUA Convention, Art 1.
[109] SUA 1988 Protocol, Art 1(3).
[110] SUA Convention, Art 3; SUA 1988 Protocol, Art 2.
[111] SUA Convention, Art 4(1).
[112] SUA Convention as amended by Protocol of 2005, Art 4(4) amending Art 3(2) and introducing Art 3*bis*.

regulatory powers. As observed earlier, in UNCLOS, Article 146, the Authority has a subsidiary regulatory power with respect to protection of human life, and this could be interpreted to include concern over the security of personnel involved in activities in the Area. The Draft Exploitation Regulations establish a requirement for a Health and Safety Plan and Maritime Security Plan.[113]

C. Marine Environment Protection

(i) Operational Vessel-Source Pollution

As observed earlier, UNCLOS, Article 145 expressly and exclusively empowers the ISA to regulate for the prevention, reduction and control of pollution and other hazards to the marine environment from activities in the Area. The provision concerns, inter alia, pollution prevention by referring to 'harmful effects of drilling, dredging, excavation, disposal of waste, construction and operation or maintenance of installations, pipelines and other devices related to such activities'. These activities may entail the use of ships as platforms for such activities. In such cases, the protection and preservation of the marine environment may necessitate the regulation of harmful wastes and emissions as a direct result of the operation of ships (eg sewage, garbage and air emissions), as distinct from harmful effects produced from the activities in the Area as described in Article 145 and as understood by the Advisory Opinion. The need for pollution prevention from activities in the Area and from shipping in the combined or coordinated operation provides a complementary interface of competencies of the ISA and IMO.

UNCLOS, Article 94 requires the flag state to regulate its ships in accordance with international standards. This rule of reference implicitly refers to maritime regulations concerning the management, recording and reporting of waste handling on board ships and other operations that produce environmental impacts, such as MARPOL and BWMC. MARPOL regulates the discharge of harmful substances from ships,[114] but excludes dumping within the meaning of the London Convention and the 'release of harmful substances directly arising from the exploration, exploitation and associated off-shore processing of seabed mineral resources'.[115]

MARPOL defines 'ship' broadly to include 'a vessel of any type whatsoever operating in the marine environment and includes hydrofoil boats, air-cushion vehicles, submersibles, floating craft and fixed or floating platforms',[116] unless

[113] See Draft Exploitation Regulations, annex VI; Draft Regulation 30 and Draft Annex VI to the Draft Regulations for Exploitation of Mineral Resources in the Area, Note by the Secretariat, ISBA Doc ISBA/26/C/17 (14 May 2020).
[114] MARPOL, Art 2(2)–(3).
[115] ibid Art 2(3)(b)(i) and (ii).
[116] ibid Art 2(4).

the flag state provides an exemption as may be permissible under an annex of MARPOL.[117] The annexes address pollution from oil (I), noxious liquid substances carried in bulk (II), harmful substances carried in packaged form (III), sewage (IV), garbage (V) and air emissions (VI). They apply to all ships, unless the regulations provide otherwise.[118] Standards are set for a broad range of wastes banned from release (eg plastics under Annex V); where release under a prescribed limited concentration is allowed (eg oil content in ballast water); where release of treated waste at a distance from the coast is permitted (eg sewage); or where the wastes are addressed by guidelines alone (eg grey water). There are also dedicated rules for garbage from fixed or floating platforms.[119]

While Annex VI applies to all ships, unless otherwise stated in specific regulations,[120] it raises a question over its scope. Regulation 3.1 appears to exclude emissions from exploitation and associated offshore processing from seabed mineral activities. These include incineration; release of gases and volatile compounds in drilling fluids and cuttings; emissions associated with the treatment, handling and storage of minerals; and emissions from marine diesel engines. Seabed mining activities may involve the use of multipurpose equipment to support both ship operations and activities more directly related to exploration and exploitation at different times. The emissions regulations otherwise applicable to all other ships include ozone-depleting substances, nitrogen oxides, sulphur oxides, particulate matter and volatile organic compounds, as well as shipboard incineration. Further, the IMO is currently developing specific greenhouse gas emission reduction measures for inclusion in the Initial IMO Strategy for the Reduction of Greenhouse Emissions from Ships.[121] The Strategy includes measures to enhance energy efficiency and fuel use. At this time, the energy efficiency regulations do not apply to platforms and drilling rigs,[122] but most other types of ships of 400 gross tons and above are captured.

(ii) Anti-fouling Systems

The AFS Convention regulates the use of anti-fouling systems, defined as 'a coating, paint, surface treatment, surface, or device that is used on a ship to control or prevent attachment of unwanted organisms'.[123] The definition of 'ship' includes a vessel of any type whatsoever operating in the marine environment and includes submersibles, floating craft, fixed or floating platforms, floating storage units (FSUs), and floating production storage and off-loading

[117] ibid annex I, reg 3.1.
[118] ibid annex I, reg 2, annex II, reg 2.1 and annex V, reg 2.
[119] ibid annex V, reg 5.
[120] ibid annex VI, chap I, reg 1.
[121] Initial IMO Strategy for the Reduction of Greenhouse Emissions from Ships, adopted by Resolution MEPC.304/72 on 13 April 2018.
[122] MARPOL, annex VI, chap IV, reg 19(2.2).
[123] AFS Convention, Art 2(2).

units (FPSOs),[124] capturing a wide range of vessels operating in activities in the Area. Ships of 400 gross tonnage and over engaged in international voyages, but excluding fixed or floating platforms, FSUs and FPSOs, are required to undergo an initial survey and subsequent surveys when anti-fouling systems are changed or replaced.[125] International voyage 'means a voyage by a ship entitled to fly the flag of one State to or from a port, shipyard, or offshore terminal under the jurisdiction of another State'.[126]

(iii) Ballast Waters

The BWMC is aimed at preventing, minimising and ultimately eliminating the transfer of harmful aquatic organisms and pathogens through the control and management of ships' ballast water and sediments.[127] States parties 'shall endeavour to co-operate under the auspices of the Organization [IMO] to address threats and risks to sensitive, vulnerable or threatened marine ecosystems and biodiversity in areas beyond the limits of national jurisdiction in relation to Ballast Water Management'.[128] The concern is the uptake of ballast water from one environment and its discharge into another, potentially transferring alien or exotic species.[129] As with other IMO conventions, the BWMC captures a range of vessels supporting activities in the Area by defining 'ship' broadly as 'a vessel of any type whatsoever operating in the aquatic environment and includes submersibles, floating craft, floating platforms, FSUs and FPSOs'.[130] It applies to vessels designed or constructed to carry ballast waters.

(iv) Dumping/Disposal of Wastes

The ISA's environmental regulatory power in Article 145 concerns

> (a) the prevention, reduction and control of pollution and other hazards to the marine environment, including the coastline, and of interference with the ecological balance of the marine environment, particular attention being paid to the need for protection from harmful effects of such activities as drilling, dredging, excavation, *disposal of waste*, construction and operation or maintenance of installations, pipelines and other devices related to such activities;
> (b) the protection and conservation of the natural resources of the Area and the prevention of damage to the flora and fauna of the marine environment. (emphasis added)

[124] ibid Art 2(9).
[125] ibid Annex IV, reg 1(1).
[126] ibid Art 2(5).
[127] BWMC, Art 1(1) and (8).
[128] ibid Art 2(9).
[129] ibid annex, reg A3(4). This contains an exception with respect to 'the uptake and subsequent discharge on the high seas of the same Ballast Water and Sediments'.
[130] ibid Art 1(12).

UNCLOS Annex III further provides:

> Rules, regulations and procedures shall be drawn up in order to secure effective protection of the marine environment from harmful effects directly resulting from activities in the Area or from shipboard processing immediately above a mine site of minerals derived from that mine site, taking into account the extent to which such harmful effects may directly result from drilling, dredging, coring and excavation and *from disposal, dumping and discharge into the marine environment of sediment, wastes or other effluents.*[131] (emphasis added)

Clearly, the Authority is the only competent international organisation in these provisions. Article 209 further supports this competence by providing that 'international rules, regulations and procedures shall be established in accordance with Part XI to prevent, reduce and control pollution of the marine environment from activities in the Area'. Article 215 reiterates this with respect to enforcement.

Article 1 defines 'dumping' as including 'any deliberate disposal of wastes or other matter from vessels … platforms or other man-made structures at sea'.[132] However, it excludes disposal of wastes from the operations of vessels, platforms and man-made structures, and includes

> wastes or other matter transported by or to vessels … platforms or other man-made structures at sea, operating for the purpose of disposal of such matter or derived from the treatment of such wastes or other matter on such vessels … platforms or structures.[133]

Although the Article 1 definition includes disposal of waste, Article 145 is unambiguous in allocating regulatory power over disposal of wastes from activities in the Area to the ISA.

The Advisory Opinion considered wastes that might be generated during exploration and exploitation. It did not consider the deliberate disposal of platforms and man-made structures following decommissioning, possibly because this action is not captured by the notions of exploration and exploitation. Article 145(a) limits the power to 'construction and operation or maintenance of installations'. It appears that 'any deliberate disposal of vessels … platforms or other man-made structures at sea' under Article 1 following termination of activities in the Area is captured by Article 210 on pollution by dumping, the London Convention and London Protocol. Although the London Convention and Protocol do not apply to the disposal of wastes from or related to the exploration, exploitation and offshore processing of seabed mineral resources, both instruments include disposal of vessels, platforms and other man-made structures at sea in the definition of dumping. The London Protocol definition

[131] UNCLOS, annex III, Art 14(2)(f).
[132] ibid Art 1(5)(a)(i).
[133] ibid Art 1(5)(b)(i).

includes 'any abandonment or toppling at site of platforms or other man-made structures at sea, for the sole purpose of deliberate disposal'.[134]

In recent years, states parties to the London Convention and London Protocol have considered alternatives to at-sea disposal.[135] Although not yet in force, the Hong Kong Convention promotes safe and environmentally sustainable ship recycling on land.[136] Also, the IMO has developed guidelines for the removal of offshore installations and structures, but they do not appear to apply to areas beyond national jurisdiction.[137] However, *Specific Guidelines for Assessment of Platforms and other Man-made Structures at Sea* have been developed under the London Convention and Protocol, as these wastes are considered permissible wastes under these treaties. These guidelines would thus apply to areas beyond national jurisdiction and were most recently updated in 2019.[138]

D. Seafarer Training Standards

While the ISA has competence for the protection of human life with respect to activities in the Area,[139] the training needs of seafarers on board ships supporting activities in the Area are likely captured by IMO training standards. Qualified and trained crews are essential for seaworthiness. The STCW Convention and accompanying STCW Code are the principal IMO instruments for standards of training and certification of seafarers, with a focus on the master, officers and engine room on sea-going vessels. They ensure that personnel are qualified and fit for their duties from the perspectives of safety of life, property safety and marine environmental protection.[140] Standards are set out for the master and the deck department, engine department, radiocommunication and radio personnel, and include provisions on firefighting, occupational safety, security, medical care and survival.

E. Accommodation of Activities in the Area

Activities in the Area are to 'be carried out with reasonable regard for other activities in the marine environment'.[141] Article 147, concerning accommodation of

[134] London Protocol, Art 1(4)(1)(4).

[135] London Convention Special Meeting Resolution LC.56(SM) on Sea Disposal of Vessels.

[136] Hong Kong Convention, Art 2(7).

[137] Guidelines and Standards for the Removal of Offshore Installations and Structures on the Continental Shelf and in the Exclusive Economic Zone adopted by Resolution A.672(16) on 19 October 1989.

[138] Specific Guidelines for Assessment of Platforms and other Man-made Structures at Sea, LC 41/17/Add.1 (11 October 2019) annex 8.

[139] UNCLOS, Art 146.

[140] STCW Convention, Art 1(2).

[141] UNCLOS, Art 147(1). See also in relation to 'reasonable regard' in the interaction with other maritime sectors: ISA, 'Deep Seabed Mining and Submarine Cables: Developing Practical Options

activities in the Area and in the marine environment, is designed to allow different ocean uses to coexist in the Area. More specifically, the ISA is empowered to regulate installations used for activities in the Area. They are to be erected, emplaced and removed in compliance with ISA rules. Their location must be notified. Further, they may not be established where interference may be caused to the use of recognised sea lanes essential to international navigation or in areas of intense fishing activity, and safety zones shall be designated around them.[142]

Article 147 does not mention artificial islands and structures in the Area, in contrast to Article 60 with respect to the exclusive economic zone (EEZ) and the continental shelf. While artificial islands in the Area are likely unrealistic, structures for use in activities in the Area are realistic. Logically, structures used in activities in the Area ought to be regulated by the Authority, but Article 147 leaves open the possibility that such structures might be subject to other international standards, for example with respect to marking.

The ISA's regulatory authority over installations may be guided by current practice. Coastal state regulation of installations and structures in the EEZ and on the continental shelf is guided by various international standards, such as the discharge of certain wastes addressed by MARPOL. The removal of abandoned or disused installations and structures is to take 'into account any generally accepted international standards established in this regard by the competent international organization'.[143] Similarly, the breadth of safety zones around the artificial islands, installations and structures is to take 'into account applicable international standards' and the breadth shall not exceed 500 metres unless 'authorized by generally accepted international standards or as recommended by the competent international organization'.[144] Consistently, all ships are required to respect the safety zones and to comply with 'generally accepted international standards regarding navigation in the vicinity'.[145]

Other users of the marine environment have a counterpart duty of reasonable regard for activities in the Area.[146] The Draft Exploitation Regulations provide that the ISA, 'in conjunction with member States, shall take measures to ensure that other activities in the Marine Environment shall be conducted with reasonable regard for the activities of Contractors in the Area'.[147] If routing measures for maritime safety in activities in the Area are needed, such as areas to be avoided, they will have to be sought from the IMO under the authority of SOLAS, Chapter V. Routing measures are typically requested by coastal states in their capacity as IMO member states and as states parties to SOLAS.

for the Implementation of the 'Due Regard' and 'Reasonable Regard' Obligations under UNCLOS' (2019) ISA Technical Study No 24.

[142] UNCLOS, Art 147(2).

[143] ibid Art 60(3).

[144] ibid Art 60(5).

[145] ibid Art 60(6).

[146] ibid Art 147(3).

[147] Draft Exploitation Regulations, reg 31(2).

It is arguable that sponsoring states or flag states acting in their capacity as states parties to SOLAS should submit routing proposals to the IMO. Since such measures would be directed to international shipping on the high seas, if and when adopted they would likely be in the form of recommendations. Sponsoring states do not enjoy jurisdiction over international shipping on the high seas. Flag states enjoy exclusive jurisdiction and control over their ships on the high seas. Although the ISA has a cooperation agreement with the IMO, reliance on the sponsoring state or flag state would likely be necessary for proposals for routing measures.

F. Liability and Compensation for Pollution of the Marine Environment

Article 235(3) UNCLOS provides states with a duty to cooperate in the implementation and further development of the international law on responsibility, liability and compensation of environmental damage, and related structures and procedures. Similarly, the London Convention and Protocol have provisions committing states parties to develop procedures for the assessment of liability.[148] This duty may be discharged through the competent international organisations having the pertinent remit.

The guidance provided by the Advisory Opinion on the meaning of 'activities in the Area' sets the scope of the ISA's commensurate power to develop a responsibility and liability regime within its remit. Within that scope, the regulatory remit includes:

> Rules, regulations and procedures shall be drawn up in order to secure effective protection of the marine environment from harmful effects directly resulting from activities in the Area or from shipboard processing immediately above a mine site of minerals derived from that mine site, taking into account the extent to which such harmful effects may directly result from drilling, dredging, coring and excavation and from disposal, dumping and discharge into the marine environment of sediment, wastes or other effluents.[149]

The power includes imposition of penalties on contractors for serious contractual violations.[150] Contractors incur 'responsibility or liability for any damage arising out of wrongful acts in the conduct of its operations, account being taken of contributory acts or omissions by the Authority'.[151] The Authority may also be held responsible or liable 'for any damage arising out of wrongful acts in the exercise of its powers and functions … account being taken of contributory acts or omissions by the contractor'.[152] In both the contractor's and the Authority's case, liability is for the actual amount of damage.

[148] London Convention, Art X; London Protocol, Art 15.
[149] UNCLOS, annex III, Art 17(2)(f).
[150] ibid annex III, Art 18.
[151] ibid Art 22.
[152] ibid Art 22.

The ISA's approach concerning liability for damage to the marine environment appears to be contractual by including a provision in the standard clauses for the exploitation contract, in accordance with Article 22 of Annex III of UNCLOS, holding the contractor liable to the Authority

> for the *actual amount of any damage*, including damage to the Marine Environment, arising out of its wrongful acts or omissions, and those of its employees, subcontractors, agents and all persons engaged in working or acting for them in the conduct of its operations under this Contract, including the costs of reasonable measures to prevent and limit damage to the Marine Environment, account being taken of any contributory acts or omissions by the Authority or third parties.[153] (emphasis added)

The IMO has developed civil liability regimes for international shipping, both for general claims and for damage to the marine environment, but with limited application to incidents on the high seas. The regimes are guided by the principles of strict and limited liability as a matter of public policy. The rationale is to encourage ship owning, enable insurability and ensure provision of vital services to maritime trade. The liability limits are updated periodically. These regimes are not as widely subscribed to by states as the IMO's pollution prevention conventions, such as MARPOL.

Under the LLMC and its 1996 Protocol, the right to limited liability is enjoyed by the shipowner (defined as the owner, charterer, manager and operator of a seagoing ship) and the insurer.[154] To deny the shipowner the right to limitation of liability, a claimant has to cross a high threshold:

> [A] person liable shall not be entitled to limit his liability if it is proved that the loss resulted from his personal act or omission, committed with the intent to cause such loss, or recklessly and with knowledge that such loss would probably result.[155]

Amended in 1996, this provision is specifically intended to establish an unbreakable defence of limitation subject to higher limits of liability.[156] The claims relevant for environmental liability concern 'the raising, removal, destruction or the rendering harmless of a ship which is sunk, wrecked, stranded or abandoned, including anything that is or has been on board such ship', 'removal, destruction or the rendering harmless of the cargo of the ship' and 'claims of a person other than the person liable in respect of measures taken in order to avert or minimize loss for which the person liable may limit his liability in accordance with this Convention, and further loss caused by such measures'.[157] The

[153] Draft Exploitation Regulations, annex 10, Standard Clauses for Exploitation Contract, s 7.
[154] LLMC, Art 1.
[155] ibid Art 4.
[156] See *The Travaux Préparatoires of the LLMC Convention, 1976 and of the Protocol of 1996*, compiled by Francesco Berlingieri (CMI undated) 121 et seq, https://comitemaritime.org/wp-content/uploads/2018/05/Travaux-Preparatoirse-of-the-LLMC-Convention-1976-and-of-the-Protocol-of-1996.pdf.
[157] LLMC, Art 2.

claims do not have geographical limits, but oil pollution claims covered by the CLC are not covered[158] and the LLMC does not apply to 'floating platforms constructed for the purpose of exploring or exploiting the natural resources of the sea-bed or the subsoil thereof'.[159] The liability limits are based on a tonnage formula.[160] Claims and defences are advanced in the domestic courts of states parties; however, states parties may modify the domestic application of the LLMC, for example by limiting its application to specific persons.[161] Thus, while some vessels engaged in supporting seabed mining, such as OSVs and bulkers, are covered, the LLMC does not apply to offshore installations and structures engaged in seabed mining.

Differently from the LLMC, the CLC and the IOPC Funds Convention (including IOPC Supplementary Fund) constitute a compensation system for claims of damage resulting from pollution of the marine environment. The operational Funds at this time are the 1992 Fund and the Supplementary Fund.[162] The CLC and Funds apply to pollution damage outside the ship from persistent oil carried on tankers as cargo or bunkers during a voyage following carriage. Only damage in the territorial sea of states parties and the EEZ is covered. However, 'preventive measures, wherever taken, to prevent or minimize such damage', which could be on the high seas, are compensable.[163] Liability is strict, with limited defences,[164] subject to limitation of liability,[165] and like the LLMC is virtually unbreakable.[166] The range of eligible claims is broad and, in addition to reasonable claims for clean up, reinstatement costs for environmental damage and preventive measures, they may include loss of income.

The Funds provide additional tiers of compensation in the event limited liability under the CLC is inadequate to meet the claims advanced.[167] The CLC ship must have insurance cover. Differently from the CLC, which constitutes the first tier of compensation, ie from the shipowner and insurer, the Funds consist of the cargo owners' share channelled through contributions levied on specified amounts of imported oil in states parties.[168] The geographical scope and types of claim that may be advanced are similar to the CLC. The levels of compensation are substantially higher in the 1992 Fund and even higher in the IOPC Supplementary Fund. In summary, the liability regimes of the CLC and IOPC Funds (including the IOPC Supplementary Fund) providing compensation for

[158] ibid Art 3.
[159] ibid Art 15(5)(b).
[160] ibid Art 6.
[161] ibid Art 15(1).
[162] International Oil Pollution Compensation Funds (2021) https://iopcfunds.org/.
[163] CLC Convention, Art II(b).
[164] ibid Art III.
[165] ibid Art V(1).
[166] ibid Art V(2).
[167] IOPC Funds Convention, Art 2.
[168] ibid Art 10.

damage from pollution to the marine environment do not extend to damage to the marine environment of the high seas and the Area, or to the cargoes of minerals extracted from the Area.

Modelled on the CLC, the Bunker Convention provides a strict liability regime for environmental damage from bunker fuel carried on ships of 1000 tons or more.[169] It has the same compulsory insurance requirement,[170] geographical scope[171] and limited defences[172] as the CLC and IOPC Funds. Thus, preventive measures on the high seas with respect to oil lost there and to mitigate impacts in the EEZ and territorial sea are compensable.[173] Shipowners and their insurers continue to enjoy the right to limit liability under any applicable national or international regime such as the LLMC.[174] In summary, the Bunker Convention is potentially applicable to ships operating and providing support to activities in the Area, but only insofar as the loss of bunker fuel threatens the EEZ and the territorial sea of neighbouring states.

Also modelled on the CLC and IOPC Funds, the HNS Convention and Protocol were adopted to address a range of hazardous and noxious substances not covered by the other compensation regimes and are similarly based on strict[175] and limited liability.[176] They have not entered into force yet. The liability regime anticipates a two-tiered system, consisting of a first tier of shipowner liability based on compulsory insurance[177] and a second tier consisting of a fund with contributions from importers of such substances.[178] The HNS Convention has a similar geographical scope of application with respect to damage to the marine environment as the CLC, IOPC Funds and Bunker Convention, and thus includes preventive measures on the high seas.[179]

V. DISCUSSION

Until now, we have discussed themes on which ISA and IMO regulation actually or potentially interact. We next consider how that interface supports the development of a comprehensive regulatory regime for activities in the Area and identify gaps and possible areas for cooperation.

The starting point is appreciating the significance of the use of ships and installations as platforms for activities in the Area and the respective jurisdictional

[169] Bunker Convention, Art 3(1).
[170] ibid Art 7.
[171] ibid Art 2(b).
[172] ibid Art 3(3).
[173] ibid Art 3(3).
[174] ibid Art 6.
[175] HNS Convention and Protocol, Art 7.
[176] ibid Art 9.
[177] ibid Art 12.
[178] ibid Art 16.
[179] ibid Art 3.

responsibilities. In addition to ISA and IMO competencies, sponsoring states are responsible for regulating contractors' activities in accordance with ISA rules, regulations and procedures, whereas flag states have exclusive jurisdiction over their ships on the high seas in accordance with IMO and other applicable regulations. The Advisory Opinion was mindful to avoid unnecessary conflict in regulating activities in the Area in a manner that could create conflict with UNCLOS provisions concerning navigation on the high seas.[180] That insight lays the ground for a symbiotic view of how activities in the Area and shipping regulation interface. The rules of reference employed in ISA instruments are evidence of this appreciation. A vital consideration in the employment of those rules to import several key IMO safety and pollution prevention regulations in the regime for the Area is their scope of application to international voyages. For example, as in the case of other IMO instruments whose application, whether in whole or in part, is confined to particular classes and tonnages of ships on international voyages, the application of AFS survey rules would have to be extended by the flag state or perhaps required by the sponsoring state.[181] At this time, it is unclear the extent to which, if at all, the mining regulations' rules of reference serve to extend the application of this (and other international standards) to all ships engaged in activities in the Area.

Accordingly, for vessels used to support activities in the Area to be made subject to the highest applicable standards, it will be important that the activities, whether while mobile or stationary, fall within the definition of 'international voyages'. If the vessels concerned operate only from and to one port, whether in the sponsoring state or some other state, they may be characterised as cabotage, thus rendering international rules intended for international voyages inapplicable. This issue could be addressed if activities in the Area are included in the notion of international voyages. Whether this determination is done by the ISA, the sponsoring state or the flag state is a matter of some complexity. Ideally, the sponsoring state should be party to the key IMO instruments concerned to be able to extend the application of those instruments to cabotage. This should cover vessels engaged in activities in the Area flagged by both the sponsoring and flag states.

The ISA's remit on the protection of human life in activities in the Area supplements existing international law, mostly developed by the IMO and ILO. The IMO and ILO have mature and comprehensive legal regimes for maritime safety, training and protection of maritime workers. IMO safety regulation provides a useful framework for addressing many of the human safety needs concerning ships used to support activities in the Area. ILO standards are critical for occupational health and safety. The ISA has recognised the value of these regimes by employing rules of reference in its exploration regulations

[180] Advisory Opinion (n 6) para 96.
[181] Under the authority of UNCLOS, annex III, Art 21(3).

and model agreements to secure the application of IMO and ILO standards. Similar observations on navigation safety can be made. The IMO rules for navigation safety protect human life and orderly use of marine spaces. Routing measures adopted by the IMO could be useful area-based management tools and the COLREGS can help minimise disruptions to mining activities and the risk of collisions.

The ISA's regulation of security is an integral part of protection of human life and could be explained as subsidiary to IMO regulation through the SUA instruments. The SUA Convention is likely applicable to vessels engaged in activities in the Area and flag states that are parties to the Convention have jurisdictional responsibilities. The implications for sponsoring states merit study. However, the SUA Protocol's limited geographical scope of application on the continental shelf leaves a gap for activities in the Area. This is an issue for possible future cooperation between the ISA and the IMO to explore options for extending the protection provided by the SUA Protocol to fixed platforms used in seabed mining in the Area.

While the ISA enjoys exclusive power over the environmental regulation of activities in the Area, the prevention and control of pollution from ships requires an understanding of the scope of multiple legal regimes. While the ISA develops a regime for activities in the Area as explained by the Advisory Opinion, the fact that ships will be used as platforms necessarily engages regimes concerning vessel-source pollution, anti-fouling systems, ballast water management and dumping. Ships will largely be subject to the MARPOL annexes. The Advisory Opinion did not explore the extent to which air emissions, as distinct from discharges at sea, are captured by the ISA's environmental regulatory power over activities in the Area. It is conceivable that 'operation of installations' includes emissions from their operation. A gap is Annex VI, on air pollution, which, as we have seen, does not apply to installations engaged in seabed mining. Emissions and energy efficiency standards do not apply to them. By contrast, should ballast water exchange in the Area be of concern, the BWMC is potentially valuable for minimising problems associated with the transfer of exotic species. If it is desirable to require all ships supporting activities in the Area to be made subject to such a standard, this could be a matter for discussion with the IMO as it is a high seas navigation issue.

Although the ISA is clearly responsible for regulating in situ disposal of wastes, the London Convention and Protocol regimes could provide guidance on how the Authority might regulate waste disposal. The London Protocol provides a framework for waste assessment that includes a waste prevention audit, consideration of waste management options, chemical–physical–biological processes, dump site selection, assessment of potential effects, monitoring and permitting.[182] Whereas Annex 2 of the London Protocol, which provides the procedure for

[182] London Protocol, annex 2.

assessment of wastes or other matter that may be considered for dumping, forms an integral part of the Protocol (*cf* London Protocol, Article 20), additional guidelines for assessment of specific wastes have also been adopted.[183] Although construction and operation as well as maintenance of installations fall within the ISA's regulatory power, the situation is less clear with respect to disposal of vessels, platforms and other man-made structures at sea. Rather, the disposal of vessels, platforms and structures at sea appears to fall under the general definition of dumping in UNCLOS and the London Convention and Protocol. Finally, waste assessment guidelines developed under the London Convention and Protocol could serve as a useful model for the development of standards and guidelines for the disposal of waste generated by activities in the Area.

IMO training regulations for seafarers cover a range of workers, but not all personnel likely to be engaged in activities in the Area. The LTC is empowered to determine whether the proposed plans of work for exploration provide for effective protection of human health and safety, and this could be understood to include the full range of personnel working at sea.[184] The ISA's supplementary power under UNCLOS, Article 146 could be used in a complementary manner to address the non-seafarer competencies needed on board ships and installations engaged in activities in the Area.[185]

The regime for accommodation of activities in the Area provides a basis for enhancing safety. If routing and reporting measures are needed to enhance safety, it is likely that the sponsoring state or flag state, as an IMO member state and SOLAS state party, would have the standing necessary to propose their adoption by the IMO. Ideally, international rules and standards for the safety of installations and structures and for navigation in their vicinity should be uniform to send a consistent message to other users of the marine environment. There may be a range of novel structures and machinery (eg excavators) employed in activities in the Area, and that may require dedicated standards and cooperation from the IMO. The IMO guidelines for the removal of offshore installations and structures, although applicable to the continental shelf and in the EEZ, and the London Convention and Protocol guidance on waste assessment could assist the ISA in discharging its responsibilities under Article 147.

Both the ISA and the IMO enjoy competencies for the development of liability regimes for compensation for pollution damage to the marine environment in their respective remits. The ISA's remit is limited to activities in the Area, including in situ transportation, whereas the IMO's concerns international shipping

[183] IMO, 'Waste Assessment Guidelines Under the London Convention and Protocol' (2014) www.imo.org/en/OurWork/Environment/Pages/wag-default.aspx. See also Revised Specific Guidelines for the Assessment of Vessels adopted by LC 38/16 (2016); Revised Specific Guidelines for Assessment of Platforms and other Man-made Structures at Sea adopted by LC 41/17/Add.1 (2019).

[184] Nodules Regulations, reg 21(4)(a); Sulphides Regulations, reg 23(4)(a); Cobalt Regulations, reg 23(4)(a).

[185] Draft Exploitation Regulations, reg 32(5).

and ex situ transportation of recovered minerals. While having limited application on the high seas, the compensation regimes for international shipping could serve to inform aspects of the liability regime for seabed mining, such as the proposed Environmental Compensation Fund in the Draft Exploitation Regulations.[186]

VI. CONCLUSION

This chapter has demonstrated that ISA and IMO competencies are highly complementary as they interface with respect to activities in the Area. The ISA's regulatory functions and UNCLOS's frequent use of rules of reference to IMO standards produce a symbiotic relationship between the two mandates. This relationship is further reflected in the rules of reference increasingly employed in the development of the regulatory regime, where IMO and potentially also ILO regulations provide complementary regulatory support on maritime safety, security and environmental protection.

As the regulatory regime for seabed mining continues to develop, it is conceivable that regulatory overlaps might emerge despite the allocation of competencies discussed in this chapter. Where necessary, they will need to be addressed on a case-by-case basis in accordance with the ISA–IMO agreement on cooperation. The more likely scenario is one that sees the ISA continually benefiting from the regulatory experience of the IMO and the London Convention and Protocol as it proceeds with the development of exploitation regulations and other supportive instruments that will be needed for their implementation, for example standards and guidelines on matters such as waste assessment.

Finally, while this chapter and ISA Technical Report No 25, on which it is based, have provided the first comprehensive studies of the interface of ISA and IMO competencies and regimes with respect to activities in the Area, more research is needed. Our analysis has raised further questions, such as: Which ISA regulations depend and rely upon or draw from IMO regulations and generally accepted practices, and how? What installations and structures employed in the Area should be considered ships to facilitate coordination between the applicable inspection regimes for seabed mining and international shipping? How should applicable IMO codes, guidelines and generally accepted practices inform, supplement or assist the development of ISA regulations? How should maritime security in seabed mining be regulated? How can international maritime labour law standards be extended and applied to activities in the Area? We invite researchers to consider possible answers to these questions.

[186] ibid s 5, Part IV. See also ISA, 'Study on an Environmental Compensation Fund for Activities in the Area' (2020) ISA Technical Study No 27.

7

What are the Limits of the Protection of Biodiversity Belonging to the Sedentary Species of the Continental Shelves within National Jurisdiction?

EKATERINA ANTSYGINA

I. INTRODUCTION

DESPITE GROWING ATTENTION being paid to the debates on the preservation of the marine environment and biological diversity, there is a potential gap in the protection of the living resources of the continental shelf (sedentary species).[1] The protection of sedentary species is of utmost importance because corals and sponges that belong to these species create structural habitats for others, including endangered and vulnerable species and species of commercial value.[2] The degradation of coral reefs can cause irreparable damage to fragile marine ecosystems.[3] Harmful fishing practices, such as bottom trawling,[4] destroy sedentary species and their habitats, and thus can inflict significant and irreversible changes on the marine environment.[5] Thus, biodiversity and genetic resources that are represented by the sedentary species

[1] Sedentary species are organisms which, at the harvestable stage, are either immobile on or under the seabed or unable to move except in constant physical contact with the seabed or the subsoil (Art 77(4) UNCLOS). Pearl oysters, lobsters, snow crabs, corals and sponges fall under this category.

[2] See, eg Pham et al, 'Removal of Deep-Sea Sponges by Bottom Trawling in the Flemish Cap Area: Conservation, Ecology and Economic Assessment' (2019) 9 *Science Reports* 15843.

[3] Victorero, Watling, Deng Palomares and Nouvian, 'Out of Sight, but Within Reach: A Global History of Bottom-Trawled Deep-Sea Fisheries from 400 m Depth' (2018) 5 *Frontiers in Marine Science* 98.

[4] Bottom trawling is a method of industrial fishing that involves dragging a large net with heavy weights across the seafloor.

[5] See Pham et al (n 2); Victorero (n 3).

or dependent on them are endangered by bottom trawling. Nevertheless, bottom trawling is by default legal fishing practice and occurs primarily on continental shelves.[6]

Article 77 of the United Nations Convention on the Law of the Sea (UNCLOS),[7] which determines the scope of rights over the continental shelf, does not contain express provisions on conservation or protection of the sedentary species. On this basis, some scholars conclude that coastal states do not have jurisdiction to protect the living resources of the shelf as far as the sovereign rights under UNCLOS, Article 77(1) are concerned.[8] Other scholars maintain that the exclusivity of the right to 'exploit', read together with Part XII in general and Article 194(5) UNCLOS in particular, implies the right to conserve the sedentary species.[9]

This legal uncertainty, which might lead to the reluctance of states to impose conservation measures, is especially striking in light of the adoption of the BBNJ Agreement.[10] The BBNJ Agreement addresses the conservation and sustainable use of marine biological diversity (including sedentary species) of areas beyond national jurisdiction. If there is to be a mechanism to protect living organisms belonging to sedentary species beyond national jurisdiction, there should also be one within states' jurisdiction.

The existence of such a mechanism is most significant for the imposition of the conservation measures on the extended continental shelves (ECSs),[11] since coastal states can protect corals and sponges within 200 nautical miles (M) by virtue of the regime of the exclusive economic zone (EEZ) under Article 61 to restore species associated with fisheries or dependent upon harvested species. Beyond 200 M, the waters superjacent the ECS belong to the high seas, where any nation can exercise the freedom of fishing, including bottom trawling. In the absence of regional fisheries management organisations (RFMOs), sedentary species of the ECS can be protected only by the coastal states. Thus, the unilateral actions on the protection of sedentary species on the ECS are especially

[6] UN General Assembly, 'The Impacts of Fishing on Vulnerable Marine Ecosystems: Actions Taken by States and Regional Fisheries Management Organizations and Arrangements to Give Effect to Paragraphs 66 to 69 of General Assembly Resolution 59/25 on Sustainable Fisheries, Regarding the Impacts of Fishing on Vulnerable Marine Ecosystems', Report A/61 (14 July 2006) 8, citing A/60/189, para 116.

[7] United Nations Convention on the Law of the Sea (Montego Bay, 10 December 1982, in force 16 November 1994) 1833 UNTS 396.

[8] Rothwell and Stephens, *The International Law of the Sea*, 2nd edn (Hart Publishing, 2017) 119.

[9] Molenaar, 'Addressing Regulatory Gaps in High Seas Fisheries' (2005) 20 *International Journal of Marine and Coastal Law* 558. See also Czybulka, 'Article 193' in Proelss (ed), *United Nations Convention on the Law of the Sea, A Commentary* (CH Beck, 2017) 1292; Mossop, 'Protecting Marine Biodiversity on the Continental Shelf Beyond 200 Nautical Miles' (2007) 38 *Ocean Development and International Law* 283, 289.

[10] Agreement under the United Nations Convention on the Law of the Sea on the Conservation and Sustainable Use of Marine Biological Diversity of Areas beyond National Jurisdiction (adopted 19 June 2023) www.un.org/bbnj/ (BBNJ Agreement).

[11] The continental shelves beyond 200 nautical miles.

important in the South China Sea, the Caribbean region and West Africa, where RFMOs are yet to be created. It might also be applicable to the Arctic Ocean in future.

The debates in the North-East Atlantic Fisheries Commission (NEAFC) on the rights of states to apply conservation measures unilaterally within the RFMOs' regulatory area indicate that states have started to consider enforcement of conservation rights beyond 200 M.[12] There is no practice on the conservation of sedentary species beyond 200 M, and this might be due to legal uncertainty on the scope of rights over the continental shelf and the lack of legal scholarship on the issue. The unwillingness of coastal states to impose protective measures can also be connected to the possibility of a dispute with other actors with conflicting rights in the absence of clarity on the existing law. Disputes on the imposition of the unilateral conservation measures on ECS might arise between the coastal and flag states, between two coastal states with overlapping ECS or between an RFMO and a coastal state.

This chapter discusses whether the regime of the continental shelf includes a right to conserve living natural resources and whether it can be a basis for the establishment of a moratorium on bottom trawl fishing on ECS. It argues that the coastal states have the right to impose measures protecting their sedentary species on the high seas superjacent their ECS according to Parts VI and XII of UNCLOS coupled with the provisions of the Convention on Biological Diversity (CBD).[13] Such measures are necessary to protect sedentary species from the adverse effects of bottom trawling.

Guided by Articles 77, 192, 194 (5) and 206 of UNCLOS and Articles 6, 7, 8, 10, 11 and 14 of the CBD, the chapter suggests the organisation of environmental impact assessments (EIAs) on the ECS in those regions where bottom trawling might occur to identify the components of biological diversity and vulnerable areas which need to be closed to bottom trawling, and the imposition of a ban on bottom trawling within the vulnerable areas so identified.

II. HARMFUL FISHING PRACTICES ADVERSELY AFFECTING SEDENTARY SPECIES

Bottom trawling is a method of industrial fishing that involves dragging a large net with heavy weights across the seafloor. It occurs primarily on continental shelves, in more environmentally sensitive areas below wave base,[14] and

[12] See Molenaar on the joint proposal by Norway and Russia to amend the NEAFC Recommendation 19:2014: Molenaar, 'Multilateral Creeping Coastal State Jurisdiction and the BBNJ Negotiations' (2020) 36 *International Journal of Marine and Coastal Law* 1, 21–22.

[13] Convention on Biological Diversity (Rio de Janeiro, New York, 5 June 1992–4 June 1993, in force 29 December 1993) 1760 *UNTS* 79.

[14] Oberle, Storlazzi and Hanebuth, 'What a Drag: Quantifying the Global Impact of Chronic Bottom Trawling on Continental Shelf Sediment' (2016) 159 *Journal of Marine Systems* 109.

ecosystems which evolved under conditions of minimal disturbance tend to be less resilient to fishing pressure.[15] While bottom trawling might not target sedentary species, it damages them and destroys their habitats. This can inflict irreversible harm on the marine environment both because the sedentary species represent biodiversity and because some of them (corals, sponges) create a structural habitat for others. The negative effects are especially noticeable for deep-sea ecosystems due to their longevity, slow growth, low reproductive rates, susceptibility to increased sedimentation, fragility and limited ability to recover from physical fragmentation.[16]

Though the problem of fishery using bottom trawling has attracted international attention and attempts to adopt an international agreement banning bottom trawling have been undertaken, there is still no comprehensive instrument on this issue. The need to combat harmful fishing practices, and to protect and conserve the marine environment, is reflected in the non-legally binding Agenda 2030 and Agenda 21.[17] Agenda 2030 suggests prohibiting certain forms of fisheries subsidies that contribute to overcapacity and overfishing (Article 14.6), enhancing the conservation and sustainable use of oceans and their resources by implementing international law as reflected in UNCLOS (Article 14c). Agenda 21 specifically mentions that coral reefs and other marine and coastal habitats are under stress or are threatened from a variety of sources, both human and natural (para 17.72). It also indicates that states should commit themselves to the conservation and sustainable use of marine living resources under national jurisdiction and, to this end, promote the development and use of selective fishing gear and practices that minimise waste in the catch of target species and minimise bycatch of non-target species (para 17.74).

The regulation of bottom trawl fishery on the high seas is done by flag states and the RFMOs or measures adopted by coastal states within their EEZs. But there is a question of whether coastal states can enforce their sovereign rights to protect sedentary species on the ECS.

III. GENERAL OBLIGATIONS TO PROTECT THE MARINE ENVIRONMENT AND BIODIVERSITY

All states have obligations to protect the marine environment under Article 192 UNCLOS. In the reply to the Request for an Advisory Opinion submitted by

[15] Fuller et al, 'How We Fish Matters: Addressing the Ecological Impacts of Canadian Fishing Gear' (Ecology Action Centre, Living Oceans Society, and Marine Conservation Biology Institute, 2008).

[16] UN GA, Report A/61 (n 6) para 50, 15.

[17] UN GA, 'Transforming Our World: The 2030 Agenda for Sustainable Development' (21 October 2015) A/RES/70/1, www.refworld.org/docid/57b6e3e44.html (Agenda 2030); United Nations Conference on Environment & Development 1992, Agenda 21, https://sustainabledevelopment.un.org/content/documents/Agenda21.pdf.

the Sub-Regional Fisheries Commission, the International Tribunal for the Law of the Sea (ITLOS) concluded that the obligation to protect and preserve the marine environment under Article 192 applies to 'all maritime areas'.[18] The obligations of Article 192 are quite wide, but they necessarily imply the protection of all species within the state's jurisdiction: coastal states have to protect, conserve and save the marine environment for future generations. The preservation requires proactive actions on the side of the states to improve the condition of the marine environment.

Article 194(5) sets up a duty of states to adopt measures to protect and preserve rare or fragile ecosystems, as well as the habitat of depleted, threatened or endangered species. The obligation of Article 194(5) requires a higher level of state involvement and more urgent actions.

Additionally, there are obligations to protect biodiversity within national jurisdiction. The CBD ensures the protection and conservation of biological diversity, the sustainable use of the components of biological diversity, and the fair and equitable sharing of the benefits from the utilisation of genetic resources. Article 2 of the CBD defines 'biological diversity' as the variability among living organisms from all sources, including terrestrial, marine and other aquatic ecosystems and the ecological complexes of which they are part; this includes diversity within species, between species and of ecosystems. The living natural resources of the shelf fall under the protection of the CBD.

Articles 6 and 7 of the CBD prescribe the Contracting Parties to develop national strategies for the conservation and sustainable use of biological diversity, to identify components of biological diversity important for its conservation and sustainable use, to monitor them and to identify processes and categories of activities that have or are likely to have significant adverse impacts on the conservation and sustainable use of biological diversity.

The Contracting Parties must also conserve biological diversity in situ, which implies the establishment of marine and coastal protected areas or areas where special measures are adopted to protect the biological diversity (Article 8). Under Article 10, the Contracting Parties must, as far as possible and as appropriate, integrate consideration of the conservation and sustainable use of biological resources into national decision-making and adopt measures relating to the use of biological resources to avoid or minimise adverse impacts on biological diversity. As bottom trawling adversely influences the sedentary species, the coastal states/Contracting Parties have to take proactive steps to prohibit it within their jurisdictions. Article 11 prescribes that Contracting Parties have to, as far as possible and as appropriate, adopt economically and socially sound measures that act as incentives for the conservation and sustainable use of components of biological diversity.

[18] Request for Advisory Opinion Submitted by the Sub-Regional Fisheries Commission, Advisory Opinion of 2 April 2015, ITLOS Reports 2015, 4, 37, para 120.

As Article 22(2) of the CBD provides, the Contracting Parties shall implement the CBD with respect to the marine environment consistently with the rights and obligations of states under the law of the sea. It would be impossible to enforce the provisions of Articles 6–8 of the CBD and the provisions of Part XII of UNCLOS without referring to the corresponding rights and obligations over the continental shelf under Part VI of UNCLOS. For example, coastal states can establish closure areas within their EEZs based on the rights of Part V and guided by the provisions of Part XII and the CBD, but they cannot unilaterally create closure areas beyond national jurisdiction (beyond the EEZ or continental shelf) because their rights for the protection of the marine environment are limited by the constraints of the corresponding regimes of the high seas and the seabed beyond national jurisdiction. The ECS is the area where tension between national and international jurisdictions is the most possible since waters suprajacent ECS belong to the high seas.

If the regime of the continental shelf does not provide for specific rights and obligations to protect the marine environment, a general obligation to protect would not be enforceable and there exists a gap in the protection of biodiversity and the marine environment on the ECS. The main challenges to the assertion that coastal states can impose protective measures on continental shelves beyond 200 M include the narrow interpretation of Article 77 UNCLOS, the obligation of coastal states not to infringe or unjustifiably interfere with freedoms of other states on the high seas (Article 78) and the right to fish on the high seas (Article 116).

IV. THE SCOPE OF RIGHTS OVER THE CONTINENTAL SHELF

Article 77 regulates the rights of the coastal state over the continental shelf and provides that a coastal state exercises sovereign rights to explore the shelf and exploit its natural resources. These rights are exclusive in the sense that if the coastal state does not explore the continental shelf or exploit its natural resources, no one may undertake these activities without the express consent of the coastal state. Article 77(1) does not expressly mention the rights to manage, protect and conserve the living natural resources.

The term 'sovereign rights' was first introduced to the regime of the continental shelf in the 1958 Convention on the Continental Shelf,[19] thus excluding any possibility to claim sovereignty over the continental shelf. During the drafting of the 1958 Convention, many governments suggested that coastal states should have sovereignty over the shelf.[20] If this approach had prevailed, there would

[19] Convention on the Continental Shelf (Geneva, 29 April 1958, in force 10 June 1964) 499 UNTS 311.

[20] See, eg Comments of the Government of the United Kingdom transmitted by a letter dated 2 June 1952 from the permanent delegation of the United Kingdom to the United Nations,

not be legal indeterminacy in respect of the protection of sedentary species. However, the International Law Commission (ILC) concluded that 'As control and jurisdiction by the coastal State would be exclusively for exploration and exploitation purposes, they cannot be placed on the same footing as the general powers exercised by a State over its territory and its territorial waters'.[21]

What is the difference between sovereignty and sovereign rights? France noted in the comments to the ILC's draft articles on the continental shelf that

> the legal consequence of the monopoly of exploitation vested in the coastal State will be the exercise of effective, though limited, sovereignty over the continental shelf and this sovereignty will be a fact even though the actual term is not employed.[22]

This statement is mostly correct if considered as applying only to the seabed, without including the superjacent waters. The regime of the continental shelf allows the exclusion of other states from the exploitation and exploration of the seabed resources, and the establishment of rights over the continental shelf does not depend on occupation, effective or notional, or any express proclamation (Article 77 UNCLOS). The only limitation to the powers of the coastal states would be the rules on the laying of submarine cables and pipelines and the authorisation of marine scientific research on the continental shelf. The coastal states still have control over the mentioned activities, but cannot prevent them without reasonable grounds.

With respect to the superjacent waters, coastal states do not have much control, but they can, for example, restrict the exercise of the freedom of navigation in the safety zones around artificial constructions. The legal construction of sovereign rights was created to accommodate the rights of other states already rooted in law and to keep a balance between the emerging regime of the continental shelf and the rights of states beyond territorial seas. Thus, when the regime of the continental shelf was taking shape, the coastal states did not get sovereignty over the continental shelf because of the rights of other states in superjacent waters.

This does not mean that the rights of coastal states are limited by exploitation and exploration. The provisions on the exclusivity of a right to exploit

Document: A/2456, Annex II Comments by Governments on the draft articles on the continental shelf and related subjects prepared by the International Law Commission at its third session in 1951 Topic: Law of the sea – régime of the high seas, extract from the Yearbook of the International Law Commission 1953, vol II, 267. Great Britain, Chile, Egypt, France, Iceland, Israel, Philippines and the Union of South Africa suggested sovereignty; Denmark, Sweden, Belgium and the USA opposed sovereignty over the continental shelf.

[21] UN GA, 'Draft Articles on the Continental Shelf and Related Subjects Prepared by the International Law Commission' (30 July 1951) A/CN. 4/49, https://legal.un.org/ilc/documentation/english/a_cn4_49.pdf.

[22] Comments of the Government of France transmitted by a letter dated 3 October 1952 from the Ministry for Foreign Affairs of France, Document: A/2456, Annex II Comments by Governments on the draft articles on the continental shelf and related subjects prepared by the International Law Commission at its third session in 1951 Topic: Law of the sea – régime of the high seas, extract from the Yearbook of the International Law Commission 1953, vol II, 250.

natural resources imply that the sole rights holder can protect resources from utilisation by third parties.[23] Czybulka maintains that the exclusivity of exploitation and exploration empowers the coastal state, inter alia, to protect and preserve the continental shelf.[24] Mossop argues that it is doubtful that any reasonable argument could be made that coastal states are forbidden from exercising their sovereign rights to conserve the living resources of the continental shelf because the exclusive right to exploit a resource implicitly involves the right not to exploit it.[25] If any unauthorised oil exploitation activities happen on the continental shelf, a coastal state can enforce its rights and prevent violations. Why should the living resources of the shelf be treated differently? The right and obligation to protect the living resources is thus tied to the right to exclude others, or else exclusivity would not be plausible. Moreover, taking into consideration the aim of UNCLOS to protect the marine environment, it is impossible to conclude that states negotiating this instrument intentionally left sedentary species within national jurisdiction without protection.

Based on a broad interpretation of Article 77 UNCLOS and the general obligations of states to protect and preserve the marine environment and biodiversity, it is possible to conclude that coastal states have the right to impose measures to prohibit bottom trawling by enforcing their sovereign rights for continental shelves beyond 200 M.[26] Bycatch of sedentary species and damage to their habitats trigger infringement of sovereign rights for exploitation and exploration of the natural resources of the shelf.

V. THE INTERPLAY OF ECONOMIC AND ENVIRONMENTAL APPROACHES TO THE PROTECTION OF SEDENTARY SPECIES

Coastal states have both economic and environmental incentives to be proactive in the protection of sedentary species. First, there is an interest of a rights holder to protect its living natural resources that have commercial value or are important as a structural habitat for species that represent commercial value. The economic outcome of bottom trawling might be questionable: as Pham et al demonstrate, the economic value of fish caught by trawling might be approximately half that of the economic value associated with the loss of sponge biomass as a result of removal by trawling.[27] Thus, it might not be beneficial

[23] Mossop, *The Continental Shelf Beyond 200 Nautical Miles: Rights and Responsibilities* (Oxford University Press, 2017) 93–122. Molenaar, 'Multilateral Creeping Coastal State Jurisdiction' (n 12) 19.

[24] Czybulka (n 9) 1292.

[25] Mossop, 'Protecting Marine Biodiversity' (n 9) 289.

[26] Antsygina, 'Prohibition of Bottom Trawling on Extended Continental Shelves: Creeping Jurisdiction or Enforcement of Sovereign Rights?' (2021) 36 *International Journal of Marine and Coastal Law* 311.

[27] Pham et al (n 2) 15843.

for a coastal state to engage in bottom trawling on its continental shelf. Even if bottom trawling is commercially beneficial, the respective coastal state is not always the recipient of those benefits: when vessels authorised by other nations engage in bottom trawling on the ECS of a coastal state, the coastal state only suffers damage.

Second, coastal states have an interest in providing a healthy environment for their populations and preserving nature for future generations. It should be noted that Article 77(1)'s regulating rights over the continental shelf or other provisions of Part VI of UNCLOS do not require coastal states to protect the living resources of the shelf. By contrast, Article 56, regulating states' rights with respect to the EEZ, specifically mentions obligations to protect and preserve the marine environment. Yet, this does not mean that, in respect of sedentary species, coastal states only enjoy rights and do not have any obligations.

These obligations follow from the aforementioned provisions of Part XII of UNCLOS and the CBD. The protection of sedentary species should not be exclusively based on the economic component, otherwise the imposition of the protective measures would solely depend on the will of a coastal state. A coastal state might not be interested in the imposition of conservation measures or might use bottom trawling in violation of its environmental obligations.

There is a collective interest of all states in the protection of sedentary species within natural jurisdiction since they are a part of biodiversity, can potentially be a source of marine genetic resources or can create a structural habitat for the species representing genetic resources. As Cassotta argues, 'the "environment" is increasingly perceived and recognized as being shared and not belonging to one single entity'.[28] The degradation of coral reefs might have long-term implications and thus adversely influence the rights of future generations. Of course, the principle of state sovereignty would limit possible ways to force a coastal state to impose conservation measures, but coastal states should fulfil the undertaken obligations under UNCLOS and the CBD which are positive, ie require proactive steps from coastal states. Thus, litigation in domestic courts can be a tool that induces coastal states to undertake conservation and protective measures on ECS.

The measures on the protection of the sedentary species should be applied with a precautionary approach.[29] The economic approach would allow for post-factum compensation for the damages incurred by bottom trawling. But in the case of living resources, it is hard to predict the consequences of damage. The United Nations Conference on Environment and Development (UNCED) maintains that a precautionary and anticipatory approach rather than a reactive one is necessary to prevent the degradation of the marine environment.[30]

[28] Cassotta, 'The Development of Environmental Law Within a Changing Environmental Governance Context: Towards a New Paradigm Shift in the Anthropocene Era' (2021) 30 *Yearbook of International Environmental Law* 54.

[29] Antsygina (n 26).

[30] UNCED Text on Protection of Oceans, UN Doct.A/CONF.151/PC/100.

Prevention should be preferred over compensation because, in the case of living resources, monetary compensation often cannot restore the situation that existed prior to the infliction of harm.[31] This principle was reflected in the United Nations Environment Programme Guidelines and Principles for Shared Natural Resources and Draft Articles on Prevention of Transboundary Harm from Hazardous Activities.[32] This principle should be adopted for the sedentary species. Agenda 21 also recommends states to integrate precautionary and anticipatory rather than reactive approaches to marine and coastal area management and development at the national, subregional, regional and global levels (paras 17.1 and 17.21).

In addition, coastal states should not limit the protective measures to endangered or vulnerable species; the economic incentive allows for the imposing of protection on any sedentary species since a coastal state has exclusive rights for them.[33] At the same time, the rights of a coastal state are not absolute and should be exercised taking into consideration the rights on the high seas.

VI. INFRINGEMENT AND UNJUSTIFIABLE INTERFERENCE WITH FISHING RIGHTS

As the ECS, which refers to national jurisdiction, lies under the waters of the high seas, there is an overlap of areas within and beyond national jurisdiction. Ideally, the two regimes would exist in parallel, regulation of the continental shelf would be under the control of a coastal state and fishing would be exercised under the regime of the high seas. In practice, the infringements are unavoidable and there might be conflicts arising out of the exercise of the freedoms of the high seas (Articles 87 and 116 UNCLOS) and sovereign rights over the ECS (Article 77), such as the use of bottom trawling. The imposition of a ban on bottom trawling on the ECS will, in turn, interfere with the freedom of fishing on the high seas.

According to the *Chagos* case, the UNCLOS does not impose a uniform obligation on a state to avoid any impairment of another state's rights; nor does it uniformly permit a state to proceed as it wishes, merely noting such rights. The extent of the regard required by UNCLOS depends upon the nature of the rights held by states, their importance, the extent of the anticipated impairment, the nature and importance of the activities and the availability of alternative approaches.[34]

[31] Draft articles on Prevention of Transboundary Harm from Hazardous Activities, with commentaries, Yearbook of the International Law Commission 2001, vol II, Part Two.

[32] ibid.

[33] Antsygina (n 26).

[34] *Chagos Marine Protected Area (Mauritius v United Kingdom)* Award of 18 March 2015, para 519.

UNCLOS created a mechanism of balancing the competing rights. According to Article 78(2), the exercise of the rights of a coastal state over the continental shelf must not infringe or result in any unjustifiable interference with navigation and other rights and freedoms of other states. Thus, the protection of sedentary species should not adversely impact the exercise of the freedom of fishing on the high seas, and hence, the imposition of a ban on bottom trawling cannot be arbitrary and requires sufficient reasons for limiting fishing practices on the high seas. At the same time, the freedom of fishing is not absolute and should be implemented with due regard for the interests of other states on the high seas under Article 87(2).

The development of the law of the sea granting more rights to coastal states beyond territorial sea (regimes of the continental shelf and the EEZ) should be considered during the balancing of the states' interests. Proelss maintains, regarding the EEZ, that

> the specific legal regime codified in Part V of the Convention is based on a shift of emphasis in favour of the coastal State which in case of conflict becomes manifest in the shape of a rebuttable presumption in favour of the coastal State.[35]

While the regimes of the continental shelf and of the EEZ have different legal bases and histories of development, the continental shelf regime is also based on the principle of adjacency, which allowed for the recognition of the exclusive rights of coastal states opposable to other nations. Ultimately, the answer to the question 'Who has the most interest in protecting sedentary species on the continental shelf?' would be 'a coastal state'. Thus, coastal states should lead the efforts on the prohibition of bottom trawling over the ECS.

The proximity to the coast is essential for the protection of the environmental and human rights of a population living along the coast. If the damage is inflicted on the marine environment, it would be the direct responsibility of a coastal state to protect its population from the negative consequences of such damage and to mitigate the impact on marine flora and fauna. Any limitation on the state's rights to control seabed activities on the continental shelves would increase the burden on a coastal state: on the one hand, it must ensure the environmental security of its population; on the other, it should mitigate the consequences of damage inflicted by bottom trawling. Thus, protective measures should not be allowed to allocate too much burden on the coastal states. However, the measures should be adequate: if there are no living resources on the ECS, there is no need to prohibit bottom trawling. The level of scientific evidence required for the establishment of a moratorium should be minimal: the presence of any sedentary species, even if not endangered or vulnerable, can be sufficient for the protection of the state's natural resources.

[35] Proelss, 'Article 56' in Proelss (n 9) 449.

The flag states also have a general obligation to protect the marine environment under Articles 192 and 194(5) UNCLOS, and the use of non-sustainable fishing practices violates those obligations.[36] There is also a customary rule on the prohibition of transboundary environmental damage. This rule is incorporated in Article 3 of the CBD and provides that a Contracting Party carries the responsibility to ensure that activities within their jurisdiction or control do not cause damage to the environment of other states or of areas beyond the limits of national jurisdiction. Hence, the use of bottom trawling on ECS might be considered a violation of the flag state's obligation not to inflict transboundary harm.

The balance of rights between the coastal and flag states can be assessed by evaluating the fishing practices in the region, the previous use of bottom trawling, the economic dependence of communities on fishing, the presence of fragile ecosystems and habitats, and ways to balance fishing and the protection of sedentary species. The outcome of the balancing test would depend on the specific circumstances. In the majority of cases, the results would be on the side of the coastal state because the prohibition of bottom trawling over the ECS would not limit other fishing practices and thus would not be unjustifiable interference or infringement.

The conducting of an environmental impact assessment before the imposition of a moratorium on bottom trawling might be a desired practice by a coastal state. There is no obligation of a coastal state under UNCLOS or the CBD to conduct such assessments before the imposition of a moratorium on bottom trawling, but it might be helpful should a flag state challenge the conservation measures.

Under Article 206 UNCLOS, when states have reasonable grounds for believing that planned activities under their jurisdiction may cause significant and harmful changes to the marine environment, they shall, as far as practicable, assess the potential effects of such activities on the marine environment. Bottom trawling above the ECS would refer to fishing on the high seas and thus would be under the control of a flag state and beyond the national jurisdiction of a coastal state. However, significant and harmful effects on sedentary species might occur within the jurisdiction of a coastal state that requests the consideration of Article 206, thus possible obligations of the flag and coastal states should be assessed.

While Article 206 refers to the pollution rather than infliction of damage in general, it is possible to use the analogy from the Chagos Marine Protected Area Arbitration and the South China Sea Arbitration, where the tribunals confirmed that Article 194, on measures to prevent, reduce and control pollution of the marine environment, is 'not limited to measures aimed strictly at controlling

[36] For more on these issues, see *South China Sea Arbitration, Philippines v China*, Award, PCA Case No 2013-19, ICGJ 495 (PCA 2016) 12 July 2016, Permanent Court of Arbitration, 378–88.

pollution and extends to measures focussed primarily on conservation and the preservation of ecosystems'.[37]

The language of Article 206 is ambiguous: while it contains the prescriptive verb 'shall', the phrase 'as far as practicable' changes the prescriptive tone. But the Arbitral Tribunal in the South China Sea Arbitration reminded that 'the International Tribunal for the Law of the Sea emphasized that "the obligation to conduct an environmental impact assessment is a direct obligation under the Convention and a general obligation under customary international law"'.[38]

The Arbitral Tribunal in the South China Sea Arbitration did not consider the obligations under Article 206 of China as a flag state, although China was engaged in harmful fishing practices. With respect to the island-building activities, China was not considered as a coastal state because the Arbitral Panel avoided the issue of sovereignty. However, the Panel found that China was in violation of Article 206 with respect to the island-building activities. This means that a state that intends to conduct potentially harmful activities should first organise an EIA and communicate its results to others. However, it might be problematic for a flag state to unilaterally organise an EIA on the ECS of another state. There is no practice of states organising EIAs before engaging in bottom trawling. However, the provisions of Articles 192 and 194(5) might require that.

The obligation of a coastal state to organise an EIA would be binding only if that state were going to conduct bottom trawling on its continental shelf. The term 'planned activities' implies that a coastal state should know about future bottom trawling activities on its ECS, which might be difficult in respect of foreign vessels due to the freedom of fishing on the high seas. Also, how can a state assess hypothetical activities if those activities are not planned by that state? Therefore, a coastal state has an obligation to organise an EIA under Article 206 UNCLOS only if it intends to engage in bottom trawling. If it does not intend to do so, there is no obligation to assess possible harm, and the coastal state can simply prohibit bottom trawling on its continental shelf based on the scientific information that there are sedentary species in the area intended for the imposition of the conservation measures.

Article 14 of the CBD also establishes an obligation to organise an EIA of the Contracting Party's proposed projects that are likely to have significant adverse effects on biological diversity with a view to avoiding or minimising such effects and, where appropriate, allow for public participation in such procedures. The problem with Article 14 is that it again regulates an EIA with respect to a Contracting Party's own projects, similar to Article 206 UNCLOS. Thus, coastal states which are not planning to engage in bottom trawling are exempt from this obligation.

[37] ibid para 945, 376; *Chagos* (n 34) para 538, 211.
[38] *South China* (n 36) para 948.

The voluntary conducting of an EIA before the imposition of a ban on bottom trawling can be beneficial for a coastal state because it can provide for a more solid scientific ground for the unilateral prohibition of bottom trawling over ECS.

VII. THE GROWING IMPORTANCE OF ENVIRONMENTAL PROTECTION IN THE ARCTIC OCEAN

The most recent adopted instrument on conservation and sustainable fishing is the 2018 Agreement to Prevent Unregulated High Seas Fisheries in the Central Arctic Ocean (CAOF).[39] The CAOF aims to prevent unregulated fishing in the high seas portion of the CAO through the application of precautionary conservation and management measures, and does not apply to sedentary species. The CAOF uses the precautionary approach to prevent the start of unregulated fishing in the high seas portion of the CAO while keeping the need for additional conservation and management measures under regular review. The precautionary approach and the intention to ensure the long-term conservation and sustainable use of living marine resources demonstrate the growing importance of the protection of the marine environment in the agenda of the states. The prohibition of bottom trawling goes along with this trend and would be a logical continuation of the CAOF.

The CAOF will apply for the initial period of 16 years to only the 10 Parties to it, and its scope is exclusively limited to 'unregulated commercial fishing'. Therefore, bottom trawling conducted by commercial fishermen authorised by the Parties[40] and other fishermen of Non-Parties will still be possible in the CAO. Hence, the imposition of a ban on bottom trawling can be a complementary measure to provide for the all-encompassing protection of Arctic sealife.

Parties to the Agreement underlined that commercial fishing is unlikely to become viable in the high seas portion of the CAO any time soon and that it is, therefore, premature to establish any additional regional or subregional fisheries management organisations or arrangements for the high seas portion of the CAO. Since there are no plans to establish an RFMO in the Arctic Ocean, the unilateral or common actions on the limitation of bottom trawling by Canada, Denmark, Russia and the USA are even more necessary. The Agreement demonstrates the growing importance of environmental protection and the necessity to implement all the possible regulations to preserve the Arctic environment.

[39] For more on the CAOF, see Schatz, Proelss and Liuc, 'The 2018 Agreement to Prevent Unregulated High Seas Fisheries in the Central Arctic Ocean: A Critical Analysis' (2019) 34 *International Journal of Marine and Coastal Law* 195.

[40] Canada, China, Denmark, the EU, Iceland, Japan, Norway, Russia, South Korea and the USA signed the CAOF.

In the CAO, there is no bottom trawling, so there are no communities that depend on this type of fishing, and the consequences of the ban for the fishing industry will not be drastic. The imposition of a moratorium on bottom trawling would not affect other types of fishing that are less damaging to the marine environment. The ban on bottom trawling will also not prevent the exploitation of the natural resources of the shelf and marine scientific research, but will merely prevent harmful practices of fishing. The benefits of the imposition of the ban will include protection of the fragile Arctic environment, prevention of overfishing and preservation of marine biodiversity. Hence, the balance of rights is on the side of the coastal states in the case of the CAO.

At the same time, there might be no sedentary species in the CAO, so there is nothing to protect. This is possible, although there is not enough data on the species living on the seabed in the CAO, some of which might be unique or commercially valuable genetic resources. Also, with global warming, the composition of the sedentary species might change because of species migrating north.[41] Because of this, the closure zones might change; hence, the monitoring of existing and new habitats and ecosystems should continue.

While the ban can be established unilaterally by the Arctic coastal states, the cooperation will enlarge the protected zone and coordinate efforts to protect the marine environment. Due to the pre-existing cooperation, the Arctic states are best placed to agree on the additional protection of the Arctic seabed and thus enhance the creation of state practice on the prohibition of bottom trawling. Environmental protection can become a factor enlarging spheres of cooperation between the Arctic states and thus growing trust between the stakeholders (once the war in Ukraine is over and Russia can participate in cooperation with the other Arctic states). The imposition of a ban will ensure the biodiversity-oriented management of ECS and will allow for the protection of marine species and ecosystems existing in the CAO. Such an initiative will serve as an example of positive action advancing environmental protection for the global community.

VIII. BIODIVERSITY BEYOND NATIONAL JURISDICTION

Another instrument that refers to the conservation of living resources is the BBNJ Agreement. The Agreement regulates the conservation and sustainable use of marine biological diversity of areas beyond national jurisdiction, in particular, marine genetic resources, including questions on the sharing of benefits, measures such as area-based management tools, including marine protected areas, EIAs, capacity building and the transfer of marine technology. The living

[41] CAFF, 'State of the Arctic Marine Biodiversity Report' (23 March 2018) CAFF www.caff.is, www.youtube.com/watch?list=PLvo6hWkBAzZyOB5wf1hE_02hZrVe7fKJ&time_continue=283&v=Fk3dW7eqACE at 4m43s-5m30s.

resources of the shelf are outside the scope of the future instrument because they refer to the resources within national jurisdiction, but the prohibition of harmful fishing practices on the ECS is in line with the objectives of Part III of the BBNJ Agreement.[42] The imposition of a ban on bottom trawling would help to preserve marine biodiversity and genetic resources in those areas where the BBNJ Agreement would not be applicable.

IX. CONCLUSION

This chapter has discussed the possibility of implementing a prohibition on bottom trawling on the high seas using rights over the ECS. Such an unusual legal construction could be useful for the protection of sovereign rights of the coastal states and protection of the marine environment on the high seas where an RFMO is yet to be created. Bottom trawling can potentially lead to permanent damage to the seabed and its inhabitants, and it is important to take timely steps to prevent environmental degradation. The enforcement of a ban on bottom trawling would be a precautionary step beneficial for the preservation of the marine environment.

A broad interpretation of Article 77 UNCLOS demonstrates that the right to conserve sedentary species follows from the provisions of Article 77(2) and Part XII of UNCLOS, and other relevant rules of international law applicable for the conservation and protection of the marine environment. The protection of sedentary species is not only within the scope of rights of coastal states, but also within the scope of their obligations pursuant to provisions of UNCLOS and the CBD. The trend in the proliferation of environmental protection and preservation agreements and the necessity of conserving sedentary species might support the imposition of conservation measures based on sovereign rights over the continental shelf.

[42] Objectives to conserve and sustainably use areas requiring protection, including through the establishment of a comprehensive system of area-based management tools, with ecologically representative and well-connected networks of marine protected areas; and to protect, preserve, restore and maintain biodiversity and ecosystems, including with a view to enhancing their productivity and health and strengthening their resilience to stressors, including those related to climate change, ocean acidification and marine pollution. UN GA, 'Draft agreement under the United Nations Convention on the Law of the Sea on the conservation and sustainable use of marine biological diversity of areas beyond national jurisdiction' (5 March 2023) 14/54, www.un.org/bbnj/sites/www.un.org.bbnj/files/draft_agreement_advanced_unedited_for_posting_v1.pdf.

8

Tight Lines at Sea: An Interdisciplinary Analysis of Fisheries, Marine Biodiversity and Institutions

NKEIRU SCOTCHER

I. INTRODUCTION: SETTING THE SCENE

FISH ARE GENERALLY considered to consist of fish stocks, crustaceans, molluscs and other aquatic animals,[1] and are renewable marine resources of a diverse nature that are exploited through fishing activity for food consumption and non-food purposes.[2] They are usually identified by species, and their distribution can be unique to certain ecosystems. Advances in genetics show that the concept of a fish stock is more complex, and species do not neatly slot into species–locale groups.[3] This is particularly pertinent to high seas or

[1] FAO, *The State of World Fisheries and Aquaculture 2020. Sustainability in Action* (2020). This definition by the biannual report of the Food and Agriculture Organisation of the United Nations (FAO) excludes aquatic mammals, reptiles, seaweed and other aquatic plants. The latest report of the FAO uses the broader term of fisheries and aquaculture products or aquatic products to define fish. See FAO, *The State of World Fisheries and Aquaculture. Towards Blue Transformation* (2022).

[2] FAO 2020 (n 1) 60–61, 64. See also FAO 2022 (n 1) 224–25, which broadened its definition in line with the 'evolving and multilateral global context of fish' to encompass consumption, domestic and international trade, processed or unprocessed, and other forms of utilisation. Whilst the majority of fish is used for food consumption purposes, fish can also be used for non-food purposes such as pharmaceuticals, where marine organisms and molecules are discovered and utilised for medication or research towards the same. Additionally, advances in genomic research using fish DNA are advancing the study of evolutionary ecology, which is the study of species, their history and their interactions. These advances can better inform management and conservation of fisheries. See further Oosting et al, 'Unlocking the Potential of Ancient Fish DNA in the Genomic Era' (2019) 12 *Evolutionary Applications* 1513.

[3] Maguire et al, 'The State of World Highly Migratory, Straddling and Other High Seas Fishery Resources and Associated Species' (2006) FAO Fisheries Technical Paper No 495, 3. This chapter further notes that fisheries are not easily defined as occurring within or beyond national jurisdiction. The authors further argue that it is misleading to designate a fishery as high seas stock because some

highly migratory fisheries, where the biology, biodiversity and stock structure of these fisheries can be divergent even within a particular fish stock.[4] Fish are also commodities in the sense that they are assets that can be physically captured, traded, processed and consumed, often on a global scale.[5] Currently, fisheries' marine capture efforts remain on the rise, as is global fish consumption, which is increasing at a rate almost twice that of global population growth.[6] Fishery, which includes aquaculture, encompasses the enterprise linked to the resource.

Fish are not only beneficial to food security and society, by helping to improve lives and support livelihoods, but are also non-food sources relevant to agriculture, such as fishmeal or fish oil, or sources of fish-derived molecules relevant to pharmaceutical industries, such as peptides.[7] The sale of fish is based on marketable rights valuable within national jurisdictions and beyond. Fish are similar to land-based assets in the sense that they are assets of marketable title and can be found within national jurisdictions. Access rights can also be licensed by the coastal state. Fish also retain their value beyond a coastal state's regime of marketable title as they can be captured beyond the national jurisdiction and their possession vests property rights with minimal constraints.[8] The mobile nature of fish and their value mean that possession is a factor underpinning the continuing issue of illegal unreported and unregulated (IUU) fishing.[9] The mobile nature of fish and fishing activities also impacts fish stocks management as states utilise the resources within their national boundaries on the one hand or access them beyond national jurisdiction as distant water fishing nations on

of these stocks can straddle different maritime zones or migrate from the high seas to areas within national jurisdiction, where they are subject to national arrangements.

[4] Ward, 'Genetics in Fisheries Management' (2000) 420 *Hydrobiologia* 191, 197–98. For instance, genetic studies comparing the highly migratory yellowfin, bigeye and albacore tuna show very pronounced differences in population structure even when they are found in similar marine regions.

[5] Fish are amongst the world's most traded commodities and, although the FAO Fish Price Index forecast was adjusted in the light of the COVID-19 pandemic to reflect a consequent fall in catches, there are concerns of tightening supply pushing up the prices of fish commodities such as tuna. See FAO, 'Food Outlook – Biannual Report on Global Food Markets: June 2020' (2020) 1 *Food Outlook* 57.

[6] Compare FAO 2022 (n 1) 1 with FAO 2020 (n 1) 65. Despite the negative impact of the COVID-19 pandemic on the sector, capture fisheries continue to grow, with global per capita consumption on the ascendant.

[7] FAO 2022 (n 1) 115; FAO, 'The State of the World's Aquatic Genetic Resources for Food and Agriculture. FAO Commission on Genetic Resources for Food and Agriculture Assessments' (2019) 11–12. Data on non-food uses of capture fisheries are often not collected alongside data for fish used for food. Therefore, data on non-food uses of fish is not well documented. For an overview of fish-derived molecules and their industrial applications, see Ramakrishnan et al, 'A Review on the Processing of Functional Proteins or Peptides Derived from Fish By-Products and their Industrial Applications' (2023) 9 *Heliyon* 14188.

[8] Brilmayer and Klein, 'Land and Sea: Two Sovereignty Regimes in Search of a Common Denominator' (2001) 33 *New York University Journal of International Law and Politics* 703, 752.

[9] ibid 753. Furthermore, this chapter highlights the view that the discussion of illegal acts in the fisheries industry, even though examined within the context of IUU fisheries, misses out on a range of offences related to fishing. See further Vrancken, Witbooi and Glazewski, 'Introduction and Overview: Transnational Organised Fisheries Crime' (2019) 105 *Marine Policy* 116, 117.

the other, or collaborate with neighbouring states to sustainably manage shared stocks. To further complicate matters, currently the governance framework[10] of fisheries beyond the boundaries of national jurisdiction is removed from the remit of issues included in the BBNJ Agreement.[11] This means that the system applicable to fish beyond national jurisdiction remains subject to multilateral efforts negotiated in the 1980s.

The English, or International Society, School[12] examines states' interaction by focusing on the institutionalisation of conventions or agreements, custom and rights, and legitimate interests. Its approach considers the interplay between state-centred power politics, the institutionalisation of mutual interests and identity among states, which leads to the creation of shared rules and norms and the identification of and focus on global identities and arrangements that transcend state relations.[13] The basic presumption of the English School approach is that the character and operation of international society evolves, and the process of this evolution is evidenced upon examination of institutions,[14] with history providing a helpful perspective to present and future issues, processes and roles.[15] It also provides us with a lens through which to identify tensions in the development of international law as an institution. The English School approach is connected to international law because of its position that international society is not just regulated by international law, but also constitutes it.[16] International law is a fundamental institution in English School analysis.[17] Its approach is relevant to this chapter because the governance of

[10] Governance entails decision-making processes and interactions by actors through legal and policy frameworks to influence and implement rules over matters of interest. This means that governance mechanisms manifest through direct state interaction or through international organisation, and include non-state actors and stakeholders. See Haas et al, 'The Future of Ocean Governance' (2021) *Reviews in Fish Biology and Fisheries* 1, 2 et seq. Here, the authors argue that the complexity of marine spaces in addition to divergent socio-ecological challenges of the same are challenging factors in balancing existing rule-based state-centric approaches with a governance framework.

[11] Agreement under the United Nations Convention on the Law of the Sea on the Conservation and Sustainable Use of Marine Biological Diversity of Areas beyond National Jurisdiction (adopted 19 June 2023) www.un.org/bbnj/. Areas beyond national jurisdiction are maritime areas that are not subject to coastal states' sovereignty or sovereign rights, namely the high seas and the seabed/ocean floor beyond the limit of national jurisdiction. See UNCLOS, Arts 86–89 and 133–37.

[12] The 'English' School is something of a misnomer as the original proponents of the approach, Hedley Bull and Charles Manning, are Australian and South African, respectively. The term 'English School' is used interchangeably with International Society perspective or school, British School and Classical approach. Scholarship on classical theories of states' relations associate the English School with the 'father' of international law, Hugo Grotius. Nonetheless, the school features in British international studies and its key concepts and approach encourages interdisciplinary scholarship.

[13] Buzan, *An Introduction to the English School of International Relations: The Societal Approach* (Polity, 2014) 12–13.

[14] ibid 35.

[15] ibid 43.

[16] ibid 103.

[17] Brems Knudsen, 'Fundamental Institutions and International Organizations: Theorizing Continuity and Change' in Brems Knudsen and Navari (eds), *International Organization in the Anarchical Society: The Institutional Structure of World Order* (Palgrave, 2019) 34–35.

fisheries is informed by global dynamics and interaction between states with other ideals of international society, such as norms. Therefore, there is an interplay of institutions which, as illuminated via an English School lens, carries implications for the assessment of tensions, challenges and opportunities looking ahead.

The legal framework governing fish and fisheries recognises that rights and associated obligations by all users of marine spaces are primarily rules-based, with the United Nations Convention on the Law of the Sea (UNCLOS)[18] as a point of departure. However, UNCLOS was of its time and prioritised the codification and extent of zones of jurisdiction for states concerned by fish stock depletion as a result of a rise in technologically advanced fishing practices.[19] Consequently, newly independent states extended their maritime zones of jurisdiction[20] to economically benefit from resources off their coasts. UNCLOS does not make a distinction between fish for trade purposes and those for scientific purposes with respect to the high seas, and its provisions on conservation and management in the high seas broadly apply to living resources.[21] As technological advances improve fishing efforts, global trends reflect coastal states' broad view of fish and fishing.[22] This indicates that, generally, when states make rules granting access rights or licences to fish within their national jurisdiction, fish and fishing are defined broadly, and there is no state practice where coastal states, in granting these rights, make a distinction between fish as a commodity or otherwise. Whilst UNCLOS had focused on arrangements within the boundaries of national jurisdiction, rules governing high seas fisheries were vague and bereft of implementation measures.[23] Fishing or fish are not defined terms in the UNCLOS, although the UN Agreement on Straddling Fish Stocks and Highly Migratory Fish Stocks (UNFSA)[24] defined fish by widening the scope of this undefined term to include molluscs and crustaceans.[25] High seas fisheries are

[18] The 1982 United Nations Convention on the Law of the Sea, 1833 UNTS 3. UNCLOS entered into force on 16 November 1994 and, as of 27 March 2023, there are 168 parties to the treaty, including the EU.

[19] Vicuña, *The Changing International Law of High Seas Fisheries* (Cambridge University Press, 2004) 45.

[20] UNCLOS, Arts 58 and 113–15 provide that the Exclusive Economic Zone extends up to 200 M. According to UNCLOS, Arts 79 and 113–15, the continental shelf can extend beyond 200 M, depending on the geological features of the coastline.

[21] UNCLOS, Arts 117 and 118. Also, according to UNCLOS, Art 192, all states are enjoined to protect and preserve the marine environment.

[22] Takei, *Filling Regulatory Gaps in High Seas Fisheries: Discrete High Seas Fish Stocks, Deep-Sea Fisheries and Vulnerable Marine Ecosystems* (Brill, 2013) 38–39.

[23] Vicuña (n 19) 51.

[24] Agreement for the Implementation of the Provisions of the United Nations Convention on the Law of the Sea of 10 December 1928 Relating to the Conservation and Management of Straddling Fish Stocks and Highly Migratory Fish Stocks, 2167 UNTS 3. The UNFSA entered into force on 11 November 2001 and there are currently 90 parties to this agreement, including the EU.

[25] UNFSA, Art 5(d) refers to fishing as one of the various human activities that target stocks and species in an ecosystem that is dependent on said stock.

also not defined in UNCLOS or the UNFSA,[26] although this activity takes place in zones defined as 'parts of the sea that are not under the jurisdiction of a state'.[27] The adoption of the UNFSA established a management regime based on precautionary principles and best scientific information,[28] but it does not share the same near-universal participation as UNCLOS.

This link between fish, fishing, the marine environment and biodiversity is acknowledged in the preamble of the UNFSA, where it notes the need to 'preserve biodiversity, maintain the integrity of marine ecosystems and minimise the risk of long-term or irreversible effects of fishing operations'.[29] As fish depend on or support numerous other species and habitats,[30] cooperation and regulated interaction among states and institutions is vital to the effective management of our oceans. This chapter highlights, in relation to fisheries and marine biodiversity, how institutions can be conceived beyond intergovernmental organisations. In light of the new BBNJ Agreement,[31] this chapter presents a systemic insight that can spur measures towards institutional change in the management of ocean spaces.

This chapter will examine fisheries and marine biodiversity[32] beyond national jurisdiction[33] using an interdisciplinary approach, with international law as a discipline *and* an institution according to the English School approach. The chapter will develop its position on tensions in ocean governance by interpreting the law as it is whilst using the English School theory of international relations to highlight the development of norms and associated practices that feature in ascertaining order[34] in the marine environment.

Institutions are vital in English School analysis, and their character is foundational in situating the framework within which issues are normatively

[26] UNCLOS, Part VII contains the provisions governing the high seas and s 2 refers to the living resources of the high seas.

[27] UNCLOS, Art 86 provides that these parts of the sea are not included in the exclusive economic zone (EEZ), territorial sea or internal waters of the state, or in the archipelagic waters of the archipelagic state.

[28] FAO (n 1) 92–95.

[29] UNFSA, Preamble, para 7.

[30] FAO (n 1) 138.

[31] BBNJ Agreement.

[32] Also known as marine biological diversity in full, this chapter will employ the short form for brevity. Marine biodiversity encompasses species such as fisheries, ecosystems and genes of various levels of biological organisation in the marine environment, over 60 per cent of which is found beyond national boundaries. For an overview of this concept, see Cochrane et al, 'What Is Marine Biodiversity? Towards Common Concepts and Their Implications for Assessing Biodiversity Status' (2016) 3 *Frontiers in Marine Science* 1, 3 et seq.

[33] Marine areas beyond national jurisdiction comprise the high seas and the Area. The high seas refer to the part of the seas not included in the EEZ (UNCLOS, Art 86) and the Area is the seabed and ocean floor beyond the limits of national jurisdiction (UNCLOS, Art 1). Within the context of this chapter, reference to zones beyond national jurisdiction will mean the high seas as considerations regarding the Area are beyond the scope of the present chapter.

[34] Order is defined as 'goal focused patterns of interactions by institutions'. See Dunne, 'The English School' in Goodin (ed), *The Oxford Handbook of Political Science* (Oxford University Press, 2011) 736–37.

examined. This chapter's approach sheds light on some key factors that define and impact challenges in reconciling fish with marine biodiversity. Institutions are defined as patterned practices that are routine in nature and based on coherent sets of ideas or beliefs.[35] They are further developed to show that behaviours or interactions that are not consistent with existing norms are not necessarily detrimental, but can be instrumental.[36] Institutions emerge from interaction and at the same time determine interaction by actors such as states and their perception of legitimate practices.[37] Therefore, institutions evolve; just as norms are not simply comprised of action but are also reasonings for action,[38] so examining institutions can bring to light the development of shared ideas that influence and impact actors' behaviour.

This chapter examines the development of institutions that have influenced specific governance measures beyond national jurisdiction by widening its analysis to governance structures[39] as influenced by states and other actors in international society.[40] The position presented herein is developed in the following sections.

First, the effects of institutions in fisheries and the historical and structural issues underpinning fisheries management are delineated. The chapter then analyses interactions and institutional changes, in particular regarding the management of fisheries beyond national jurisdiction.

Second, the interactions regarding marine biodiversity beyond national jurisdiction are examined, highlighting how the development of institutions on marine biodiversity responded to change, as evidenced in treaty law and case law jurisprudence.

Finally, the chapter compares possibilities for reconciling institutional tensions. The benefits of harmonising institutions cannot be underestimated. In stressing the linkages between fisheries and marine biodiversity, this closing section questions whether the separation of fish from the remit of multilateral efforts such as the BBNJ Agreement can meet sustainability goals, which are at the heart of a growing consensus in the management of ocean spaces.

[35] Holsti, *Taming the Sovereigns: Institutional Change in International Politics* (Cambridge University Press, 2004) 21.

[36] Spandler, 'The Political International Society: Change in Primary and Secondary Institutions' (2015) 41 *Review of International Studies* 601, 606.

[37] ibid 606.

[38] Holsti (n 35) 23.

[39] Governance structures can be explained as the continuum of decision-making organisations such as international organisations, institutions, agreements, norms and regimes that together present an institutional framework in relation to an issue or area of focus. See FAO, 'Fisheries and Aquaculture Topics. Fisheries and Aquaculture Governance. Topics Fact Sheets' (FAO Fisheries Division, 2021) www.fao.org/fishery/governance/en accessed 3 March 2021.

[40] International society in relation to international law is defined as an association of states or actors based on certain institutions and bound by certain rules. See Bull, *The Anarchical Society: A Study of Order in World Politics*, 3rd edn (Palgrave Macmillan, 2002) 13.

II. INSTITUTIONALISING FISHERIES

Institutions, defined as patterned practices based on a coherent set of ideals in international society,[41] can be primary or secondary. The distinction between the two types[42] is based on two key factors: the examination of actors' functions as defined by core principles and the nature of the participating actors. Primary institutions are characterised by coherent principles that have evolved based on actors' common and shared goals. These institutions censure the legitimacy and obligation-inducing nature of certain principles in the international legal system.[43] Moreover, principles can become legally binding, making them rules that are specific or general and norms that are subject to acknowledgement and support in order to become law.[44] Secondary institutions are products of interactions and are designed, usually by states, to address specific issues.[45] Concurring with the argument that primary institutions are foundational whilst secondary ones are derivative,[46] this section examines fisheries through discourse on the evolutionary character of institutions.[47] The development of rules governing fisheries has been subject to norms and principles just as issues in international relations are underpinned by ideals unique to a particular era.[48] Interactions between institutions with respect to fisheries highlight tensions that endure

[41] These practices or interactions evolve and change, making international society a broad framework marked by the presence of and interaction between institutions. See Brems Knudsen (n 17) 38. Whilst international society was formed by imperial and colonial powers and the submission of the colonised states to Western states' ideals, newly independent states adopted the basic structure of international society and in some interactions utilised its tools in self-advocacy. See Onuma, 'When Was the Law of International Society Born?' (2000) 2 *Journal of the History of International Law* 1, 64–65.

[42] This distinction is an ongoing process. See Buzan (n 13) 16–17.

[43] Reus-Smit, 'The Politics of International Law' in Reus-Smit (ed), *The Politics of International Law* (Cambridge University Press, 2004) 20.

[44] Onuf, 'The Constitution of International Society' (1994) 5 *European Journal of International Law* 1, 10.

[45] Buzan (n 13) 17. Holsti also makes the distinction between primary and secondary institutions using the terms 'foundational' and 'procedural' institutions, respectively. See Holsti (n 35) 24–27. In applying this approach to the context of fisheries in the high seas, an RFMO is an example of a secondary institution.

[46] Holsti (n 35) 24–29. Primary and derivative institutions have also been used to make this distinction. Focusing on primary institutions, Schouenborg further categorises primary institutions based on function and proposes categories that can be used as a conceptual framework to differentiate them. See Schouenborg, 'A New Institutionalism? The English School as International Sociological Theory' (2011) 25 *International Relations* 26, 30–39.

[47] Buzan, 'Revisiting World Society' (2018) 55 *International Politics* 125, 132. Some examples of primary institutions include territoriality, sovereignty and international law. Secondary institutions are most intergovernmental bodies formed by states to address specific issues, eg the FAO, the International Maritime Organization and the UN generally.

[48] Holsti (n 35) 18–22. According to Holsti, institutions as actions and interactions between states guided by rules, norms and principles, underpinned by ideas and beliefs unique to the particular era, can be identified using three criteria: (i) patterned practices; (ii) ideas and/or beliefs that necessitate the above practices; and (iii) significance of norms.

to the present, it being argued that the development of institutions governing commodified fish and fisheries in the maritime domain continues to play a significant role in governance frameworks over marine spaces.

A. Interactions and Changes

The institutions of sovereignty, territoriality and international law are significant to an analysis of fisheries because they remain persuasive in states' interactions with respect to resources in our oceans and they continue to evolve in tandem with uses and users of marine spaces. Sovereignty is essential in any analysis of state interaction as it confers on the state rights that are autonomous and independent from interference.[49] This is vital to the establishment of legal personality and in international relations as it assists in the recognition and characterisation of actors as they interact with each other. Territory demarcates title and delimits the boundary of states' competence.[50] As an institution, territory is concerned with the determination of the limits of states' full competences. International law as an institution in the English School means interactions or patterns of legitimacy.[51] The relationship between the three institutions is seen in the fact that the evolution of legal concepts that could impact the right to fish is influenced by circumstances and interests beyond legal rules.[52] These circumstances could be geographical, for instance where areas of high seas (which are beyond national jurisdiction) are surrounded entirely by maritime zones under the national jurisdiction of one coastal state, and freedom of fishing in such enclaves in accordance with Article 87 UNCLOS negatively impacts the entire ecosystem and the interests of neighbouring coastal states.[53] Influencing circumstances could be political[54] or caused by climate

[49] *The Case of the SS 'Lotus' (France/Turkey)* Judgment, PCIJ Reports 1927, Series A No 10, 14.

[50] *Island of Las Palmas Case (The Netherlands/The United States)* Permanent Court of Arbitration, 2 RIAA 829–71, 838. Here, the Court stated that sovereignty is epitomised by the state's 'independence with regard to a portion of the globe'.

[51] Schouenborg (n 46) 37.

[52] Vicuña, 'The International Law of High Seas Fisheries: From Freedom of Fishing to Sustainable Use' in Stokke (ed), *Governing High Seas Fisheries* (Oxford University Press, 2001) 24.

[53] For instance, in the central sea of Okhotsk, there is the 'Peanut Hole' enclave, which is beyond the 200 M limit of Russia and rich in pollock stocks. See Oude Elferink, 'Fisheries in the Sea of Okhotsk High Seas Enclave – the Russian Federation's Attempts at Coastal State Control' (1995) 10 *International Journal of Marine and Coastal Law* 1, 5 et seq. The above is one of four pockets in the Arctic Ocean, the largest of which is approximately 2.8 million square kilometres of high seas in the central Arctic and is completely enclosed. See further Molenaar, 'Participation in the Central Arctic Ocean Fisheries Agreement' in Shibata et al (eds), *Emerging Legal Orders in the Arctic* (Routledge, 2019) 136.

[54] For instance, in Africa, the principle of self-determination underpinned self-rule claims and independence of former colonies. However, concerns about further secessionist movements and territorial revisions led to African states' reliance on the principle of *uti possidetis*, which maintains colonial boundaries. So, whereas the right to self-determination is not confined to a decolonisation process, it was in this instance in conflict with the principle of territorial integrity. See Majinge,

change.[55] Notwithstanding the interests that impact the readjustment of rules and rights applicable in the high seas, institutional interaction is ongoing in its reflection of norms and adjustment of rules between actors.[56] These institutions upon which fisheries governance is based also evolve or change. Holsti posits that institutional changes are evidenced through several means, such as increased or decreased complexity, transformation or obsolescence.[57] This chapter develops this argument to contend that changes in relation to high seas fisheries highlight tensions but also the plurality of approaches needed to resolve these tensions.

In the late nineteenth century, the concept of states' territorial limits at sea was established in contradiction to the prior view that ocean spaces were common property and free for all.[58] This transformation from unrestricted freedom to an increase in states' competences formed the basis for claims establishing a continuous and measurable breadth of water near coasts.[59] As they expanded seaward, states' territories curtailed unrestricted freedom of fishing.[60] For instance, the 1882 Convention between Belgium, Denmark, France, Germany, the UK and the Netherlands introduced rules governing the conduct of the ratifying states with respect to fishing activities beyond the limits of national jurisdiction.[61] Here,

'Uti Possidetis and State Secession in International Law: An Examination of the Evolving Legal Practice in Africa' (2010) 18 *African Yearbook of International Law Online* 81, 82 et seq.

[55] For instance, a recent study in the Irish Sea highlighted how climate change is causing the attenuation of finfish following declines in cod, herring and sole stocks but growing mollusc and crustacean fisheries. See Bentley et al, 'Retrospective Analysis of the Influence of Environmental Drivers on Commercial Stocks and Fishing Opportunities in the Irish Sea' (2020) 29 *Fish Oceanography* 415, 416.

[56] Holsti (n 35) 22. Another instance where norms play a significant part in ocean affairs is that of maritime boundary delimitation. The law of maritime delimitation proceeds from the axiomatic norm of territorial sovereignty of states regardless of divergent territorial claims over a disputed boundary. Moreover, in the delimitation process, the disputed area is first determined. This is essentially a determination of title to maritime territory and the basis of a state's claim to a disputed area. In treaty law, UNCLOS, Art 76(1) defines the continental shelf as the seabed which follows the natural prolongation of the land territory to the continental margin or 200 M from the low water mark of the baseline. In case law, the International Court of Justice (ICJ) made specific reference to this axiomatic norm in *Continental Shelf Case (Libyan Arab Jamahiriya/Malta) Judgment* ICJ Reports 1985, 13.40–41, para 49.

[57] Holsti (n 35) 58. Holsti also lists novelty or replacement, addition or subtraction and reversion as additional ways in which change is materialised in the international system.

[58] Heinzen, 'The Three-Mile Limit: Preserving the Freedom of the Seas' (1959) 11 *Stanford Law Review* 597, 620–34. Here, the author explains the origins of the territorial sea limit and argues that the origins of a defined limit in determining areas of coastal states' jurisdiction lie in Nordic state practice in the 18th century.

[59] The utility of a continuous belt of water surrounding a coastline was made apparent during the Seven Years' War between France and Great Britain, where both states fought over colonial territories. By the end of the 18th century, practice was established. States such as Sweden and its neighbouring states had established national measures declaring a four-mile limit of waters within coastal jurisdiction. See Kalijarvi, 'Scandinavian Claims to Jurisdiction over Territorial Waters' (1932) 26 *American Journal of International Law* 57, 60.

[60] Vicuña, 'The International Law of High Seas Fisheries' (n 52) 24. See also Takei (n 22) 14–15.

[61] The Convention for the Regulation of the Policiing of the North Sea Fisheries of 6 May 1882. See United Nations, *Laws and Regulations on the Regime of the High Seas*, Legislative Series Vol 1 (1951) 179–85, Art 1. This treaty was terminated in 1964 upon the expansion of the limits of

the states accepted that whilst the oceans are necessary mediums for trade and communications,[62] the policing and protection of the resources found therein, even beyond national lines, was deemed acceptable.

The 1958 Convention on Fishing and Conservation of the Living Resources of the High Seas[63] is notable as the first convention on fisheries in the light of conservation concerns due to expanding fishing capacity of fleets from distant water fishing states,[64] and here this chapter highlights institutional change and an emerging consensus on the need for conservation of resources beyond the limits of national jurisdiction. Evidenced during the discourse leading to the adoption of the 1958 Convention, sovereignty and territoriality were reimagined. This is evident in the participation of more elements of cooperation in balancing competing interests in fisheries through the codification efforts during the period of 1945–60.[65] However, the principle that 'the land dominates the sea'[66] was established alongside freedoms such as the right for states to fish freely beyond the limits of their national jurisdiction.

Granted that UNCLOS represents an accommodation of sovereignty and territoriality[67] in its delimitation of geographical and substantive competences of coastal states, transformative change is notable in the concept of functional jurisdiction as applicable in the exclusive economic zone (EEZ),[68] which introduces a qualification to territoriality.[69] However, the issue of impact beyond national jurisdiction remained and the framework established by UNCLOS indicates that states accepted the possibility of regulated interaction beyond the boundaries of national jurisdiction. Founded on the growing norm of ecosystem approaches – that interconnected resources do not follow lines of

national jurisdiction beyond the initial limit of 3 M. For an in-depth examination of the importance of this treaty and lessons that could be learned from its rules on enforcement and compliance in the fisheries domain, see Bangert, 'The Effective Enforcement of High Seas Fishing Regimes: The Case of the Convention for the Regulation of the Policing of the North Sea Fisheries of 6 May 1882' in Bangert, Goodwin-Gill and Talmon (eds), *The Reality of International Law: Essays in Honour of Ian Brownlie* (1999) 1–20.

62 Anand, *Origin and Development of the Law of the Sea: History of International Law Revisited* (Martinus Nijhoff, 1982) 86. Although there were supporters of the view that maritime spaces can be appropriated, most states prioritised the preservation of freedoms, such as those of fishing and navigation.

63 559 UNTS 285. This treaty entered into force 20 March 1966.

64 Vicuña, 'The International Law of High Seas Fisheries' (n 52) 25.

65 Takei (n 22) 16, where the author provides a comprehensive overview of this period.

66 This principle is established in maritime boundary delimitation and means that coastal states' maritime rights derive from their sovereignty over land. The idea being that, due to the geologically factual nature of a coastal state's continental shelf, its right to seaward maritime spaces is a given. See *North Sea Continental Shelf (Federal Republic of Germany/Denmark; Federal Republic of Germany/Netherlands)* ICJ Reports 1969, 3, paras 95–96; *Case Concerning Maritime Delimitation and Territorial Questions between Qatar and Bahrain* Merits, Judgment, para 185.

67 UNCLOS, Arts 2–11 see the limitation of sovereignty to internal waters, archipelagic waters and the territorial sea. See also Oxman, 'The Territorial Temptation: A Siren Song at Sea' (2006) 100 *American Journal of International Law* 830, 835.

68 UNCLOS, Arts 56–75.

69 Gavouneli, *Functional Jurisdiction in the Law of the Sea* (Martinus Nijhoff, 2007) 65–66.

national jurisdiction – institutional change occurred in the form of an addition to the already growing regulatory framework. The UNFSA was adopted a year after UNCLOS came into force and regulates fisheries that are highly migratory in nature, in addition to stocks that straddle jurisdictions.[70] As noted in the preamble of the UNFSA, fisheries management measures beyond the EEZ were necessary to stem overutilisation of fisheries stock. The objective was to ensure better enforcement of conservation rules by flag states,[71] port states[72] and coastal states, again concentrating on the users of the resources and how to modify behaviour and introduce obligations for the conservation of the resource.

Maintaining biological unity of fisheries is essential with respect to its conservation and sustainable use in high seas fisheries even with treaty law constraints,[73] and cooperation underpins measures between states as they exercise the right to fish on high seas. The provisions of the UNFSA on conservation and management epitomise principles that reflect institutional change and that impact fisheries beyond the EEZ.[74] The objective of the UNFSA is to ensure conservation of sustainable use of the fisheries that straddle territorial boundaries and are highly migratory.[75] To this end, it sets out the general principles necessary to achieve its objective: providing rules that govern coastal and flag states' behaviour in the high seas, with reference to biodiversity in the marine environment and measures that consider the ecosystem.[76] Although the precautionary approach is not defined in the UNFSA, the treaty in its annex[77] provides guidelines for applying precautionary reference points to conservation and management measures that shall apply to states.[78] Declarations such as the 1992 Rio Declaration, which declared that measures managing marine living resources in the high seas 'must be integrated in content and precautionary and anticipatory in ambit',[79] show how the conservation of fish as marine living resources became an environmental challenge.[80] This view is bolstered by the

[70] The argument being that effective management measures must take into account the connection between fisheries found within the EEZ and those beyond national jurisdiction. See Juda, 'Rio Plus Ten: The Evolution of International Marine Fisheries Governance' (2002) 33 *Ocean Development and International Law* 109, 115.

[71] States with fishing vessels that engage in fishing activities in ocean areas beyond the states' waters. According to UNCLOS, Art 92, all ships must sail under the flag of one state.

[72] States where fishing vessels can dock to perhaps offload fished load or to refuel.

[73] Franckx, 'Pacta Tertiis and the Agreement for the Implementation of the Provisions of the United Nations Convention on the Law of the Sea of 10 December 1982 Relating to the Conservation & Management of Straddling Fish Stocks & Highly Migratory Fish Stocks' (2000) FAO Legal Papers Online No 8, 13.

[74] Vicuña, 'The International Law of High Seas Fisheries' (n 52) 32.

[75] UNFSA, Art 2.

[76] UNFSA, Arts 5, 5(d) and 5(g).

[77] UNFSA, Annex II.

[78] UNFSA, Art 6.

[79] Declaration of the United Nations Conference on Environment and Development, UN DOC A/CONF.151/26, Vol I (14 June 1992), Agenda 21.

[80] Takei (n 22) 76.

acknowledgement that a state should not only assess risks with regard to its territory, but also take into account risk that is transboundary.[81] The UNFSA provides for a conservation and management link between the coastal state and the flag state exercising its right to fish on the high seas[82] and provides a basis for regional cooperation through regional fisheries management organisations (RFMOs) between flag states and coastal states. Additionally, the FAO Compliance Agreement[83] focuses on the flag state to encourage its assertion of authority over its flagged vessels in the event that a vessel fails to meet its obligations with respect to conservation and management of high seas resources. In addition to the FAO Code of Conduct,[84] which provides guidance to assist states and non-state actors as they put in place rules to govern and sustainably manage fisheries in the high seas, these mechanisms represent secondary institutions consciously designed by states.

B. Tensions and Priorities

States' duties to preserve the marine environment are not subject to boundary limits,[85] and whilst, on the face of it, the emergence of principles rooted in sustainability presents less of an obstacle to state sovereignty,[86] the fact that fewer states are party to the FAO Compliance Agreement and the UNFSA than are party to UNCLOS reveals institutional tensions. In the high seas, freedoms (sovereignty) are subject to principles evidenced through patterns of legitimacy (international law), with the added dimension of states' competence over their vessels (territoriality).

Applied to fisheries, distance from the shore dictates the extent to which the coastal state has sovereignty or sovereign rights over the natural resources and when flag state jurisdiction commences. Norms relating to territory exist in concomitance with those related to sovereignty or the capacity of states to

[81] *The Gabcikovo Nagymaros Project (Hungary/Slovakia)* ICJ Reports 1997, 7, para 140.

[82] UNFSA, Art 7. Annex I of the UNFSA provides guidelines for the collection and sharing of data between states in the interest of conservation and management.

[83] 1993 Agreement to Promote Compliance with International Conservation and Management Measures by Fishing Vessels on the High Seas 2221 UNTS 91, entered into force 24 April 2003 (FAO Compliance Agreement). There are currently 42 parties to the agreement, including the EU.

[84] 31 October 1995. FAO Code of Conduct for Responsible Fisheries, www.fao.org/publications/card/en/c/e6cf549d-589a-5281-ac13-766603db9c03 (CCRF). A non-binding instrument that can be adopted by state and non-state actors, it was adopted by the 28th Session of the Conference of the FAO in Resolution 4/95 on 31 October 1995 and sets out governing principles and related norms that represent paradigm-shifting flexible processes that have contributed to institutional changes in fisheries governance. See Friedrich, 'Legal Challenges of Nonbinding Instruments: The Case of the FAO Code of Conduct for Responsible Fisheries' (2008) 9 *German Law Journal* 1539, 1540.

[85] UNCLOS, Art 192. This obligation is open-ended and not dependent on maritime zones. It was conceived to apply to the marine environment as a whole.

[86] Duncan, 'A Reappraisal of Sovereignty in the Light of Global Environmental Concerns' (2001) 21 *Legal Studies* 376, 398.

monitor and control these spaces.[87] With fisheries, this works when fish occur within national jurisdiction, though only up to a point. Ecological connectivity not only links coastal zones in terms of challenges such as climate change or pollution, but also maritime zones in terms of stocks connectivity and distribution.[88] International law measures governing fish exploitation beyond national jurisdiction have not conclusively resolved these tensions because the ecological connectivity of fish is not sufficiently prioritised over norms of territorial or sovereign interests.

Attempts by UNCLOS, the UNFSA, the FAO Compliance Agreement and non-binding instruments draw attention to the need to protect marine environments through sustainable conservation and management. However, the continued construction of fish as a free resource that can be freely exploited beyond national jurisdiction stymies the reimagining of conservation and management of fisheries in line with present realities. Issues of priorities are also present when we examine the management of these resources by RFMOs, a consciously designed institution.[89] For instance, Article 5 of the BBNJ Agreement provides that the agreement shall not undermine measures in accordance with UNCLOS and other relevant instruments, although it has been argued that, as worded, compatibility with the UNFSA is open to divergent interpretations.[90] This raises further issues relating to fisheries governance beyond national jurisdiction contrary to the BBNJ Agreement's objective to respect the competences of global, regional, subregional and sectoral bodies that are already in existence in the context of UNCLOS.

However, over 90 per cent of fish biodiversity beyond national jurisdiction is unassessed, with a significant percentage lacking any stock or species information.[91] Stock governance mechanisms in the high seas are premised on the condition that no state has sovereignty over the resources. Coastal and flag states' interests, bolstered by institutions such as sovereignty, underpin the weak enforcement of conservation measures by RFMOs, a lack of compliance amongst the member states of the RFMOs and the general inadequacy of RFMOs.[92] RFMOs are without 'teeth' and therefore even more in need of a framework that could reinforce existing efforts on fish species or other species belonging to the same ecosystem.

[87] Holsti (n 35) 97.

[88] Popova et al, 'Ecological Connectivity Between the Areas Beyond National Jurisdiction and Coastal Waters: Safeguarding Interests of Coastal Communities in Developing Countries' (2019) 104 *Marine Policy* 90, 92–93.

[89] Also known as secondary institutions.

[90] Haas et al, 'Regional Fisheries Management Organizations and the New Biodiversity Agreement: Challenge or Opportunity?' (2021) 22 *Fish and Fisheries* 226, 229.

[91] Crespo et al, 'High-Seas Fish Biodiversity Is Slipping Through the Governance Net' (2019) 3 *Nature Ecology & Evolution* 1273, 1274. This does not include non-fish species such as sea birds and marine invertebrates.

[92] Cullis-Suzuki and Pauly, 'Failing the High Seas: A Global Evaluation of Regional Fisheries Management Organizations' (2010) 34 *Marine Policy* 1036, 1041–42.

Finally, focus on fish as a commodity shows that distant water fishing states (usually developed economies) benefit the most.[93] Institutional tensions are also revealed upon examination of monitoring, enforcement and compliance rules within national boundaries in comparison to flag state measures beyond national boundaries. Whilst there is a broad view in relation to what constitutes fish or even fishing activity,[94] this broadness is not replicated in measures or rules applicable beyond national jurisdiction. This divergence means that the goals of the main actors are linked to the commodification of fisheries at the expense of conservation. Therefore, although these types of interaction between institutions still represent order defined as 'patterns of activity that sustains the goals of international society',[95] sovereignty remains dominant, despite there being recognition that a change is vital in the interests of the conservation and sustainable use of fish.

III. INSTITUTIONALISING MARINE BIODIVERSITY

Prior examination of primary institutions impacting fisheries beyond national jurisdiction has highlighted that whilst constitutive of state actors who act in relation to one another, institutional tensions continue to influence the extent to which conservation and management occur. This begs the question whether marine biodiversity itself has been impacted by institutions and the extent to which the development of principles and rules concerning marine biodiversity are influenced. In developing the discourse on institutions, standards of behaviour between actors have driven the debate and informed rule development. As noted earlier, these standards of behaviour or norms have been impacted by ideals of the era. Interactions between actors are constitutive of norms which are necessary in reimagining the governance of marine resources. Therefore, multilateral efforts leading to agreements such as the BBNJ Agreement can still be readdressed through interactions between actors towards general rules or encouragement of more discursive measures, such as minimum terms and standards.

IV. AN EMERGENCE

In addition to the institution of international law, which ensures that rules are binding in character, the development of environmental stewardship as an

[93] Asche et al, 'Fair Enough? Food Security and the International Trade of Seafood' (2015) 67 *World Development* 151, 157–58. Distant water fishing states are those whose vessels can traverse long distances far from their coastal areas to engage in fishing activities either in a host country's EEZ or in high seas areas.

[94] For instance, it is established and supported by case law jurisprudence that fishing support vessels for research or bunkering are considered fishing vessels for the purpose of rules on fish exploitation. See *The M/V 'Virginia G' Case (Panama v Guinea-Bissau). Judgment* ITLOS Case No 19, 68.

[95] Bull (n 40) 8.

institution is significant because of its shift from piecemeal to collective action in realising humanity's shared interest in the global commons.[96] Environmental stewardship, whilst persuasive in states' interactions with respect to resources in our oceans, continues to evolve in tandem with uses and users of marine spaces. The recognition within the English School approach that non-state actors can interact just as much as state actors with respect to challenges is well analysed.[97] Accordingly, the emergence of environmental stewardship was founded on the principle that environmental challenges were no longer a national issue but a collective one in need of global management measures.

In addition to the UNFSA, other landmark conventions, such as the 1973 Convention on International Trade in Endangered Species,[98] have provided support for environmental stewardship as an emerging norm.[99] Normatively, transformative change with respect to marine biodiversity underpinned the 1992 Rio Declaration[100] and actors' declaration that marine biodiversity challenges are global challenges. Marine biodiversity within the overarching framework of biodiversity is defined in the Convention for Biological Diversity (CBD) as part of the variability among living organisms within marine ecosystems.[101] The first international convention to deal with conservation and sustainable use of biological diversity, the CBD recognises that environmental challenges are a collective issue. The treaty's jurisdictional scope, as well as primarily applying within national jurisdiction, reaches processes and activities of contracting states beyond national jurisdictions.[102] The CBD prescribes for the transposition of state action in a broader ecosystem context and whilst not undermining the institutions of sovereignty and territoriality, it envisages a broader state responsibility towards sustainable use of living resources.[103] The CBD concerns

[96] Falkner R, *Environmentalism and Global International Society* (Cambridge University Press 2021) 104–27; Falkner and Buzan, 'The Emergence of Environmental Stewardship as a Primary Institution of Global International Society' (2019) 25 *European Journal of International Relations* 131, 132; Holsti (n 35) 18–24.

[97] Buzan, *From International to World Society? English School Theory and the Social Structure of Globalisation* (Cambridge University Press, 2004) 91–128; Falkner, 'Global Environmentalism and the Greening of International Society' (2012) 88 *International Affairs* 503, 507.

[98] The 1973 Convention on International Trade in Endangered Species 993 UNTS 243. Known as CITES, this treaty entered into force 1 July 1975 with 183 parties, including the EU. The application of CITES to ocean governance issues arising from its provisions regarding the introduction of species from the sea is possible, but issues remain as to its coherence with the existing legal framework governing marine spaces. See Franckx, 'The Relationship between CITES, FAO and Related Agreements: Legal Issues' (FAO, 2011) FAO Fisheries and Aquaculture Circular No 1062, 21–26.

[99] Falkner, 'Global Environmental Responsibility in International Society' in Vetterlein and Hansen-Magnusson (eds), *The Rise of Responsibility in World Politics* (Cambridge University Press, 2020) 12–20. Falkner provides an in-depth overview of the development of environmental stewardship from the end of the Second World War up to the 1992 Rio Conference.

[100] See n 79.

[101] The 1992 Convention on Biological Diversity 1760 UNTS 79. Hereinafter referred to as CBD, it entered into force on 29 December 1993. There are currently 196 parties to the convention, including the EU.

[102] CBD, Art 4.

[103] Juda (n 70) 129.

biodiversity in all ecosystems and, through the Conference of the Parties to the convention (COP),[104] concluded the Jakarta mandate on marine and coastal biodiversity.[105] The mandate supported the recommendations by the Subsidiary Body on Scientific, Technical and Technological Advice to cover integrated marine and coastal management, mariculture, alien species, living resources and marine protected areas.[106] Here, there is a clear coordination of efforts in a multidisciplinary way recognising that principles are generalisable if grounded in scientific facts and sustainable, and that conservation-focused measures are best served by evidence-based research. The discussions during the COP at Jakarta were dominated by fisheries issues;[107] however, the mandate emphasised and declared the need for an ecosystems approach with respect to conservation and sustainable utilisation of marine spaces.

Yet, despite the provisions of Article 4, the CBD binds states within their national boundaries and is advisory beyond national jurisdiction, and this raises the question of its applicability to marine biodiversity beyond national boundaries.[108] In reiterating that institutions are patterned practices based on a coherent set of ideas, this chapter posits that the evolution of the institution of environmental stewardship beyond national jurisdiction is foreseeable. Institutions are more than rational constructs by actors; the relationships between states, non-states and institutions are mutually constructive.[109] A broader understanding of challenges is an indicator that an institution is undergoing change.[110] Upon examination of the institution of environmental stewardship, such a broader understanding of challenges is evidenced in the development of protected areas, which are geographical areas designated or regulated and managed as such for sustainable objectives.[111] During the seventh COP,[112] a broader interpretation of the marine and coastal protected area (MPA) was endorsed, enabling a high level of protection to be afforded to an area within the MPA.[113] Additionally,

[104] In accordance with CBD, Art 23.

[105] CBD, *Final Report of the Second Meeting of the Confernce of the Parties to the Convention on Biological Diversity. Jakarta, Indonesia* UNEP/CBD/COP/2/19 (6–17 November 1995).

[106] CBD (n 105). See also Juda (n 70) 118.

[107] Goote, 'The Jakarta Mandate on Marine and Coastal Biological Diversity' (1997) 12 *International Journal of Marine and Coastal Law* 377, 383.

[108] Garcia, Rice and Charles, 'Bridging Fisheries Management and Biodiversity Conservation Norms: Potential and Challenges of Balancing Harvest in Ecosystem-Based Frameworks' (2016) 73 *ICES Journal of Marine Science* 1659, 1660.

[109] Brems Knudsen (n 17) 28.

[110] ibid 39.

[111] CBD, Art 2.

[112] CBD, *Seventh Ordinary Meeting of the Conference of the Parties to the Convention on Biological Diversity. Kuala Lumpur, Malaysia* Decision VII/5 Marine and Coastal Biological Diversity (9–20 February 2004) www.cbd.int/meetings/COP-07.

[113] Jakobsen, *Marine Protected Areas in International Law: An Arctic Perspective* (Brill Nijhoff, 2016) 8. The encouragement of states to consider expanded protected areas are also part of the Aichi Biodiversity Target No 11. See further www.cbd.int/doc/strategic-plan/targets/T11-quick-guide-en.pdf.

like the CBD, the UN General Assembly (UNGA) resolution for the development of the BBNJ Agreement[114] recognised the utility of a global approach to better address the conservation and sustainable use of marine biodiversity. The BBNJ Agreement, within the broad framework of conservation and sustainable use of marine biodiversity beyond national jurisdiction, also aims to address, inter alia, issues concerning marine genetic resources, environmental impact assessments and capacity building. To this end, the BBNJ Agreement sets out principles necessary to achieve its global objective[115] whilst providing detailed measures that integrate principles such as the precautionary principle and the ecosystem approach.[116] It also provides for coordination in the development and framework of MPAs.

V. BEYOND TENSIONS

The character of the institutions and the norms underpinning mutually constructive interactions play a part in the recognition of broader challenges and subsequent evolution of marine biodiversity governance. Ecological considerations with respect to marine biodiversity have widened the scope of management measures governing fisheries to include, amongst others, considerations of fish not only as commodities, but also as contributors to ecosystem structures and function.[117] The UN's proclamation of a decade of ocean science for sustainable development from 2021 to 2030 is founded on the recognition of the need for a global effort towards the sustainable use of marine spaces, and goal 14 is particularly relevant with respect to marine biodiversity.[118] It is now accepted that the relationship between fish and marine biodiversity is synergistic and the challenges they face are complementary. Whilst the nature of fish as commodities is established, they are also repositories of biological resources that can be utilised in myriad industries. Upon examination of the institution of international law and the patterns of legitimacy with respect to marine biodiversity, inter-institutional linkage[119] is ongoing with UNCLOS, the UNFSA, the FAO measures and the CBD.

[114] UNGA, *Resolution 69/292 – Development of an International Legally Binding Instrument under the United Nations Convention on the Law of the Sea on the Conservation and Sustainable Use of Marine Biological Diversity of Areas Beyond National Jurisdiction* UN Doc A/RES/69/292 (6 July 2015) https://daccess-ods.un.org/tmp/1387849.00307655.html.

[115] BBNJ Agreement, Art 2.

[116] ibid Art 5.

[117] Friedman, Garcia and Rice, 'Mainstreaming Biodiversity in Fisheries' (2018) 95 *Marine Policy* 209, 210.

[118] At the seventieth session of the UNGA, the 2020 Agenda was adopted with 17 goals to achieve sustainable development. UNGA, *Transforming Our World: The 2030 Agenda for Sustainable Development* UNGA Res A/RES/70/1 (21 October 2015) https://undocs.org/en/A/RES/70/1.

[119] In this instance, linkages between secondary institutions.

Marine biodiversity does not respect national boundaries, and its protection and management beyond national jurisdiction also affects biodiversity within national boundaries. Here, there is recognition that the conservation of the marine environment must be founded on the interaction between states and non-state actors towards common goals. The development of principles and the interaction of actors in relation to marine biodiversity are influenced by the institution of environmental stewardship. There is purchase in meeting gaps in a multi-level way which utilises a wider range of actors so that global and diverse regional frameworks can operate with an immediacy that is not the case with international agreements.[120] Just as marine biodiversity is multi-spatial and multi-temporal,[121] so its conservation and sustainable use has to be based on measures that are iterative in order to adapt to and accommodate the intricacies of resource use sustainably.

VI. CONCLUSIONS: WHAT LIES BENEATH AND BEYOND

At present, the notion of fish and fisheries continues to evolve and encompasses various interests, activities and ecosystems in our oceans. As genetic resources, fish can comprise stocks hitherto unlisted in the Aquatic Sciences and Fisheries Information System used by the FAO, but can be in the form, inter alia, of genes, foundational or brood stocks, or embryos. Currently, the status of known fish stocks is concerning as they continue to be fished at unsustainable levels. In light of the above, this chapter notes that global efforts to sustainably manage resources beyond national boundaries recognise the nature of the resource as transboundary, but challenges are founded on a tension between institutions. On the one hand, areas beyond national jurisdiction are better managed collectively by multilateral measures as these zones are not within any state's sovereignty or sovereign rights. However, fish that occur in these areas, whilst forming part of marine biodiversity, are exploited by a range of actors subject to flag states' jurisdiction. The question remains how to balance the rights of states and their responsibilities in areas beyond national jurisdiction.

In seeking to highlight the interactions of states and non-state actors that underpin the situation with respect to fish beyond national jurisdiction, this chapter applied the English School approach to international relations. Utilising this interdisciplinary approach, the chapter analysed institutions and noted a tension between states' sovereignty and the responsibility of ensuring that the marine environment is better managed. The chapter also emphasised how these

[120] For instance, a notable contentious issue in the negotiations leading to the BBNJ Agreement is that of marine genetic resources. See Papastavridis, 'The Negotiations for a New Implementing Agreement Under the UN Convention on the Law of the Sea Concerning Marine Biodiversity' (2020) 69 *ICLQ* 585, 586.

[121] See Cochrane et al (n 32) 3.

institutions have evolved in order to show that it is only in the realm of interaction that international society can find a plurality of solutions commensurate with the challenges it faces. The particular concern of this chapter has been institutions and the nature of institutional change. Here, the systemic implications for fish, fisheries and marine biodiversity governance based on these institutional interactions were drawn out, in addition to the emergence and ongoing evolution of an institution with an environmental focus.

The chapter explored the potential issues that can arise when applying concepts of sovereignty and territoriality to a resource that does not fit into the same spatial parameters by historically following the emergence of UNCLOS, the UNFSA, the FAO Compliance Agreement and the CBD. Institutional changes were also illustrated, in particular by tracing the impact of norms in the development of mutually constructed interactions between actors. In terms of determining practical approaches that cohere with evolving management needs, this chapter supports an understanding that the development of fish, fisheries and marine biodiversity are linked and, although institutional interactions with respect to fish, fisheries and marine biodiversity have developed separately, they are now nearing convergence.

The shared structures between fish, fisheries and marine biodiversity stress the utility of governance mechanisms that bridge the gaps between them. This chapter argued that multilateral efforts can and should address missed opportunities to address the gaps of implementation existing in fisheries management. An ecosystem is not fixed, and such fluidity necessitates equally dynamic efforts to resolve the challenge of sustainable use of resources in our marine spaces. It remains to be seen to what extent the BBNJ Agreement will address institutional gaps in the management of ocean spaces in practice, but there is purchase in states and non-state actors coordinating their efforts in a multi-level format. Here, the state can coordinate measures with regional institutions, and regional institutions can coordinate with global institutions either in a top-down or bottom-up way.

Applying the English School approach to this issue is not meant to present the reader with a clear solution; rather, it is intended to highlight the ongoing institutional tensions that underpin mutually constructive interactions between states and non-state actors in relation to fish, fisheries and marine biodiversity. Whilst the establishment and efficacy of sustainable policies at the national level are dependent on factors such as effective national jurisdiction, capacity and political will, states' preferences are not set in stone and traditional institutions can change. Additionally, this chapter outlined the emergence of a new institution without the imperial undercurrents that beset the concepts of sovereignty and territoriality. It also foregrounded possibilities for more inclusive discourse on the management of marine spaces and highlighted ways in which institutions can change and be changed by the actors. Such possibilities have implications not just in respect of fisheries and marine biodiversity, but also in terms of our ocean spaces as a whole.

9

Bioprospecting under the Nagoya Protocol and the Sustainable Development Goals

PETER GOTTSCHALK

I. INTRODUCTION

THE DEVELOPMENT OF policy and law in the field of marine bioprospecting requires the integration of several different legal regimes: the law of the sea, the rules on access and benefit sharing of the Nagoya Protocol (NP)[1] and intellectual property law. The NP is central to bioprospecting in that it sets out a system for access to and fair sharing of benefits arising from the use of genetic resources. Achieving sustainability is a main challenge for the development of policy and law in the field of marine bioprospecting. To do so, all relevant legal frameworks should support the sustainability goals of UN 2030 Sustainable Development Agenda (Agenda 2030).[2] While, for example, the NP in its Preamble recognises the important contribution to sustainable development that the Protocol should make, it does so without specifying how this should happen. Agenda 2030 sets out more concrete Sustainable Development Goals (SDGs). Marine bioprospecting relates to several goals in Agenda 2030, especially SDG 9, comprising inclusive and sustainable industrialisation and fostering innovation, SDG 14, on conservation and sustainable use of the oceans, and goal 15, on protection of biodiversity. SDG 15.6 relates particularly clearly to the NP by encouraging states to 'Promote fair and equitable benefits arising from the utilization of genetic resources and promote appropriate access to such resources, as internationally agreed'.

While Agenda 2030 itself is non-binding, it makes several references to international law. A crucial question is how law can support and contribute

[1] Nagoya Protocol on Access to Genetic Resources and the Fair and Equitable Sharing of Benefits Arising from Their Utilization to the Convention on Biological Diversity (29 October 2010).

[2] Agenda 2030, Preamble; 'Transforming Our World: The 2030 Agenda for Sustainable Development', resolution adopted by the General Assembly on 25 September 2015, A/RES/70/1.

to fulfilling the Agenda. Also pertinent is the extent to which the Agenda may impact on the design of law. While the Agenda describes the goals as 'universal' and 'integrated and indivisible', states have a large discretion in making priorities, integrating the goals in national planning, etc.[3] At the same time, the importance of an *integrated approach* is highlighted.[4]

Generally, international environmental law interacts closely with science, technology and medical research. The NP addresses several issues relating to research and technology transfer. In fact, how we generate and manage new knowledge and technology are central issues from a sustainability perspective. Several of the SDGs contain elements of innovation, knowledge production and technology development. Especially, emerging technologies like biotechnology, genetically modified organisms, nanotechnology and synthetic biology raise difficult issues along the value chain, from basic research and research and development (R&D) to commercialisation and other forms of knowledge diffusion and technology transfer.

Long before Agenda 2030 was adopted, Sands noted that it is the second and third objectives of the Convention on Biological Diversity (CBD) – ie sustainable use of the components of biological diversity, and the fair and equitable sharing of the benefits arising out of the utilisation of genetic resources – that take it into the field of sustainable development.[5] Access and benefit sharing (ABS) is by definition about fairness (fair and equitable benefit sharing), as well as about economy and ecology. The NP is also expected to contribute more broadly to the achievement of sustainable development.[6] In other words, the third objective – ABS – is not to be pursued in isolation from the broader framework established by the CBD; it is linked to the other two objectives – conservation of biological diversity and sustainable use of the components of biological diversity.[7]

This chapter addresses the sustainability challenges in developing a legal framework for marine bioprospecting, primarily at the national level, though it also briefly considers the global situation. Discussions about marine bioprospecting have mainly focused on the global context, in particular in the recent negotiations for a legal instrument on biodiversity beyond national jurisdiction (BBNJ),[8] rather than the local context (territorial waters and economic zones). The chapter discusses the relevant SDGs, the synergies and conflicts

[3] Agenda 2030, paras 54–59.

[4] Le Blanc, 'Towards Integration at Last? The Sustainable Development Goals as a Network of Targets' (2015) 23 *Sustain Development* 176.

[5] Sands, 'International Law in the Field of Sustainable Development' (1994) 65 *British Yearbook of International Law* 303, 335; Convention on Biological Diversity (Rio de Janeiro, 5 June 1992).

[6] Morgera, Tsioumani and Buck, *Unraveling the Nagoya Protocol. A Commentary on the Nagoya Protocol on Access and Benefit-sharing to the Convention on Biological Diversity* (Brill/Nijhoff, 2014) 50. In fact, the Preamble refers to the Millennium Development Goals, but by now this reference should reasonably mean Agenda 2030.

[7] ibid 54–56.

[8] UNGA Resolution 72/249 of 24 December 2017.

between the goals, and how the conflicts could be managed in the context of a legal framework for marine bioprospecting.[9]

The argument put forward is that Agenda 2030 can be used to formulate policy and law for marine bioprospecting, but also that the SDGs should provide input to the cooperation under the BBNJ Agreement. The importance of addressing interactions with other international processes such as Agenda 2030 are underscored by, inter alia, the Kunming–Montreal Global Biodiversity Framework.[10]

II. WHAT IS MARINE BIOPROSPECTING?

There is no official definition of bioprospecting, but in the context of the CBD it has been described as 'the process of identifying unique characteristics of marine organisms for the purpose of developing them into commercially valuable products'.[11] In fact, most suggested definitions are similar. Farrier and Tucker note that the end focus of bioprospecting is on the design and development of pharmaceuticals and other commercial applications.[12] Further, bioprospecting is often a transnational activity,[13] making international cooperation necessary, even for the design of a national policy on marine bioprospecting.[14] The fact that bioprospecting is defined as a process aimed at commercial products points to the practical problem of distinguishing basic scientific research from commercial research R&D. The sharing of benefits concerns not just commercial research, but also scientific knowledge.[15]

III. THE LEGAL FRAMEWORK FOR MARINE BIOPROSPECTING

The CBD has three objectives:

> the conservation of biological diversity, the sustainable use of its components and the fair and equitable sharing of the benefits arising from the utilization of genetic resources, including by appropriate access to genetic resources and by appropriate transfer of relevant technologies, taking into account all rights over those resources

[9] Breu et al, 'Where to Begin? Defining National Strategies for Implementing the 2030 Agenda: The Case of Switzerland' (2019) 16 *Sustainability Science* 183.

[10] Kunming–Montreal Global Biodiversity Framework, CBD/COP/DEC/15/4, Annex, para 26, s D (Relationship with the 2030 Agenda for Sustainable Development).

[11] Mossop, 'Marine Bioprospecting' in Rothwell et al (eds), *The Oxford Handbook on the Law of the Sea* (Oxford University Press, 2015) 825.

[12] Farrier and Tucker, 'Access to Marine Bioresources: Hitching the Conservation Cart to the Bioprospecting Horse' (2001) 32 *Ocean Development and International Law* 213.

[13] Morgera et al (n 6) 4–5.

[14] ibid 7–10 ('asymmetries').

[15] Leary et al, 'Marine Genetic Resources: A Review of Scientific and Commercial Interest' (2009) 33 *Marine Policy* 183, 184.

> and to technologies, and by appropriate funding, thereby contributing to the conservation of biological diversity and the sustainable use of its components.[16]

The ABS regime as it is elaborated in the CBD and the NP addresses a complex set of issues.[17] The core of the regime consists of ABS obligations (Article 15 CBD), but several other related issues are addressed, such as scientific research (Article 18 CBD), commercial R&D and technology transfer (Article 16 CBD). In addition, intellectual property (especially patent law) has always been part of the ABS debate, although not legally part of ABS.

Further, the United Nations Convention on the Law of the Sea (UNCLOS) also contains international obligations regarding, for example, development and transfer of marine technology (Part XIV).[18] Some of the issues have been further elaborated in the BBNJ negotiations.

International obligations of scientific cooperation and transfer of marine technology can thus be found under UNCLOS and the CBD,[19] and under the NP. Articles 8 and 9 NP ('Special considerations') address the issue of 'research contributing to conservation and sustainable use of biodiversity'.[20]

It should be noted that the relationship between UNCLOS and CBD was also addressed at the CBD in Rio, and resulted in Article 22(2) CBD, which states: 'Contracting Parties shall implement this Convention with respect to the marine environment consistently with the rights and obligations of States under the law of the sea.' This issue also appeared in the NP negotiations, under Article 4 NP.[21]

International law is generally regarded as a legal system, although one that is less well organised than national legal systems.[22] The international legal system has expanded in an uncoordinated fashion in the last half century, giving rise

[16] CBD, Art 1.

[17] The objective of the Nagoya Protocol reads (Art 1 NP): 'The objective of this Protocol is the fair and equitable sharing of the benefits arising from the utilization of genetic resources, including by appropriate access to genetic resources and by appropriate transfer of relevant technologies, taking into account all rights over those resources and to technologies, and by appropriate funding, thereby contributing to the conservation of biological diversity and the sustainable use of its components.'

[18] United Nations Convention on the Law of the Sea (Montego Bay, 10 December 1982).

[19] Ntona, 'The Transfer of Marine Technology as Benefit-Sharing', https://benelexblog.wordpress.com/2015/11/04/the-transfer-of-marine-technology-as-benefit sharing/.

[20] NP, Art 8(a) states: 'In the development and implementation of its access and benefit sharing legislation or regulatory requirements, each Party shall: (a) Create conditions to promote and encourage research which contributes to the conservation and sustainable use of biological diversity, particularly in developing countries, including through simplified measures on access for non-commercial research purposes, taking into account the need to address a change of intent for such research.'

[21] Morgera, 'Fair and Equitable Benefit-Sharing in a New Instrument on Marine Biodiversity: A Principled Approach Towards Partnership Building?' (2018) 5 *Maritime Safety and Security Law Journal* 48.

[22] International Law Commission, 'Report of the Study Group on Fragmentation of International Law: Difficulties Arising from the Diversification and Expansion of International Law' (2003) UN Doc A/CN.4/L.644.

to a fragmented system. Part of the fragmentation problem is the emergence of special types of law, which has, in turn, caused problems of coherence in international law. Political scientists have sometimes described these kinds of problems of density or fragmentation as 'regime complexes'.[23] International negotiations, such as the BBNJ negotiations, have to address such problems. However, international negotiations often fail to avoid norm conflicts, for example due to 'chilling effects',[24] and international law is poorly equipped to deal with conflicts of norms.[25] The result can be continued problems of coherence in international law.

Article 4 NP refers to the concept of mutual supportiveness for the management of relationships between different legal norms. Thus, the NP's relationship with UNCLOS, intellectual property laws, etc should be governed by the concept of mutual supportiveness. However, the meaning of the concept is not clear. Managing trade-offs between SDGs in Agenda 2030 would be a way to achieve both mutual supportiveness (synergies) and sustainable development.[26] The fairly broad freedom of choice enjoyed by states when implementing the NP makes this an important policy issue. International negotiations informed by policy analysis (policy coherence) are therefore suggested as a solution. Achieving the goals of Agenda 2030 will thus require extensive international cooperation in the case of marine bioprospecting, especially in the context of the BBNJ negotiations, but also cooperation at the state level.

IV. SUSTAINABLE DEVELOPMENT: AGENDA 2030

As mentioned above, a main challenge for the development of policy and law in the field of marine bioprospecting is to achieve sustainability. How should policy and law for marine bioprospecting be formulated and designed to do this? The main idea behind this chapter is that the overarching goal of achieving sustainability can help us design coherent policy and law for marine bioprospecting.

For quite some time, the image of sustainable development has been conceptualised as consisting of three more or less overlapping circles, each representing dimensions of sustainability: ecological, social and economic sustainability. This conceptualisation is, however, changing. With the adoption of Agenda

[23] Raustiala and Victor, 'The Regime Complex for Plant Genetic Resources' (2004) 58 *International Organization* 277.

[24] Eckersley, 'The Big Chill: The WTO and Multilateral Environmental Agreements' (2004) 4 *Global Environmental Polititics* 24.

[25] Borgen, 'Resolving Treaty Conflicts' (2005) 37 *George Washington International Law Review* 573.

[26] Sanwal, 'Trends in Global Environmental Governance: The Emergence of a Mutual Supportiveness Approach to Achieve Sustainable Development' (2004) 4 *Global Environmental Polititics* 16; Morgera et al (n 6) 106–08. It is not far-fetched to argue that 'mutual supportiveness' and 'synergistic' should mean more or less the same thing.

2030, the image of sustainable development is more that of a network. This is still connected to the idea of sustainability as consisting of three dimensions, but they are scattered throughout the goals and targets. In the three dimensions model, sustainability meant balancing the three dimensions against each other. This newer networked image affects how we should approach links, or interactions, between SDGs and systemic impacts.[27] In fact, how the SDGs interact with each other has emerged as a key question in the implementation of Agenda 2030.[28] While the goals of the Agenda are described as 'integrated and indivisible',[29] both synergies (co-benefits) and conflicts (trade-offs) between the goals and targets can be identified.

A. Which SDGs are Relevant to Marine Bioprospecting?

The idea is that ABS can be conceptualised as a cluster – tight couplings within the network – of sustainability targets situated within Agenda 2030.[30] Agenda 2030 addresses ABS from several perspectives, 'particularly their harvesting and the associated redistributional dimensions' (targets 2.5, 2.a and 15.6).[31] As noted above, target 15.6 requires states to 'Promote fair and equitable benefits arising from the utilization of genetic resources and promote appropriate access to such resources, as internationally agreed'. The central goals in the marine bioprospecting cluster are SDGs 14 (oceans) and 15 (biodiversity). Closely related is SDG 9 (promote innovation). However, the cluster of SDGs relevant to marine bioprospecting policy is much larger. Despite a considerable amount of research on the SDGs, it seems target 15.6 (ABS) has largely passed under the radar. No clear cluster can be identified. The use of the concept of 'access and benefit sharing' in target 15.6 'hides' many linkages in the sense that there are many linkages inherent to the concept of ABS which are not immediately visible. This is not uncommon in the articulation of goals, targets and indicators,[32] including environmental ones.[33] As ABS appears in legal texts

[27] *Forskning för Agenda 2030: Översikt av forskningsbehov och vägar framåt* (Formas, 2018) 44 ('Att förstå och beforska kopplingar mellan hållbarhetsmål' ['To understand and research linkages between sustainability goals']).

[28] Weitz et al, 'Towards Systemic and Contextual Priority Setting for Implementing the 2030 Agenda' (2017) 13 *Sustainability Science* 1.

[29] Agenda 2030, Preamble.

[30] Le Blanc (n 4).

[31] Dupuy and Viñuales, *International Environmental Law* (Cambridge University Press, 2018) 240.

[32] Fukuda-Parr and McNeill, 'Knowledge and Politics in Setting and Measuring the SDGs: Introduction to Special Issue' (2019) 10 *Global Policy* 5.

[33] Elder and Høiberg Olsen, 'The Design of Environmental Priorities in the SDGs' (2019) 10 *Global Policy* 70; Elder and Zusman, 'Strengthening the Linkages Between Air Pollution and the Sustainable Development Goals' (July 2016) IGES Policy Brief (they conclude that there is still room

such as the CBD, the NP and the International Treaty on Plant Genetic Resources for Food and Agriculture (ITPGR), the regime is much more comprehensive and complex. As an issue area, ABS is not neatly delimited and defined. The question is how far the expression 'as internationally agreed' in target 15.6 can be stretched through interpretation. The SDGs makes no explicit reference to the NP, but, as is common in Agenda 2030, it connects to legally binding rules. The 'international agreements' mentioned intarget 15.6 obviously include at least the CBD, the NP and ITPGR.[34] But what about international agreements entered into after 2015, such as the BBNJ? And although Agenda 2030 is closely aligned with international law, it is not an international treaty subject to the interpretive rules of the Vienna Convention on the Law of Treaties.

Target 15.6 does not make any explicit distinction based on where ABS takes place, geographically or legally, but the reference to international law should probably be interpreted as meaning that at present it does not apply to areas beyond national jurisdiction (compare Article 3 NP).[35] Should a specialised ABS regime concerning marine genetic resources in areas beyond national jurisdiction emerge from the BBNJ Agreement, this could mean that ABS applies to both genetic resources from the seabed beyond national jurisdiction (the Area) and genetic resources from the water column beyond national jurisdiction (the high seas).[36]

Since Agenda 2030 links strongly to international law, and given that a legal framework for marine bioprospecting should satisfy the legal requirements set out in, for example, UNCLOS,[37] I suggest that the best approach is to start mapping the legal framework for marine bioprospecting. In that sense, Agenda 2030 can also help us identify legal gaps and give direction to legal design. There are some obvious gaps in the current legal framework for the oceans. Among other things, it does not contain any rules for marine bioprospecting on the high seas. This could be one reason why there are no such targets in SDG 14. In territorial waters, the NP applies.[38] The NP also provided input into the BBNJ negotiations, even though the Protocol's approach does not fit the principle of the common heritage of mankind that applies to the deep seabed.[39]

to incorporate air pollution more concretely and systematically in the SDG implementation process, especially at the regional, national, and local levels).

[34] NP, Art 4 can provide guidance about other access and benefit sharing agreements.

[35] Salpin, 'The Law of the Sea: A Before and an After Nagoya?' in Morgera et al (n 6) 153–54.

[36] Morgera et al (n 6) 106–08.

[37] Spijkers, 'The Cross-fertilization Between the Sustainable Development Goals and International Water Law' (2016) 25 *RECIEL* 39; Kim, 'The Nexus Between International Law and the Sustainable Development Goals' (2016) 25 *RECIEL* 15; Salpin (n 35) 149–83.

[38] Papastavridis, 'The Negotiations for a New Implementing Agreement Under the UN Convention on the Law of the Sea Concerning Marine Biodiversity' (2020) 69 *ICLQ* 585.

[39] Morgera (n 21).

B. Which SDGs are Relevant to Consider in the Regulation of Marine Bioprospecting?

In view of the universal nature of Agenda 2030, the simple answer is all SDGs; they are interdependent and interlinked ('integrated and indivisible'). However, in reality, the Agenda leaves considerable room for making priorities and adaptation to local contexts. This, in turn, brings a challenge of achieving policy coherence.[40] Sustainability science has approached this problem in different ways. For example, Weitz et al treat Agenda 2030 as an indivisible whole.[41] On the other hand, an approach where goals and targets with relevance to marine bioprospecting are identified and prioritised seems a better option, even though such an approach might appear at odds with the principle of indivisibility.[42] It must, however, be emphasised that much of the research in the field of sustainability science indicates that, while in general there are several synergies between the 17 goals, the number of conflicts and trade-offs are relatively few.[43] For example, in light of global asymmetries, the NP should contribute to SDG 10 on the reduction of inequality within and among countries.[44]

Since the issue here is about *marine* bioprospecting, it would seem obvious to take SDG 14 as a starting point. However, this SDG contains nothing about marine bioprospecting or ABS. Target 14.c sets out to 'Enhance the conservation and sustainable use of oceans and their resources'. In the literature, references are made to the concept of the 'blue economy',[45] without specifying more precisely how the concept could be used. The wording ('conservation and sustainable use') brings to mind the objectives of the CBD, but without any mention of the third objective, ie ABS. Target 14.c also makes clear that the goals and targets should be achieved by implementing international law as reflected in UNCLOS. In addition, reference is made to paragraph 158 of 'The Future We Want' (the outcome document of the 2014 UN Conference on Sustainable Development),[46]

[40] See SDG 17.14 ('Enhance policy coherence for sustainable development').

[41] Weitz et al (n 28).

[42] Breuer, Janetschek and Malerba, 'Translating Sustainable Development Goal (SDG) Interdependencies Into Policy Advice' (2019) 11 *Sustainability* 1, 11.

[43] Ekener and Katzeff, 'Kunskapsöversikt över ömsesidiga beroenden' (Naturvårdsverket, 2018) 7 ['Knowledge Overview of Mutual Dependencies' (Swedish Environmental Protection Agency, 2018)].

[44] Morgera et al (n 6) 7 ('Asymmetries and the ethical rationale for ABS').

[45] Sturesson, Weitz and Persson, 'SDG 14: Life Below Water. A Review of Research Needs', Technical annex to the Formas report Forskning för Agenda 2030: Översikt av forskningsbehov och vägar framåt (Stockholm Environment Institute, 2018) 16 and 30.

[46] Para 158 states: 'We recognize that oceans, seas and coastal areas form an integrated and essential component of the Earth's ecosystem and are critical to sustaining it, and that international law, as reflected in the United Nations Convention on the Law of the Sea, provides the legal framework for the conservation and sustainable use of the oceans and their resources … and to effectively apply an ecosystem approach and the precautionary approach in the management, in accordance with international law, of activities having an impact on the marine environment, to deliver on all three dimensions of sustainable development.'

which takes note of the 'fragmented governance regime for the oceans'. In the Formas report, it is noted that 'blue carbon and bioprospecting of oceans are issues of particular concern for the high seas but which are not included in SDG 14'.[47]

This analysis takes a particular target, namely target 15.6, as its 'entry point'.[48] Using a goal or target as an entry point is a way to identify and prioritise interactions and then focus on connections specific to this entry point. Since SDG 15 is about life on land,[49] it may at first seem to have little relevance to SDG 14, but there are strong links between SDG 14 and 15.

SDG 14 seeks to ensure the sustainable use of the oceans, seas and marine resources. This goal is generally considered important for achieving the other SDGs and it has received considerable interest from a sustainability point of view.[50] Le Blanc et al have made a preliminary mapping of SDG 14 in relation to the other SDGs.[51] Singh et al find that of the other 16 SDGs, all except SDG 17 are associated with SDG 14, though to different degrees and with different relationships.[52] In most cases, the authors find, SDGs can be largely complementary and even mutually dependent. SDG 14 also makes reference to international law, in this case explicitly to UNCLOS.[53] Le Blanc et al conclude that 'while many interlinkages identified here have the potential to be addressed through synergies, some of them involve trade-offs'.[54]

Policy and law in the field of marine bioprospecting should also contribute to fulfilling target 14.a ('Increase scientific knowledge, develop research capacity and transfer marine technology'). Generally, it is said that we lack scientific knowledge about the oceans, but that also depends on whether we are discussing shallower areas or the deep ocean.[55] In any case, distinguishing between research projects that do or do not contribute to conservation and sustainable use will be a practical challenge.[56] Salpin discusses the provisions of UNCLOS related

[47] Sturesson et al (n 45) 16 and 30.

[48] Alamco et al, 'Analysing Interactions Among the Sustainable Development Goals: Findings and Emerging Issues From Local and Global Studies' (2020) 15 *Sustainability Science* 1561, 1564.

[49] 'Protect, restore and promote sustainable use of terrestrial ecosystems, sustainably manage forests, combat desertification, and halt and reverse land degradation and halt biodiversity loss'.

[50] 'Conserve and sustainably use the oceans, seas and marine resources for sustainable development'; Singh et al, 'A Rapid Assessment of Co-benefits and Trade-Offs Among Sustainable Development Goals' (2018) 93 *Marine Policy* 223; Le Blanc, Freire and Vierros, 'Mapping the Linkages Between Oceans and Other Sustainable Development Goals. A Preliminary Exploration', DESA Working Paper No 149 (ST/ESA/2017/DWP/149); Ntona and Morgera, 'Connecting SDG 14 With the Other Sustainable Development Goals Through Marine Spatial Planning' (2017) 93 *Marine Policy* 214.

[51] Le Blanc et al (n 50).

[52] Singh et al (n 50) 225.

[53] Target 14.c: 'Enhance the conservation and sustainable use of oceans and their resources by implementing international law as reflected in the United Nations Convention on the Law of the Sea.'

[54] Le Blanc (n 4) 26.

[55] Leary et al (n 15) 184–88.

[56] Morgera et al (n 6) 181.

to marine scientific research (MSR), including whether the NP is 'a deterrent' to MSR or whether they are 'working in tandem'.[57]

SDG 17 should also be mentioned here. This goal focuses on means of implementation, ie partnerships for the goals, and in particular the possibility for research and knowledge cooperation across borders. Target 17.10 makes reference to the world trading system: 'Promote a universal, rules-based, open, non-discriminatory and equitable multilateral trading system under the WTO [World Trade Organization] including through the conclusion of negotiations within the Doha Development Agenda.' This also includes the WTO Agreement on Trade-Related Aspects of Intellectual Property Rights (TRIPS), since it forms part of the multilateral trading system under the WTO. SDG 17 is concerned with means for the implementation of Agenda 2030. Interestingly, technology is mentioned as one of those means (targets 17.6, 17.7 and 17.8). For the purposes of marine bioprospecting, SDG 17 should also be linked to other technology transfer 'obligations' in Agenda 2030 (targets 14.a and 15.6).

C. Interactions (Links) between SDGs

As Weitz et al make clear, 'The dynamics of how exactly targets interact with each other is an empirical question'.[58] While analysis often starts with one SDG as an 'entry point', in this case target 15.6, the second step is to count the number of interactions, map them and then 'discuss synergies and trade-offs from the perspective of that issue area'.[59] Systemic impacts should be taken into consideration.[60] The idea is briefly the following: if progress is made on target *x*, how does this influence progress on target *y*? Here, we are specifically interested in: if progress is made on, for example, SDG 3 (health), how does this influence progress on target 15.6? How influence works in the other direction is also of interest; if progress is made on target 15.6, how does this influence progress on targets regarding biodiversity conservation and sustainable use of the oceans (SDG 14)? For example, if we assume that the result of the marine bioprospecting project is a pharmaceutical product, protected by a patent and some kind of benefit-sharing agreement that contribute to the achievement of target 15.6, it should probably also contribute to the achievement of SDG 3 (health; especially target 3.B).

Despite the fact that 'Numerous efforts have been made to conceptualize and assess interactions amongst the SDGs',[61] more extensive research on the

[57] Salpin (n 35).
[58] Weitz et al (n 28) 532.
[59] ibid 532.
[60] ibid 532 ('the systemic properties of the system as a whole are poorly understood').
[61] ibid 532; Breuer et al (n 42).

interactions between the different SDGs is still lacking.[62] The interactions have been conceptualised in different ways, for example by using network theory.[63] While the SDGs are integrated and their implementation should be guided by a principle of indivisibility, Agenda 2030 itself does not provide guidance on what indivisibility means in practice, how the SDGs interact or how to assess these interactions. Although one cluster is analysed here, the overall aim is to contribute to the fulfilment of all SDGs.

Nilsson and Weitz emphasise that 'a comprehensive approach to achieve policy coherence should start with a problem definition'.[64] In fact, an essential means of implementation for all the goals is target 17.14, on policy coherence.[65] Most of the legal and policy problems relating to marine bioprospecting are well known.[66] The development of policy and law in the field of marine bioprospecting presents considerable problems for the policy- and lawmaker since it requires the integration of several different legal regimes: the law of the sea, the NP, intellectual property laws, etc. In addition to the different legal frameworks that will have to be taken into account, the various jurisdictional zones established under UNCLOS must be considered. Policy coherence for sustainable development means: (i) to foster synergies and minimise trade-offs between sustainability goals; (ii) to reconcile domestic policy objectives with internationally agreed objectives; and (iii) to address the transboundary and long-term effects of policies.[67]

The SDGs are best seen as a whole, a web, with interlinkages between more than two or three goals.[68] Here, I use the idea of 'SDGs as a network of targets' to conceptualise the different SDGs relevant to marine bioprospecting, including ABS. While there are several links that could be addressed, I focus on two such links as illustrations:[69] the link between ABS and biodiversity conservation; and that between ABS and science, technology and innovation.

[62] Bennich, Weitz and Carlsen, 'Deciphering the Scientific Literature on SDG Interactions: A Review and Reading Guide' (2020) 728 *Science of the Total Environment* 1; Nilsson et al, 'Mapping Interactions Between the Sustainable Development Goals: Lessons Learned and Ways Forward' (2018) 13 *Sustainability Science* 1489.

[63] Le Blanc (n 4) 176–87.

[64] Nilsson and Weitz, 'Governing Trade-Offs and Building Coherence in Policy-Making for the 2030 Agenda' (2019) 7 *Politics and Governance* 254, 256.

[65] Target 17.14: 'Enhance policy coherence for sustainable development.'

[66] Vierros et al, 'Who Owns the Ocean? Policy Issues Surrounding Marine Genetic Resources' (2016) 25 *ASLO* 29; Rimmer, 'The Sorcerer II Expedition: Intellectual Property and Biodiscovery' (2009) 6 *Macquarie Journal of International and Comparative Environmental Law* 147; see also Morgera et al (n 6) 3; Wright et al, 'The Long and Winding Road Continues: Towards a New Agreement on High Seas Governance' (IDDRI, 2015) Study No 01/16.

[67] Morales, 'Why Is Policy Coherence Essential for Achieving the 2030 Agenda?' (UN System Staff College Blog, 10 September 2018) www.unssc.org/news-and-insights/blog/why-policy-coherence-essential-achieving-2030-agenda/.

[68] Ekener and Katzeff, 'Kunskapsöversikt över ömsesidiga beroenden' (Naturvårdsverket, 2018); Le Blanc (n 4).

[69] Le Blanc (n 4); Swain and Ranganathan, 'Modeling Interlinkages Between Sustainable Development Goals Using Network Analysis' (2021) 138 *World Development*.

D. How Should the Link between ABS and Biodiversity Conservation be Conceptualised?

It is clear that the third objective of the CBD, like the objective of the NP, is not to be pursued in isolation from the broader framework established by the CBD.[70] In accordance with Article 1 NP, the Protocol will indirectly contribute to the conservation of biodiversity. There are potentially several links between ABS and conservation or sustainable use. These links could be synergistic, but they could just as well imply trade-offs between ABS and conservation or sustainable use. ABS as set out in international law – although not in target 15.6 – creates a link between ABS on the one hand and conservation of biodiversity and sustainable use on the other. Benefit sharing is thought of as a financial 'contribution' to the conservation of biodiversity and the sustainable use of its components,[71] but so too are the promotion and encouragement of research activities, for example, seen as 'contributions'. This is a legal, normative link that needs to be empirically confirmed.[72] If it works in that way, it would be synergistic; the achievement of target 15.6 would contribute to conservation of biodiversity and sustainable use.

Even though an assumption is often made that ABS will contribute to (or at least incentivise) conservation, it is not at all certain that this will happen in practice. One idea is that bioprospecting, if properly regulated, particularly through intellectual property rights, will incentivise and thereby fund biodiversity conservation.[73] In fact, ABS is 'assumed' to create strong incentives for biodiversity conservation 'quasi-automatically'.[74] Morgera et al argue that ABS for genetic resources may be seen as 'one of the frontrunners for linking economic activities more clearly to the services provided by healthy ecosystems'.[75]

Policy and law on deep sea prospecting developed primarily with regard to non-living matter, especially deep seabed mining.[76] It is reasonable to assume that marine bioprospecting is less damaging to the marine ecosystem than seabed mining of minerals, as it is about sampling and acquiring genetic knowledge,[77] but things would be different if production for commercial exploitation required some kind of harvesting of marine genetic resources.

[70] Morgera et al (n 6) 54.

[71] ibid 54.

[72] Weitz et al (n 28) 532 ('The dynamics of how exactly targets interact with each other is an empirical question').

[73] Farrier and Tucker (n 12) 218; Morgera et al (n 6) 10–14 ('An incentive-based approach to biodiversity conservation and the economic rationale for ABS'); Chiarolla, Lapeyre and Pirard, 'Bioprospecting Under the Nagoya Protocol: A Conservation Booster?' (IDDRI, November 2013).

[74] Oberthür and Rosendal, *Global Governance of Genetic Resources: Access and Benefit Sharing After the Nagoya Protocol* (Routledge, 2015) 244–45. Morgera (n 21) 10.

[75] Morgera et al (n 6) 12.

[76] Vierros et al (n 66) 29–35.

[77] Hunt and Vincent, 'Scale and Sustainability of Marine Bioprospecting for Pharmaceuticals' (2006) 35 *AMBIO* 57, 60.

E. Science, Technology and Innovation: SDSG 9

Interest in marine bioprospecting depends on a healthy ecosystem, but in order to retain or restore a healthy ecosystem we need knowledge about it. As has already been pointed out, Agenda 2030 highlights in several places the role of 'science, technology, and innovation' for the achievement of the goals. The importance of technology (R&D) is highlighted throughout the Agenda, without explicitly mentioning intellectual property's role in achieving the goals.[78] Transfer of technology is also mentioned in several places.[79]

One of the most controversial issues in the relationship between the CBD and TRIPS concerns the patenting of biological material.[80] In fact, the conclusion of the CBD did put the issue of ABS on the agenda,[81] and the CBD has started to have an impact on patent law in different ways. Policy discussions have taken place especially in the context of TRIPS and public health. Related to innovation policy and ABS more broadly is the discussion about the human right to science.[82]

Science, technology and innovation are essential for the sustainable use of marine resources,[83] and the aim of bioprospecting is often a patented invention (as noted above, most definitions of marine bioprospecting presuppose a commercial purpose).[84] Although intellectual property has been a debated issue in ABS and the negotiations that led up to the NP, it is not explicitly regulated within the ABS context. And while intellectual property is not mentioned in Agenda 2030, it should be addressed in the context of SDG 9 (promote innovation). In any case, the role of technology and its development is highlighted throughout Agenda 2030.[85] According to Chon, Agenda 2030 also directly

[78] Schneider et al, 'How Can Science Support the 2030 Agenda for Sustainable Development? Four Tasks to Tackle the Normative Dimension of Sustainability' (2019) 14 *Sustainability Science* 1593; Haugen, 'Why Are Intellectual Property Rights Hardly Visible in the United Nations Sustainable Development Goals?' in Rognstad and Ørstavik (eds), *Intellectual Property and Sustainable Markets* (Edward Elgar Publishing, 2021) 12–37.

[79] eg Agenda 2030, para 41, targets 7a, 9.4, 9c, 14a, 17.6–17.7; para 70, 'Technology Facilitation Mechanism'.

[80] Morgera et al (n 6) 8 (the tension between international law on intellectual property rights and on biodiversity is still unresolved).

[81] Bentley and Sherman, *Intellectual Property Law* (Oxford University Press, 2009) 355–56 ('While the Convention may not have an immediate impact on patent law, it does represent a change of attitude towards the way natural resources are exploited which may impact upon the way patents are viewed. In particular it may help to undermine the pro-patent attitudes that have dominated for the last forty or so years. The impetus provided by the Convention on Biological Diversity to reconsider the aims and functions of the patent system has been reinforced by the growing body of literature that question the often taken-for-granted assumption that technological development is both desirable and neutral').

[82] Boggio and Ho, 'The Human Right to Science and Foundational Technologies' (2018) 18 *American Journal of Bioethics* 69; Hubert, 'The Human Right to Science and Its Relationship to International Environmental Law' (2020) 31 *European Journal of International Law* 625.

[83] Le Blanc et al (n 50) 24.

[84] Rimmer (n 66).

[85] Schot and Steinmueller, 'Three Frames for Innovation Policy: R&D, Systems of Innovation and Transformative Change' (2018) 47 *Research Policy* 1554.

addresses this linkage between intellectual property and development through SDG 9, together with its targets and indicators.[86] It is especially the patenting of marine resources that is at stake. Patentability of marine resources is a matter for patent law and the patent offices. A fundamental policy issue is whether privatisation of such knowledge should be allowed and whether patenting should be allowed at all (these issues relate to technology transfer). Nevertheless, patenting of biological material is controversial,[87] and raises several policy issues that are not unique to marine genetic resources.

Patenting in the field of marine genetic resources is a controversial issue.[88] Craig Venter's Explorer expedition[89] illustrated some of the difficult policy problems raised in marine bioprospecting regarding both basic research (open access to data; data in the form of digital sequence information (DSI) and commercialisation (patents)). Whether access to data should be open or restricted in different ways is an important policy issue. Open access to data is probably important for biodiversity conservation and ecological sustainability overall, but concerns are raised that open access to data could bypass benefit-sharing obligations, as debates about DSI in the ITPGR and the NP show.[90]

In the context of science, technology and innovation, it is to be noted that the 'utilisation' of genetic resources includes the 'conduct of research and development on the genetic and/or biochemical composition of genetic resources, including through the application of biotechnology as defined in Article 2 CBD' (Article 2 NP). However, it is generally recognised that there are difficulties in distinguishing between bioprospecting for scientific use and for commercial use.[91]

Nilsson et al point out that 'For the ocean, knowledge gaps are large in relation to all interactions … These gaps have various causes and are often specific to the issues of marine resources, and some cannot be immediately addressed without more research'.[92] For example, there is weak support for the idea that marine bioprospecting would boost biodiversity conservation, although Article 9 NP makes such an assumption.[93] We generally have little knowledge about marine ecosystems, including potential economic values.[94] For example, the potential

[86] Chon, 'Recasting Intellectual Property in Light of the UN Sustainable Development Goals: Toward Knowledge Governance' (2019) 34 *American University International Law Review* 768.

[87] See, eg Bentley and Sherman (n 81) 355–56.

[88] Leary et al (n 15) 189–92.

[89] Rimmer (n 66).

[90] Nehring, 'Digitising Biopiracy? The Global Governance of Plant Genetic Resources in the Age of Digital Sequence Information' (2022) 43 *Third World Quarterly* 1970.

[91] See, eg Rosendal, Myhr and Tvedt, 'Access and Benefit Sharing Legislation for Marine Bioprospecting: Lessons From Australia for the Role of Marbank in Norway' (2016) 19 *Journal of World Intellect Property* 86.

[92] Nilsson et al (n 62) 1495.

[93] Chiarolla et al (n 73). NP, Art 9 states: 'The Parties shall encourage users and providers to direct benefits arising from the utilization of genetic resources towards the conservation of biological diversity and sustainable use of its components.'

[94] Leary et al (n 15).

for commercial use of marine genetic resources is uncertain.[95] Further, effective follow-up would require more specific ABS indicators.[96] There is currently only one ('rough') indicator for ABS,[97] and that seems insufficient.

V. CONCLUSIONS

This chapter addressed the sustainability challenges in developing a legal framework for marine bioprospecting. It discussed the relevant SDGs, the synergies and conflicts between the goals, and how the conflicts could be managed in the context of a legal framework for marine bioprospecting. As a general matter, implementation should aim to strengthen synergies and avoid trade-offs. An important question is what kind of measures could be undertaken in order to overcome, avoid or reduce the trade-offs. After all, the main problem with sustainability decision-making is how to achieve one goal without impairing the achievement of other goals. In other words, 'Attaining the SDGs will largely depend on whether policy can tackle trade-offs and leverage synergies within this broad agenda'.[98] Finally, it should be emphasised that the approach discussed in this chapter remains tentative and calls for further development.

[95] Leary, 'Marine Genetic Resources in Areas Beyond National Jurisdiction: Do We Need to Regulate Them in a New Agreement?' (2018) 5 *Maritime Safety and Security Law Journal* 22.

[96] See Agenda 2030, paras 72–91, which sets up a system for follow-up and review.

[97] Indicator 15.6.1: 'Number of countries that have adopted legislative, administrative and policy frameworks to ensure fair and equitable sharing of benefits'; compare Aichi target 16; Fukuda-Parr and McNeill (n 32) 5–15 ('Essential to the way a concept is defined is the choice of measurement method. One of the most striking findings of this research is how frequently the indicators watered down the ambition of the goals – by either narrowing down or distorting meaning'); Aichi target 16 will be replaced by Target 13 in the Kunming–Montreal Global Biodiversity Framework, CBD/COP/DEC/15/4, Annex, para 26, s D.

[98] Nilsson and Weitz (n 64) 257.

10

Regulation of Marine Bioprospecting in Iceland

SNJÓLAUG ÁRNADÓTTIR

I. INTRODUCTION

THE PROSPECTING OF biological diversity, or bioprospecting, refers to systematically searching for genes, organisms or biochemical information in the natural environment for the purpose of developing 'commercially-valuable products for pharmaceutical, agricultural, cosmetic and other applications'.[1] It relates to commercial development, as opposed to purely scientific purposes. Marine bioprospecting is the targeted and systematic search for components, bioactive compounds or genes within marine organisms. This search is directed at organisms, molecules and genes that can potentially be exploited for commercial purposes, often through the pharmaceutical industry. Marine bioprospecting can contribute to the development of new drugs for, inter alia, cancer and diabetes,[2] and various products in other industries.[3] The organisms used in marine bioprospecting may come from the sea, coastal areas, the seabed or even beneath the seabed. The result of this process can be a purified molecule that is produced biologically or synthetically.

The ocean covers approximately 70 per cent of the planet's surface and makes up around 97 per cent of the biosphere.[4] The diversity of marine life is immense and extends far beyond human knowledge. Scientific advances are expanding this knowledge to previously uncharted territory. Thus, unsurprisingly, there is growing interest in marine bioprospecting worldwide. Icelandic authorities have seen a rise in applications for marine bioprospecting, and the bio-industry is

[1] UN Development Programme, 'Bioprospecting: Overview', www.sdfinance.undp.org/content/sdfinance/en/home/solutions/bioprospecting.html.

[2] Abida et al, 'Bioprospecting Marine Plankton' (2013) 11 *Marine Drugs* 4594, 4598.

[3] See more examples in s II.

[4] Sands and Peel, with Fabra and MacKenzie, *Principles of International Environmental Law*, 4th edn (Cambridge University Press, 2018) 455.

becoming very important to the Icelandic economy. Marine biotechnology is booming and is predicted to reach $6.4 billion globally by 2025.[5]

Iceland is obligated, under the Convention on Biological Diversity (CBD),[6] to promote the conservation and sustainable use of biological diversity, and equitable sharing of benefits arising from the use of genetic resources. The Nagoya Protocol deals specifically with access to genetic resources and fair and equitable sharing of benefits arising from their utilisation.[7] Iceland is not a party to the Protocol, but provisions therein can inform the interpretation of the CBD, potentially impacting the obligations of those not bound by the Protocol. Moreover, Iceland must protect the marine environment in accordance with Part XII of the United Nations Convention on the Law of the Sea (UNCLOS)[8] and conduct environmental impact assessments before allowing activities within its national jurisdiction that may cause significant and harmful changes to the marine environment.[9] These obligations must be implemented in domestic law, administrative acts and policies. Yet, there is currently no comprehensive Icelandic legislation governing marine bioprospecting.

The marine environment is now under unprecedented pressure due to climate change. The oceans have engulfed over 90 per cent of all excess heat and 20–30 per cent of anthropogenic CO_2 emissions from the 1980s, which leads to ocean warming and acidification.[10] This is threatening marine ecosystems and their habitats,[11] leading to a loss of biodiversity and the relocation of certain species.[12] Corals are particularly vulnerable,[13] and fish stocks are expected to migrate and decline.[14] The international community is increasingly guided by the precautionary principle in relation to activities that potentially harm the marine environment, and has responded to these threats with the conclusion of a new agreement promoting biological diversity in areas beyond national jurisdiction.[15] Indeed, ongoing environmental degradation should incentivise

[5] Blasiak et al, 'Corporate Control and Global Governance of Marine Genetic Resources' (2018) 4 *Science Advances* 1.

[6] CBD (adopted 5 June 1992, entered into force 29 December 1993) 1760 UNTS 79, 143.

[7] Nagoya Protocol on Access to Genetic Resources and the Fair and Equitable Sharing of Benefits Arising from their Utilization to the Convention on Biological Diversity (adopted 29 October 2010, entered into force 12 October 2014) (CBD), CoP Decision X/1, 'Access to Genetic Resources and the Fair and Equitable Sharing of Benefits Arising From Their Utilization' (Nagoya, 29 October 2010) Annex I.

[8] United Nations Convention on the Law of the Sea (adopted 10 December 1982, entered into force 16 November 1994) 1833 UNTS 3.

[9] UNCLOS, Art 206.

[10] International Panel on Climate Change (IPCC), '2019: Summary for Policymakers' in Pörtner et al (eds), *IPCC Special Report on the Ocean and Cryosphere in a Changing Climate* (World Meteorological Organization, 2019) paras A.2 and A.2.5.

[11] ibid paras A.5 and A.5.2.

[12] ibid para A.6.3.

[13] ibid para A.6.4.

[14] ibid para B.8.

[15] UN, 'UN Delegates Reach Historic Agreement on Protecting Marine Biodiversity in International Waters' (5 March 2023) https://news.un.org/en/story/2023/03/1134157.

states to carefully regulate all activities affecting the marine environment. In that spirit, and to satisfy international obligations, Iceland should formulate a policy and set of rules to govern marine bioprospecting, and not simply respond to applications on a case-by-case basis.

This chapter explores Icelandic activities qualifying as marine bioprospecting; relevant rules of international law; and Icelandic law relating to marine bioprospecting (or lack thereof); and suggests key components for new Icelandic legislation governing marine bioprospecting. The purpose is to contribute to the development of the law in this field and determine how marine biotechnology may be appropriately regulated in Iceland.

II. MARINE BIOPROSPECTING IN ICELAND

Marine genetic resources are being increasingly utilised in Iceland. The use of such resources has developed into a major industry, and Icelandic companies are making a big impact on a global scale. Since 1983, this use has mostly involved the production of biotechnology, biochemicals and medical products from by-products of the fisheries sector that were previously discarded. Renowned Icelandic companies in this field include Zymetech, which manufactures (among other things) the Bio Effect skincare products and ColdZyme/Precold, which has been shown to combat the virus that causes COVID-19.[16] Lýsi hf is involved in research and sells various products obtained from fish oils in Iceland and abroad.[17] Finally, Kerecis, established in 2010, produces regenerative tissue from fish skin and fatty acids which is used worldwide by hospitals, healthcare facilities and others for the treatment of wounds and in surgeries. The technology developed by Kerecis is patented in over 40 countries, the company's operational headquarters are in the USA and all products are manufactured in Ísafjörður, Iceland.[18] These companies rely on genetic resources from living resources, but the use of genetic resources from microbes is also underway. In particular, algae are being harvested by companies such as VAXA Technologies, Hafkalk, Rækt, Lava Seaweed and Blue Lagoon International ehf for the purposes of research and for the production of animal feed, food supplements and skin care products.[19]

The growth of the bio-based industry has led to an increase in bioprospecting activities in marine areas. Scientists are showing an interest in unique and

[16] Dineshwori, 'This Mouth Spray Can Deactivate Coronavirus by 98.3%, Say Experts' (The Healthsite, 23 July 2020) www.thehealthsite.com/news/this-mouth-spray-can-deactivate-coronavirus-by-98-3-say-experts-758785/; Zymetech, www.cmocro.com/company/Zymetech+ehf./index.html.

[17] Lýsi (Cod Liver Oil), www.lysi.is/.

[18] Kerecis, www.kerecis.com/about-us/.

[19] VAXA Technologies, www.vaxa.life/; Hafkalk, www.hafkalk.com/; Rækt, www.raekt.is/en/; Lava Seaweed, https://lavaseaweed.is/; Blue Lagoon International ehf, https://arsskyrsla2019.bluelagoon.is/en/.

unexplored maritime areas under Iceland's jurisdiction, such as the hydrothermal vent site (geothermal cones) at the sea floor in Eyjafjordur to the north of Iceland.[20] It is also interesting to note that more than 20 per cent of Icelandic patent applications filed from 2010 to 2020 relate to the fisheries sector and over half the patents currently in force relate to the fishing industry. Furthermore, the content of patent applications has changed in recent years as derivative products from fisheries and aquaculture have become increasingly prominent.[21]

This raises complicated issues because, while states are urged to promote scientific research and protect the marine environment under the law of the sea, and the CBD and Nagoya Protocol facilitate access and equitable sharing of benefits arising from the utilisation of genetic resources, intellectual property must also be protected. Indeed, the growth of the bio-based industry requires harmony among all of these factors. There is currently no legal framework governing bioprospecting in Icelandic maritime zones, but the National Energy Authority of Iceland has issued licences for research on marine microbes by reference to Rules No 234/1999 on the Granting of Licences for Research and Utilisation of Microbes that May be Processed in Geothermal Vents (Rules on Geothermal Vents).[22]

III. RELEVANT RULES OF INTERNATIONAL LAW

The CBD governs conservation and sustainable use of biodiversity, and the utilisation of marine genetic resources. The Nagoya Protocol to the CBD is also highly relevant to the subject matter at hand, although it is not directly binding on Iceland, which has not ratified it. Furthermore, marine bioprospecting in Iceland only takes place in maritime zones within the national jurisdiction, which makes the legal regimes of the territorial sea, the exclusive economic zone (EEZ) and the continental shelf directly applicable. UNCLOS also entails rules governing protection of the marine environment and marine scientific research generally, without geographic limitations.

The following sections will consider the most important developments in international law relevant to the regulation of marine bioprospecting. They provide an analysis of the rules applicable under the CBD; relevant rules of the Nagoya Protocol; and relevant rules of UNCLOS. It should be mentioned that the Agreement on Trade Related Aspects of International Property Rights[23] is relevant to fair and equitable access and benefit sharing under the CBD and

[20] See National Energy Authority, 'Licence for Research of Geothermal Cone Areas in Eyjafjörður' (Reykjavik, 22 August 2017) Reference No OS2017080013/50.4.3, https://orkustofnun.is/gogn/Leyfi/OS-2017-L023-01_EarthLifeScienceInst_Eyjafj-orverur.pdf.

[21] Memo prepared by the Icelandic Intellectual Property Office (6 November 2020).

[22] See National Energy Authority (n 20).

[23] Annex 1C of the Marrakesh Agreement Establishing the World Trade Organization (adopted 15 April 1994, entered into force 1 January 1995) 1867 UNTS 154.

Nagoya Protocol. However, it primarily relates to the utilisation of genetic resources derived from traditional knowledge, which is not a contentious issue in Iceland. Therefore, this chapter will not particularly consider international or domestic rules relating to intellectual property rights.

A. The Convention on Biological Diversity

The CBD entered into force in 1993 and was ratified by Iceland in 1994. It contains no definition of bioprospecting, but defines biological resources as genes, (parts of) organisms or biotic components of ecosystems that can be useful or valuable to humankind.[24] It defines genetic material as material, originating from, inter alia, plants, animals or microbes, that contains 'functional units of heredity'. Finally, genetic resources are genetic material that is potentially valuable.[25]

The objectives of the CBD are conservation of biological diversity, sustainable use of the components of biological diversity and utilisation of genetic resources on the basis of fair and equitable benefit sharing, which includes giving appropriate access to relevant resources and technology.[26] Article 3 CBD acknowledges that states have sovereign rights to utilise the resources within their jurisdiction in accordance with national policies, but also affirms that states have an obligation to ensure that such activities do not cause transboundary harm. The CBD urges states to provide access to genetic resources and emphasises that activities must be 'environmentally sound'.[27] Access to genetic resources is subject to 'mutually agreed terms' and 'prior informed consent' by the party giving access.[28] Article 15 CBD also promotes cooperative scientific research[29] and obligates states to adopt national law, administrative acts or policies to facilitate the sharing of research and benefits arising from the exploitation of genetic resources. This relates to commercial and non-commercial benefits.[30] Moreover, this measure is meant to facilitate the sharing of the costs, in addition to the benefits, arising out of the utilisation and conservation of biological diversity. Access to genetic resources and benefit sharing is often misconstrued as relating only to economic gain, but non-monetary benefits are an important aspect, too.[31] Examples of non-monetary benefits include acknowledgements in academic publications and access to technology, facilities and research data.[32]

[24] CBD, Art 2.
[25] ibid Art 2.
[26] ibid Art 1.
[27] ibid Art 15(2).
[28] ibid Arts 15(4) and (5).
[29] ibid Art 15(6).
[30] ibid Art 15(7).
[31] Lallier et al, 'Access to and Use of Marine Genetic Resources: Understanding the Legal Framework' (2014) 31 *Natural Product Reports* 607, 612.
[32] Moran et al, 'Biodiversity Prospecting: Lessons and Prospects' (2001) 30 *Annual Review of Anthropology* 505, 516.

Article 8(j) CBD provides that states parties shall endeavour to 'respect, preserve and maintain knowledge, innovations and practices of indigenous and local communities embodying traditional lifestyles relevant for the conservation and sustainable use of biological diversity'. Parties shall encourage the broader use and equitable sharing of traditional knowledge, innovations or practices, but with the consent and participation of holders of that knowledge. This provision employs permissive language. Consequently, parties to the CBD and stakeholders disagree on whether this entails a legal requirement to acquire prior informed consent from indigenous and local communities for access to traditional knowledge.[33]

The CBD clearly necessitates domestic implementation. This is explicitly stated on several occasions. For example, Article 15(1) CBD stipulates that the access to genetic resources is determined by reference to national legislation, and Article 15(7) refers to the obligation to 'take legislative, administrative or policy measures'. The CBD further obligates contracting states to develop, in accordance with their capabilities,

> national strategies, plans or programmes for the conservation and sustainable use of biological diversity or adapt for this purpose existing strategies, plans or programmes which shall reflect, inter alia, the measures set out in this Convention relevant to the Contracting Party concerned.[34]

These states shall 'Integrate, as far as possible and as appropriate, the conservation and sustainable use of biological diversity into relevant sectoral or cross-sectoral plans, programmes and policies'.[35] Furthermore, contracting states are obligated to 'Identify components of biological diversity important for its conservation and sustainable use' as far as is possible and appropriate, to be able to employ conservation measures in relevant areas.[36] Obligations relating to protected areas or in situ and ex situ conservation are described in Articles 8 and 9 CBD.

It is of particular relevance for this chapter that contracting states shall also 'Identify processes and categories of activities which have or are likely to have significant adverse impacts on the conservation and sustainable use of biological diversity, and monitor their effects through sampling and other techniques'.[37] New and emerging practices, such as those relating to bioprospecting in the ocean, seabed or subsoil, should be particularly identified in this regard so that states may apply the conservation measures described in Articles 8 and 9 CBD to appropriate activities, and ensure sustainable use of vulnerable resources, as

[33] ibid 218; Kamau, Fedder and Winter, 'The Nagoya Protocol on Access to Genetic Resources and Benefit Sharing: What Is New and What Are the Implications for Provider and User Countries and the Scientific Community?' (2010) 6(3) *LEAD* 246.

[34] CBD, Art 6(a).

[35] ibid Art 6(b).

[36] ibid Art 7(a).

[37] ibid Art 7(b).

per Article 10 CBD. Indeed, contracting states must, insofar as is appropriate and possible, consider sustainable development of biological resources when making decisions at the national level; prevent or minimise threats to biological diversity; and promote cooperation between the private and public sectors when developing methods for the sustainable use of these resources.[38] Furthermore, states must take economic and social measures to incentivise 'conservation and sustainable use of components of biological diversity'.[39]

The CBD carries other obligations. These relate to, inter alia, research and training relating to conservation and sustainable use of biological resources;[40] public education and awareness;[41] impact assessments and mitigation of harm;[42] and transfer of technology.[43] Another provision of particular relevance is Article 22, concerning the relationship between the CBD and the law of the sea, which provides that implementation of the CBD shall not infringe the rights and obligations that states have under UNCLOS or consonant customary law.

Finally, it will be noted that the ecosystem approach is the principal framework of action to be used under the CBD.[44] The CBD does not explicitly refer to, or define, the ecosystem approach, but, according to a decision of the states parties, it is 'a strategy for the integrated management of land, water and living resources that promotes conservation and sustainable use in an equitable way'.[45] This is further clarified by the Malawi Principles for the Ecosystem Approach, which were adopted in 1998 and presented at the Fourth Meeting of the Conference of the Parties to the CBD.[46] The principles provide, among other things, that 'Ecosystem managers should consider the effects of their activities on adjacent and other ecosystems'.[47] According to the states parties to the CBD, the ecosystem approach does not operate to the preclusion of other management and conservation approaches, but rather integrates them to tackle complicated situations.[48] The joint commissions of the OSPAR and Helsinki Conventions have explained that application of the ecosystem approach involves the

> integrated management of human activities based on the best available scientific knowledge about the ecosystem and its dynamics, in order to identify and take action on influences which are critical to the health of marine ecosystems, thereby achieving

[38] ibid Art 10.
[39] ibid Art 11.
[40] ibid Art 12.
[41] ibid Art 13.
[42] ibid Art 14.
[43] ibid Art 16.
[44] ibid CoP Decision II/8, 'Preliminary considerations of components of biological diversity particularly under threat and action which could be taken under the Convention' (Jakarta, 17 November 1995) para 1.
[45] ibid CoP Decision V/6 'Ecosystem approach' (Nairobi, 26 May 2000).
[46] ibid CoP Decision IV/1B (Bratislava, 4–15 May 1998) referring to UNEP/CBD/COP/4/Inf.9 'Report of the workshop on the ecosystem approach' (hereinafter Malawi Principles).
[47] Malawi Principle 3.
[48] CBD, CoP Decision V/6 (n 45).

sustainable use of ecosystem goods and services and maintenance of ecosystem integrity.[49]

The relevance of the ecosystem approach extends further than the CBD. It has become particularly relevant for the management of marine resources[50] and applies to numerous ocean instruments.[51] Indeed, Karmenu Vella, the European Commissioner for the Environment, Marine Affairs and Fisheries, recently explained that an ecosystem approach is necessary for sustainable use of oceanic resources and our common future.[52] Moreover, the UN General Assembly (UNGA) noted, on 30 December 2020, that ecosystems must be protected in a response to the ongoing environmental degradation[53] and that states must cooperate and take all appropriate measures when responding to the impacts on marine ecosystems in areas within and beyond national jurisdiction.[54]

B. The Nagoya Protocol

The Nagoya Protocol entered into force in 2014 and now has 140 states parties.[55] Iceland is not one of them. Even so, the Protocol elaborates on certain obligations enshrined in the CBD and can, therefore, be useful for interpreting that convention. Indeed, it serves the function of effectively implementing the objectives of the CBD, specifically those outlined in Articles 8(j) and 15.[56] The Nagoya Protocol was adopted under the framework of the CBD, following a call for

[49] Helsinki and OSPAR Commissions, 'Statement on the Ecosystem Approach to the Management of Human Activities "Towards an Ecosystem Approach to the Management of Human Activities"', First Joint Ministerial Meeting of the Helsinki and OSPAR Commissions (Bremen, Germany, 25–26 June 2003) Annex 5, Ref. §6.1, www.ospar.org/site/assets/files/1232/jmm_annex05_ecosystem_approach_statement.pdf.

[50] Langlet and Rayfuse (eds), *The Ecosystem Approach in Ocean Planning and Governance: Perspectives from Europe and Beyond* (Brill Nijhoff, 2019) 2.

[51] See Convention on the Conservation of Antarctic Marine Living Resources (adopted 20 May 1980, entered into force 7 April 1982) 1329 UNTS 47, Art 2(3)(c); Convention for the Protection of the Marine Environment of the North-East Atlantic (adopted 22 September 1992, entered into force 25 March 1998) 2354 UNTS 67, Annex V, Art 3(1)(b)(iv); Convention on the Protection of the Marine Environment of the Baltic Sea (adopted 9 April 1992, entered into force 17 January 2000) 2099 UNTS 195, see Art 15; Agreement for the Implementation of the Provisions of the United Nations Convention on the Law of the Sea of 10 December 1982 relating to the Conservation and Management of Straddling Fish Stocks and Highly Migratory Fish Stocks (adopted 4 August 1995, entered into force 11 December 2001) 2167 UNTS 3, Art 5; FAO Code of Conduct for Responsible Fisheries, FAO COP Resolution 4/95 (31 October 1995) esp Arts 6, 9(2) 9(3)(1) 12(5) and 12(10)–(11).

[52] Langlet and Rayfuse (n 50) 1, referring to a speech at a side event to the UN Oceans Conference in June 2017, co-organised with the United Nations Environment Programme, the UNEP/MAP, the Food and Agriculture Organisation and the General Fisheries Commission for the Mediterranean.

[53] UNGA Res 75/239, 'Oceans and the Law of the Sea' (31 December 2020) para 198(a).

[54] UNGA (n 52) para 198(d).

[55] UN Treaty Collection, 'Parties to the Nagoya Protocol' (2023) www.cbd.int/abs/nagoya-protocol/signatories/.

[56] Nagoya Protocol, Art 4(4).

action by the World Summit on Sustainable Development, to ensure the implementation of rules concerning access and benefit sharing and to elaborate on those mechanisms.[57] It promotes the adoption of global frameworks to ensure consistency and predictability for stakeholders in different national settings.[58]

Article 5 of the Nagoya Protocol explains that benefit sharing extends to the utilisation of genetic resources, including related applications and commercialisation. Benefits shall be shared between the state of origin and the party acquiring the resources in conformity with the CBD, on mutually agreed terms.[59] States must also adopt laws, rules or policies to ensure that benefits arising from utilisation of genetic resources are shared with indigenous or local communities if such communities have an entitlement to the resources under domestic law. These arrangements shall also be on mutually agreed terms.[60] Similar measures must be taken to ensure equitable benefit sharing in relation to the utilisation of traditional knowledge involving genetic resources.[61] The Protocol confirms that benefits can include, inter alia, monetary benefits; collaboration in education, giving priority to certain research interests; and 'Joint ownership of relevant intellectual property rights'.[62]

Article 6 of the Nagoya Protocol details the requirements of prior informed consent. States shall take appropriate measures to ensure 'legal certainty, clarity and transparency of their domestic access and benefit sharing legislation or regulatory requirements'.[63] Rules governing access to genetic resources shall be fair and informative of the process. Applicants for access to genetic resources shall be provided with clear, written decisions in a timely and cost-effective manner, and successful applications shall result in the issuance of permits or similar evidence of the prior informed consent.[64] A specific process concerning prior informed consent involving indigenous or other communities should be set up where relevant under domestic legislation.[65] Moreover, domestic rules should clearly regulate the establishment of documented, mutually agreed terms. These should provide for, inter alia, dispute settlement, consideration for intellectual property rights and, where applicable, third-party use or change of intent (signifying a shift from research to commercial interests).[66]

Benefit sharing must be established with prior informed consent on mutually agreed terms whenever the marine activities occur in areas under national

[57] Report of the World Summit on Sustainable Development, Johannesburg, South Africa, 26 August–4 September 2002 (United Nations publication, Sales No E.03.II.A.1 and corrigendum) ch I, resolution 1, annex, para 44(o).

[58] Lallier et al (n 31) 612.

[59] Nagoya Protocol, Arts 5(1) and (3).

[60] ibid Art 5(2).

[61] ibid Art 5(5).

[62] ibid Art 5(4), Annex I.

[63] ibid Art 6(3)(a).

[64] ibid Art 6(3), sub-paras (b)–(e).

[65] ibid Art 6(3)(f).

[66] ibid Art 6(3)(g).

jurisdiction. That includes internal waters, the territorial sea, the EEZ and the continental shelf. Consequently, the rules of the CBD and the Nagoya Protocol concerning marine bioprospecting extend to maritime zones, which are also governed by the law of the sea. UNCLOS entails a set of rules concerning scientific research that can apply in conjunction with the CBD and the Nagoya Protocol. In fact, those interested in marine bioprospecting may have to acquire two distinct permits from different authorities within a single state, one authorising marine scientific research as per UNCLOS and another relating to access and benefit sharing in accordance with the CBD and the Nagoya Protocol.[67] It may, in some instances, be difficult to determine where the threshold lies when marine scientific research becomes marine bioprospecting, and this depends on the domestic legislation of the state where the activities take place.[68] However, while the mechanisms referred to in the Nagoya Protocol govern access to and exploitation of marine genetic resources regardless of whether they are acquired in situ or ex situ, UNCLOS only becomes applicable when the resources are accessed in situ, ie when the activities take place within maritime zones under national jurisdiction.[69]

The following subsection explores the law of the sea as it relates to the regulation of marine bioprospecting.

C. The Law of the Sea

Iceland ratified UNCLOS in 1985 and it entered into force in 1994. UNCLOS largely reflects customary international law and entails several provisions that are directly applicable to marine bioprospecting in areas within, and beyond, national jurisdiction. It makes no mention of genetic resources, but governs the conservation, exploitation and research of 'living', 'natural' and 'biological' resources.[70] It is important to take note of these rules because states can satisfy the requirements of the CBD and the Nagoya Protocol as they relate to marine bioprospecting while simultaneously violating obligations under UNCLOS, or vice versa.[71]

UNCLOS affords coastal states sovereign rights over exploration, exploitation, conservation and management of genetic resources in the EEZ. This zone extends 200 nautical miles (M) from baselines along the coast, and includes the water column, seabed and subsoil.[72] Coastal states also have jurisdiction over marine scientific research and protection of the marine environment in

[67] Lallier et al (n 31) 615.
[68] ibid 615.
[69] ibid 613.
[70] ibid 613.
[71] ibid 613.
[72] See UNCLOS, Arts 56(1)(a), 57.

the EEZ.[73] Moreover, sovereign rights to explore and exploit resources of the seabed and subsoil can reach further out to sea where the natural prolongation of the continental margin extends beyond 200 M, but never more than 350 M from baselines, or 100 M from the 2500 metre isobath.[74] The resources subject to the regime of the continental shelf include 'sedentary species, that is to say, organisms which, at the harvestable stage, either are immobile on or under the seabed or are unable to move except in constant physical contact with the seabed or the subsoil'.[75] This encompasses marine microbes. Consequently, coastal states can have jurisdiction over the exploration and exploitation of these resources to a distance of 200 M from relevant coastlines, or to the outer edge of the continental margin as determined on the basis of Article 76(8) UNCLOS. However, where neighbouring states have overlapping claims, these entitlements are delimited on the basis of Articles 74 and 83 UNCLOS.

Part XIII of UNCLOS is devoted to marine scientific research. It provides a general right for all states to engage in marine scientific research, with due consideration for other states.[76] It also encourages states and international organisations to facilitate marine scientific research and to cooperate to that end.[77] Marine scientific research is subject to general principles laid down in Article 240 UNCLOS, which provide, inter alia, that it shall be used for peaceful purposes and in conformity with obligations to protect and preserve the marine environment.[78] Part XIII of UNCLOS also contains rules concerning dissemination of the information derived from marine scientific research, particularly to developing states;[79] it emphasises the exclusive right of coastal states to regulate and authorise marine scientific research in the territorial sea;[80] and it provides that while coastal states have a general right to govern marine scientific research in the EEZ and on the continental shelf, they shall normally permit marine scientific research in these areas if the proposed activities are consistent with UNCLOS.[81]

Furthermore, states shall ensure through domestic rules and procedures that consent for marine scientific research in the EEZ and on the continental shelf is not unduly delayed or denied.[82] However, Article 246(5) UNCLOS lists scenarios in which consent for marine scientific research may be withheld, for example if the project directly impacts exploration or exploitation of natural

[73] ibid Art 56(1)(b).
[74] ibid Arts 76 and 77(1).
[75] ibid Art 77(4).
[76] ibid Art 238.
[77] ibid Arts 239 and 242(1).
[78] The obligation to prevent damage to the marine environment when conducting marine scientific research is also reiterated in UNCLOS, Art 242(2).
[79] ibid Art 244.
[80] ibid Art 245.
[81] ibid Art 246, paras (1)–(3).
[82] See ibid Art 246(3).

resources, or if it involves 'the use of explosives or the introduction of harmful substances into the marine environment'. Despite the general assumption of consent for research in the EEZ or on the continental shelf, coastal states must be given detailed descriptions of proposed projects at least six months before they commence, and they are entitled to be represented in such projects.[83]

UNCLOS rules governing marine scientific research often refer to protection of the marine environment. This is obviously an important factor to be considered when regulating projects in the marine environment, regardless of whether they qualify as scientific research or bioprospecting. Indeed, UNCLOS codifies obligations concerning environmental protection that apply irrespective of activities or maritime zones. All states are obligated 'to protect and preserve the marine environment'.[84] Article 194 UNCLOS further obligates states to take positive action to prevent marine pollution from any source. Pollution of the marine environment extends, inter alia, to the indirect introduction 'of substances or energy into the marine environment' if it is likely to harm marine life and impair the quality of the oceans.[85] This definition of marine pollution has been interpreted broadly, to encompass, for example, pollution caused by greenhouse gas emissions[86] and destructive fishing techniques.[87] Therefore, it can surely extend to environmental harm resulting from marine bioprospecting.

Boyle has explained that the environmental obligations of UNCLOS Part XII relate not only to fish stocks and marine mammals, or economic and private interests, but to marine biodiversity generally. This is supported by reference to Articles 61 and 117 UNCLOS, which outline the obligations to conserve living resources, and to the CBD.[88] The International Tribunal for the Law of the Sea has also explained, in the Fisheries Advisory Opinion, that the reference to the 'marine environment' in Article 192 UNCLOS includes conservation of the living resources of the sea and other marine life.[89] Moreover, the arbitral tribunals in *Philippines v China* and *Chagos Marine Protected Area* confirmed that Article 194(5) UNCLOS 'is "not limited to measures aimed strictly at controlling marine pollution," which while "certainly an important aspect of environmental protection … is by no means the only one"'.[90]

Article 194 UNCLOS 'extends to measures focused primarily on conservation and the preservation of ecosystems', and marine protected areas are

[83] ibid Art 248.

[84] ibid Art 192.

[85] ibid Art 1(1)(4).

[86] Boyle, 'Law of the Sea Perspectives on Climate Change' in Freestone (ed), *The 1982 Law of the Sea Convention at 30: Successes, Challenges and New Agendas* (Martinus Nijhoff, 2013) 157, 158.

[87] *South China Sea (Philippines v China)* (Merits) (2016) XXXIII RIAA 153, para 970.

[88] Boyle (n 86) 158; see also Boyle, 'Law of the Sea Perspectives on Climate Change' (2012) 27 *International Journal of Marine and Coastal Law* 831, 832.

[89] Request for an advisory opinion submitted by the Sub-Regional Fisheries Commission (Advisory Opinion) [2015] ITLOS, 54 ILM 890, paras 120 and 216.

[90] *South China Sea* (n 87) para 945, referring to *Chagos Marine Protected Area (Mauritius v United Kingdom)* (2015) XXXI RIAA 359, paras 320 and 538.

among those measures.[91] The CBD defines protected areas as geographically defined areas which are 'designated or regulated and managed to achieve specific conservation objectives'.[92] These broad obligations are relevant to the governance of marine bioprospecting for two reasons: first, because such activities can involve intrusive methods that are harmful to the marine environment and marine biodiversity, or otherwise disturb the delicate balance of marine ecosystems; and second, because the obligation and decision to permit certain activities may be influenced by pre-existing protective measures, such as marine protected areas.

Article 206 UNCLOS is also relevant for the regulation of marine bioprospecting. It stipulates that states are under an obligation to assess the potential effects of planned activities within their maritime zones if there is reason to believe that such activities 'may cause substantial pollution of or significant and harmful changes to the marine environment'. The tribunal in the *South China Sea* dispute explained that while the language concerning the obligation to perform an environmental impact assessment is permissive, this provision contains an absolute obligation to communicate the results of an impact assessment to the competent international organisation.[93] This means that marine bioprospecting must be subject to an environmental impact assessment procedure if it is likely to result in substantial pollution or significant adverse effects to the marine environment.

The law of the sea is a rapidly developing field of law, currently responding to various environmental threats, such as habitat destruction and loss of biodiversity. A major developmental milestone occurred on 4 March 2023, with the conclusion of the Agreement on the Conservation and Sustainable Use of Marine Biological Diversity of Areas Beyond National Jurisdiction (BBNJ Agreement).[94] This instrument has no direct bearing on marine bioprospecting in areas within national jurisdiction. However, Part II of the BBNJ Agreement regulates activities concerning marine genetic resources and benefit sharing in areas beyond national jurisdiction which will become highly relevant to marine bioprospecting in such areas once it enters into force. If ratified by Iceland, this agreement will apply to marine bioprospecting activities subject to Icelandic jurisdiction on the high seas or in the international seabed area, but have no direct applicability to activities taking place within Iceland's maritime zones. Even at this stage, and despite being inapplicable to areas within national jurisdiction, it can shed light on international developments and approaches to the conservation of marine biodiversity and use of biotechnology.

[91] *Chagos Marine Protected Area* (n 90) para 538.

[92] CBD, Art 2.

[93] *South China Sea* (n 87) para 948.

[94] Agreement under the United Nations Convention on the Law of the Sea on the Conservation and Sustainable Use of Marine Biological Diversity of Areas beyond National Jurisdiction (adopted 19 June 2023).

Marine bioprospecting has already begun in areas beyond national jurisdiction, but it is not specifically regulated by UNCLOS and arguably falls within a 'legal lacuna'.[95] The BBNJ Agreement governs the use of marine genetic resources and offers practical rules concerning access to, and sharing of benefits from, marine genetic resources in areas beyond national jurisdiction. Moreover, it codifies rules on area-based management tools, including marine protected areas, environmental impact assessments, capacity building and transfer of technology.[96] It stipulates that activities concerning marine genetic resources may be carried out by all states,[97] and that they shall be for the benefit of humankind as a whole, 'particularly for the benefit of advancing the scientific knowledge of humanity and promoting the conservation and sustainable use of marine biological diversity'.[98] The BBNJ Agreement also sets up a clearing-house mechanism and stipulates that various items of information must be conveyed to it prior to in situ collection of marine genetic resources in areas beyond national jurisdiction.[99] States are obligated to ensure, through domestic legislative, administrative or policy acts, that their subjects report to the clearing-house mechanism.[100]

IV. ICELANDIC LEGISLATION TO GOVERN MARINE BIOPROSPECTING

Many countries have adopted a legal regime for this activity that allows for screening of research, open access to data and the sharing of benefits, but Iceland is not one of them. Nonetheless, marine bioprospecting is well underway, and it is important that legislation is developed to ensure that Iceland satisfies international obligations relating to the governance of these activities and provides the legal certainty necessary to attract investors.

The following subsections discuss relevant domestic instruments and propose key components for new legislation governing marine bioprospecting in Icelandic maritime zones.

A. Governing Law and Need for Further Regulation

The Icelandic Parliament has enacted legislation to implement some of its obligations under the CBD. Certain provisions of the Nature Conservation Act from

[95] Heiðar, 'Conservation and Sustainable Use of Marine Biological Diversity Beyond Areas of National Jurisdiction: A Third Implementing Agreement Under the Law of the Sea Convention?' in *Liber Amicorum: In Honour of a Modern Renaissance Man His Excellency Guðmundur Eiríksson* (Universal Law Publishing, 2017) 87, 94–95.

[96] See BBNJ Agreement, Parts III–V.

[97] ibid Art 11(1).

[98] ibid Art 11(6).

[99] ibid Art 12(2).

[100] ibid Art 12(1).

1999 were meant to reflect these commitments.[101] For example, Articles 41, 37, 50 and 65 are based on the obligations enshrined in Articles 6(b), 8(d) and 8(h) CBD. This legislation has now been replaced by a new Nature Conservation Act from 2013, which has a chapter dedicated to the import and distribution of alien species.[102] Article 61 is based on Article 37 of the predecessor and governs special protection of certain ecosystems and geological monuments. Additionally, Article 13 and Chapter VIII of the new Nature Conservation Act govern the designation of protected areas and the making of action plans. The Act also contains a general codification of the principle of prevention – the precautionary principle – and provides that decisions shall be made on the basis of the best available science, an ecosystem approach, and with consideration for the overall impact on the area.[103] Furthermore, it stipulates that the developer shall, as appropriate, bear the cost of preventing or limiting damage to nature resulting from each project.[104]

Article 34 of the Law on Exploration and Utilisation of Ground Resources[105] also implements certain elements of the CBD. In fact, it was intended to provisionally satisfy Articles 15–19 CBD, concerning access to genetic resources; access to and transfer of technology; exchange of information; technical and scientific cooperation; and handling of biotechnology and distribution of its benefits. Article 34 of the Act on Exploration and Utilisation of Ground Resources is limited to microorganisms in geothermal areas, and in geographic terms it is limited to land territory and a narrow belt of sea extending 115 metres from the coast, known as 'netlög' or netting limits.[106] According to official remarks of the Icelandic Minister for the Environment in 1999, this was meant to be supplemented with specific legislation concerning genetic resources, access and benefit sharing.[107] This law stipulates that the National Energy Authority can issue licences for exploration and exploitation, and impose restrictions or limitations on the licensee.[108] Furthermore, it refers to the need to agree, on mutual terms with the landowner, on compensation before a resource is utilised or, alternatively, expropriation.[109] The Rules on Geothermal Vents were enacted in 1999 by the Minister of Innovation. Their objective is, inter alia, to ensure compliance with the CBD.[110] They are also limited to geothermal vents and a maximum distance of 115 metres from the coast.[111]

[101] Official response of then Minister of the Environment, Siv Friðleifsdóttir, to a question about Icelandic implementation of the CBD (Parliament 1999–2000) www.althingi.is/altext/125/s/0932.html.
[102] Nature Conservation Act, Law no 60/2013, ch XI.
[103] ibid Arts 6–10.
[104] ibid Art 11.
[105] Law no 57/1998 on Exploration and Utilisation of Ground Resources.
[106] ibid Art 1.
[107] Above n 101.
[108] Law on Exploration and Utilisation of Ground Resources (n 105) Arts 4–6.
[109] ibid Art 7.
[110] Rules on Geothermal Vents, Art 1.
[111] ibid Arts 1, 2.

Icelandic institutions (such as the Icelandic Institute of Natural History) have also been guided by the provisions of the CBD when establishing policies and planning future projects. The Icelandic government has sought to implement its obligations, inter alia, through specific projects, some of which are international or regional, while others are required by domestic law but adjusted to fit the requirements of the CBD.[112] The Icelandic government adopted the Iceland National Biodiversity Strategy in 2008. It promotes the conservation and sustainable use of biodiversity, and includes measures to conserve species, restore habitats and establish new protected areas.[113] Iceland has also concluded an Action Plan with 49 immediate and long-term actions to implement the National Biodiversity Strategy. These are partly incorporated into Iceland's National Nature Conservation Strategy, which is updated every five years.[114]

It seems that, to date, Iceland has not fully complied with the requirements of the CBD. For example, the Icelandic government has not submitted all required national reports to the CBD. The most recent national report submitted by Iceland was the Fourth National Report, covering the 2005–09 period.[115] Moreover, existing Icelandic legislation implements some, but not all, of the provisions of the CBD, and the implementation does not provide the level of detail necessary to ensure legal certainty for users of genetic resources. The Rules on Geothermal Vents provide specific guidance on the research and utilisation of microbes from geothermal vents and are useful for that purpose. However, no such rules govern the exploration or utilisation of marine genetic resources beyond 115 metres from the coast, and the number of activities in the field certainly justify the adoption of specific rules for marine bioprospecting. In fact, limited attention has been afforded to the marine environment in the implementation of the CBD, and where Iceland's national reports to the CBD discuss the marine environment, they mostly do so in the context of fisheries.

It is relevant to note that the Law Concerning Iceland's Ownership of Seabed Resources confirms that the state possesses all resources on, in or under the seabed beyond 115 metres from the low-water line.[116] These 115 metre netting limits mark the extent of private ownership over coastal territory. This legislation further provides that Icelandic authorities have the exclusive right to regulate utilisation, conservation and management of seabed resources under national jurisdiction.[117] Furthermore, the Law on Planning of Marine and Coastal Areas was adopted in 2018 with the objective of providing a basis for diverse utilisation of marine resources through an ecosystem approach, with consideration for the

[112] Official response of then Minister of the Environment (n 101).
[113] Iceland's Fourth National Report to the CBD (2005–2009) 21, www.cbd.int/doc/world/is/is-nr-04-en.pdf.
[114] ibid.
[115] ibid.
[116] Law no 73/1990 Concerning Iceland's Ownership of Seabed Resources, Art 1.
[117] ibid Art 4.

effects of climate change and sustainable development as guiding principles.[118] This legislation governs the policies for marine and coastal planning but not the utilisation and protection of marine living resources of the sea and seabed.[119] It does, however, refer to the need for legal certainty and stipulates that permits for marine activities shall be consistent with relevant zonal plans.[120]

Marine scientific research in Iceland's maritime zones is subject to approval by the Icelandic government.[121] This legislation provides no definition of marine scientific research, so it is unclear to what extent it may apply to marine bioprospecting. Applications by foreign states and competent international organisations to conduct marine scientific research in the EEZ or on the continental shelf shall normally be approved if they involve peaceful efforts to promote knowledge of the marine environment.[122] There is no explicit reference to private entities, domestic or foreign, or to other maritime zones. Article 9(2) of the Law on Planning of Marine and Coastal Areas provides that permit applications may be rejected if they are directly related to the study or exploitation of organic or inorganic resources; involve drilling on the continental shelf, the use of explosives or substances harmful to the environment; or lead to the construction, operation or use of structures.

Applications for research permits under the Law on Maritime Zones must be submitted to relevant authorities[123] six months prior to the commencement of research activities. Icelandic authorities are given four months to decide whether to reject a research application,[124] and each application must be accompanied by detailed information regarding: (i) the nature and objectives of research; (ii) the research method, ie the name, size, type and make of vessels and a description of the research equipment used; (iii) the exact location of the areas to be investigated; (iv) the beginning and end of the research period; (v) the name of the research organisation, the name of its director and the manager of the research mission; and (vi) the planned participation of the Icelandic government in the research.[125]

The Law on Prevention of Coastal and Marine Pollution covers all kinds of commercial activities in the marine environment.[126] It is relevant for the implementation of UNCLOS obligations concerning protection of the marine environment and has implications for marine bioprospecting insofar as it involves dumping, within the meaning of Article 210 UNCLOS and the

[118] Law no 88/2018 on the Planning of Marine and Coastal Areas, Art 1(b).
[119] ibid Art 2.
[120] ibid Art 8.
[121] Law no 41/1979 on Maritime Zones, Art 9(1).
[122] ibid Art 9(2).
[123] This is customarily the Foreign Ministry.
[124] Law on Maritime Zones Act, Art 10(2).
[125] ibid Art 10(1).
[126] Law no 33/2004 on Prevention of Coastal and Marine Pollution, Art 2.

London Dumping Convention[127] and Protocol.[128] Dumping is prohibited under Article 9 of the Law on Prevention of Coastal and Marine Pollution, but Iceland's Environment Agency can grant permission for the dumping of natural, inactive substances, ie solid minerals that have not been chemically processed and are composed of materials that are unlikely to be released into the ocean.[129] Placement of substances or objects in Icelandic maritime zones is not considered dumping, and consequently is not prohibited, if the placement is for legitimate purposes other than disposing of the material.[130] This legitimate purpose could be marine scientific research.

The Ministry of the Environment, Energy and Climate recently had to decide whether marine scientific research relating to carbon dioxide removal in Iceland's maritime zones constituted dumping, in the context of Article 9 of the Law on Prevention of Coastal and Marine Pollution. The Environment Agency held that these activities, which involved the farming of macroalgae, should be prohibited. That decision was appealed to the Ministry of the Environment, Energy and Climate, which found that the activity was for a legitimate purpose, as demonstrated by the fact that a licence to conduct said marine scientific research had already been issued by the Foreign Ministry.[131] This demonstrates that marine bioprospecting can be exempt from the dumping prohibition if it receives a research licence under Article 9 of the Law on Maritime Zones.

B. Key Components of New Legislation

Marine bioprospecting must be regulated in Iceland. The new rules should aim to satisfy all the requirements of the Nagoya Protocol, inter alia, to clarify and make transparent the domestic legal process for access and benefit sharing, and to make the procedure for accessing marine genetic resources equitable and non-arbitrary.[132]

A preliminary step in adopting new regulation for marine bioprospecting in Iceland would be to identify legal gaps and determine the scope of the new rules. There might be overlaps with existing legislation, but fragmentation should be avoided as far as possible. For example, in determining the scope of the new rules, a distinction should be made between marine scientific research as per UNCLOS and marine bioprospecting, which is subject to the CBD and

[127] Convention on the Prevention of Marine Pollution by Dumping of Wastes and Other Matter (adopted 29 December 1972, entry into force 30 August 1975) 1046 UNTS 120.

[128] Protocol to the Convention on the Prevention of Marine Pollution by Dumping of Wastes and Other Matters (adopted 7 November 1996, entry into force 24 March 2006) 36 ILM 1.

[129] Law on Prevention of Coastal and Marine Pollution, Art 3(27)(b).

[130] ibid Art 3(27)(a).

[131] Decision of the Ministry of the Environment, Energy and Climate in the case of Running Tide (25 April 2023).

[132] Nagoya Protocol, see particularly Arts 6(a) and (b).

the Nagoya Protocol. These international obligations impose different requirements and can justify different treatment, eg in terms of the right to withhold consent and the right of participation. Also, a decision should be made regarding the connection between the new legislation and existing rules governing the use of genetic and ground resources extending to 115 metres from the coast.[133]

The new rules could be an Act of Parliament or administrative rules. However, given the broad legal gaps, it seems advisable that a new legal framework be adopted to regulate the exploration and exploitation of genetic resources in Icelandic maritime zones, or beyond the 115 metre netting limits. More detailed rules could be concluded on that basis and they should be comparable to the Rules on Geothermal Vents, which implement the CBD in the context of a closely related subject matter, ie the granting of licences for research and utilisation of microbes in geothermal vents on land and to the 115 metre mark. Indeed, the Rules have been repeatedly referenced by the Energy Authority in its granting of licences for marine bioprospecting.[134]

The following subsections will explore two key issues in more detail: namely, access and benefit sharing; and conservation and sustainable use of marine genetic resources.

(i) Access and Benefit Sharing

The Rules on Geothermal Vents are relevant as a point of reference for the regulation of marine bioprospecting because they entail the most detailed Icelandic rules on bioprospecting. They create a framework for the granting of permits for research and utilisation of microorganisms found in geothermal vents; and they ensure proper monitoring of research and utilisation. Moreover, the Rules promote access to research; technological development; and fair and equitable sharing of benefits arising from the utilisation of microorganisms, in line with the objectives of the CBD.[135] They afford the Minister for Industry (after consultation with the Minister for the Environment, Energy and Climate) the responsibility to grant permission to research and utilise microorganisms in geothermal areas.[136] The Minister for Industry may grant, on the basis of the Rules, a licence for research or utilisation, and a distinction is made between exclusive licences for applied research, general licences for practical research and general research permits for basic research. Utilisation licences relate to the production of certain microorganisms and can be obtained by anyone who has previously received an exploration licence. In general, before a utilisation licence is issued, the researcher must secure an agreement with the owner of the geothermal area on compensation for the use. It is also possible to set as a

[133] ie Law on Exploration and Utilization of Ground Resources; Rules on Geothermal Vents.
[134] See National Energy Authority (n 20).
[135] Rules on Geothermal Vents, Art 1.
[136] ibid Art 1.

condition for granting a utilisation licence that a patent has been obtained for the specific use.[137] Finally, Article 3 of the Rules on Geothermal Vents explicitly states that licences for utilisation shall be granted on the basis of Articles 15–19 CBD.

The Rules on Geothermal Vents entail very few rules on the practical aspects of access and benefit sharing. More detailed rules should be adopted to implement the relevant rules of the CBD and the Nagoya Protocol. For example, permission to utilise genetic resources could trigger an obligation to deposit certain data on open-access platforms, including 'databases, repositories or gene banks'.[138] The existing Rules provide that research results submitted to the Icelandic Institute of Natural History or other public bodies are treated as confidential for two years after the expiration of each research permit. This can increase to five years if the research leads to the issuance of a licence to utilise. This arguably strikes a balance between users wanting to acquire patents for their discoveries and those interested in access to research results because the time limit prevents information being withheld indefinitely, pending patent applications. Indeed, the main challenges involved in access and benefit sharing relate to the balancing of these rights, which requires that competing interests, arising under different areas of law, are reconciled.

The Conference of the Parties to the CBD has acknowledged that the implementation of the rules on access and benefit sharing can be complicated as it requires not only the adoption of domestic laws, administrative acts and policies, but also institutional arrangements and 'the designation of checkpoints'.[139] Furthermore, the Nagoya Protocol calls for participation of indigenous peoples, local communities and stakeholders, in addition to cooperation between different ministries and institutions.[140] Iceland has the competent national authorities to handle institutional arrangements, but should elaborate on these arrangements and checkpoints in the legislation. The absence of any indigenous population in Iceland simplifies the task, but coordination may be required between several institutions and sectors of government, including the Ministry of Industry and Innovation, the Ministry for the Environment, Energy and Climate, the Institute of Natural History, the National Energy Authority and the Icelandic Intellectual Property Office.

It can be useful to look to neighbouring countries and apply regional approaches in the implementation of the CBD and Nagoya Protocol.[141] Some lessons might be drawn, for instance, from Norway, because the Norwegian government presented a revised proposal for regulating extractions and

[137] ibid Art 3.

[138] Such a provision can be found in the BBNJ Agreement, Art 12.

[139] CBD, 'Report of the Compliance Committee Under the Nagoya Protocol on Access to Genetic Resources and the Fair and Equitable Sharing of Benefits Arising From Their Utilization on the Work of Its Second Meeting' (August 2018) UN Doc CBD/NP/MOP/3/2 31, Annex I, paras 2–3.

[140] ibid Annex I, para 5.

[141] See ibid Annex I, paras 6–7.

utilisation of genetic material (the Bioprospecting Regulations) for consultation in 2017. The purpose of this regulation was to implement Article 1 CBD and the Nagoya Protocol, and it was revised on the basis of a proposal put forth in 2012/13. It differed from the previous proposal in respect of benefit sharing and reporting obligations, and involved a simplified application procedure for repeat users.[142] The Norwegian proposal aimed to regulate marine bioprospecting in all maritime zones under Norwegian jurisdiction[143] and provide, inter alia, for equitable sharing of benefits arising out of their utilisation. One of the driving factors was the fact that foreign actors had been deterred from participating in Norwegian bioprospecting projects due to uncertainty about the Norwegian rules.[144] The lack of legal certainty in Iceland invites the same risk.

The proposed Norwegian regulation has met with some opposition, and the authorities have described challenges in concluding the rules due to rapid technological developments; difficulties in defining genetic material; and complications with producing final products from genetic material. The proposed regulation promotes the use of genetic material for the benefit of Norway and the international community. It establishes a low threshold for bioprospecting, but refers to the requirement of environmentally sound use. The regulation proposes a two-tier permit system, involving extraction and utilisation of genetic material from nature and distribution of genetic material from public collections. The authorities giving permits are enabled to set conditions for non-economic benefit sharing; this may include sharing scientific information about the ecosystem related to the extraction and depositing material for public collection. A processing fee may also be charged.[145] The Icelandic Energy Authority has set similar conditions for licensing marine bioprospecting in Iceland and the new rules should govern this competence. The Norwegian proposal also provides for financial and non-financial distribution of benefits when handing out material from public collections.[146]

The Norwegian proposal provides that the extraction of biological material from nature only requires a permit if it is for the purpose of utilising the genetic material.[147] A permit, under the proposed Norwegian regulation, shall provide (with accompanying documents) proof of a decision on prior informed consent and on the determination of mutually agreed terms in accordance with Article 6(3)(e) of the Nagoya Protocol.[148] The proposed Norwegian regulation further provides that genetic material can be disseminated through public

[142] Regjeringen, 'Forskrift om uttak og utnytting av genetisk material' (3 October 2017) Reference no 7/3078-1, www.regjeringen.no/no/dokumenter/forskrift-om-uttak-og-utnytting-av-genetisk-materiale/id2564099/, see eg § 7 of the proposed regulation.

[143] ibid § 2 of the proposed regulation.

[144] ibid.

[145] ibid § 7 of the proposed regulation.

[146] ibid § 7 of the proposed regulation.

[147] ibid § 4 of the proposed regulation.

[148] ibid § 8(f) of the proposed regulation.

collections for standardised processing fees. This can involve the negotiation of agreements on distribution of benefits, which are overseen by competent authorities. The applicant must be provided with a written decision on the delivery and distribution of benefits, in both Norwegian and English. The Ministry of Climate and the Environment shall be notified of these arrangements.[149]

This proposed regulation has been criticised by several interested parties and institutions. For example, the Norwegian Patent Office has argued that it is unclear what constitutes 'benefits' and how they will be shared. It explains that potential revenue from biotechnology is often an uncertain and distant reality, involving high risks and initial losses. For these reasons, it can be difficult to determine appropriate benefits before extraction even occurs. The Norwegian Patent Office has also expressed the view that practical aspects of benefit sharing should be explained in more detail and that those rules should be compatible with those in competing states. Several other provisions require further clarification according to the Norwegian Patent Office, eg those concerning conditions for the granting of permits.[150] These criticisms should be borne in mind when rules on marine bioprospecting are implemented in Iceland. However, it should also be noted that, as desirable as legal certainty generally is, a level of flexibility is also needed to allow for mutually agreed terms.

(ii) Conservation and Sustainable Use

While Iceland must facilitate access to, and sharing of benefits arising from, marine genetic resources, it should also emphasise the conservation and sustainable use of marine resources. It is imperative that Iceland minimise pollution of the marine environment because the state is so heavily dependent on oceanic resources. In fact, sustainable use of marine resources is a priority for Iceland for both economic and environmental reasons.[151] According to Iceland's Fourth National Report to the CBD, 'Iceland is the world's twelfth largest fishing nation', and fisheries are one of the country's main economic sectors, accounting for 36.7 per cent of all exports in 2009.[152] The Icelandic marine environment is also home to zoo- and phytoplankton and rich benthic communities.[153] The Benthic Invertebrates of Icelandic Waters project has resulted in the collection of 2035 benthic fauna species, some of which have not been discovered elsewhere.[154] It is vital to the Icelandic economy that marine resources are sustainably managed,

[149] ibid § 11 of the proposed regulation.

[150] Patentstyret, 'Svar til høringsnotat om forslag til forskrift om uttak og utnytting av genetisk material (bioprospekteringsforskriften)' (Oslo, 27 September 2017) www.regjeringen.no/contentassets/570a68df36764fdbb1eb27a148a4920e/patentstyret.pdf?uid=Patentstyret.pdf.

[151] Iceland's First National Report to the CBD (1992–1998) 42, www.cbd.int/doc/world/is/is-nr-01-en.pdf accessed 1 March 2021.

[152] Iceland's Fourth National Report to the CBD (n 113) 14.

[153] ibid 14.

[154] ibid 15.

but protection of the marine environment can also impact the market value of marine produce generally because 'product wholesomeness' (minimum impact of pollution) is increasingly important to consumers.[155] This may be relevant to the fact that Iceland's marine biotechnology industry is largely connected to health and wellness, as outlined in section II above.

New Icelandic legislation concerning marine bioprospecting could incorporate environmental principles and new approaches in international law. Some of these are featured in the CBD and various ocean instruments, such as the precautionary principle, best available science and the ecosystem approach. The ecosystem approach is featured in the CBD and in many ocean instruments,[156] and could be incorporated into new legislation governing marine bioprospecting in Iceland. It could have the effect of requiring authorities to consider the overall effect of proposed activities before giving permission. This could be an important aspect because marine genetic resources are fundamental to many ecosystems. Furthermore, the precautionary principle is central to the ecosystem approach[157] and particularly relevant in this field, where scientific knowledge is sparse. The precautionary principle is already reflected in related Icelandic legislation, eg in Articles 4 and 6 of the Law on Exploration and Utilisation of Ground Resources, which specify that use of organisms is prohibited without special permission from Iceland's National Energy Authority. A similar approach could be taken for marine bioprospecting beyond 115 metres from the coast. However, according to the CBD, the new rules should promote, rather than restrict, access. They should not serve the purpose of excluding users or limiting activities, but instead encourage environmentally sound uses, the conservation and sustainable use of genetic resources, and the equitable sharing of benefits.

Another issue that merits highlighting is the designation of marine protected areas. States parties are urged to establish protected areas under the CBD, and this is a central tool in the new BBNJ Agreement. Furthermore, international jurisprudence confirms the relevance of marine protected areas as measures to implement the environmental obligations enshrined in UNCLOS. Iceland has prioritised the establishment and management of protected areas in its implementation of the CBD[158] and could continue to do so in the planning of coastal and marine areas. However, the right of access to genetic resources within such areas might have to be contemplated in new legislation concerning marine bioprospecting in Iceland.

Finally, Icelandic authorities are bound to assess the environmental impacts of activities that may reasonably be expected to cause significant adverse effects on the marine environment. This is a direct obligation under UNCLOS[159] and

[155] Iibid 18.
[156] Sands et al (n 4) 457.
[157] Helsinki and OSPAR Commissions (n 49).
[158] See Iceland's Fourth National Report to the CBD (n 113) Annex III, 36–39.
[159] UNCLOS, Art 206.

its importance is further emphasised by the BBNJ Agreement,[160] but the obligation is not clearly implemented in domestic law. The new rules could specify that potentially harmful bioprospecting should be subject to the domestic environmental impact procedure. A simple reference to the Icelandic Law Concerning Environmental Impact Assessments should suffice.[161]

V. CONCLUSION

A clear and well-grounded regulatory framework is necessary to facilitate increased marine bioprospecting and sustainable utilisation of marine genetic resources. Yet, there is no comprehensive legal regime in Iceland on licences, collection, export, utilisation or sharing of benefits of these resources. This chapter has explored the most relevant international obligations under the CBD, the Nagoya Protocol and UNCLOS, along with recent developments in the law of the sea, specifically those relating to protection of the marine environment and utilisation of marine resources. This chapter has demonstrated that certain principles are imperative to the equitable governance of marine bioprospecting in Iceland. First, Iceland is obligated to implement the provisions of the CBD and UNCLOS as these instruments are directly applicable to Iceland. They relate to marine bioprospecting insofar as the CBD governs the sustainable use of genetic resources, access and benefit sharing, while UNCLOS governs marine scientific research and protection of the marine environment. Second, the Nagoya Protocol implements certain provisions of the CBD and is therefore relevant for the interpretation and implementation of CBD provisions on access and benefit sharing.

The following principles have emerged from the foregoing analysis and should guide the process of codifying new rules governing marine bioprospecting in Iceland: fair and equitable access to genetic resources; equitable sharing of benefits arising out of the utilisation of genetic resources; sustainable use and conservation of genetic resources; legal certainty and predictability; best available science; the precautionary principle; the ecosystem approach; and the principle of environmental impact assessments. The principles relating to protection of the marine environment do not necessarily need to be explicitly implemented in the new rules, but they should be considered in the codification process.

Icelandic authorities have acknowledged the need to implement rules on marine bioprospecting. Indeed, Iceland must clarify the domestic legal process and make it more predictable to incentivise environmentally sound uses of marine genetic resources. New Icelandic rules governing marine bioprospecting

[160] BBNJ Agreement, Art 28.
[161] Law no 106/2000 Concerning Environmental Impact Assessments.

could build on Rules on Geothermal Vents and take note of the ongoing codification process in Norway. However, the Icelandic rules should seek to provide more detail than those precedents. For example, they should explain what the non-monetary benefits may be, using the reference list found in the Nagoya Protocol Annex.

The new rules should provide for the screening of research and make intrusive, or potentially intrusive, activities subject to prior and ongoing environmental impact assessments. Permits should be granted on the basis of a precautionary, ecosystem-based approach to ensure the conservation of marine biodiversity. Meanwhile, environmentally sound uses of marine genetic resources should be encouraged and facilitated. Those extracting marine genetic resources should be required to deposit certain data on open-access platforms and access to research results should be promoted. Research results should only be allowed to remain confidential for a limited time pending patent applications to prevent undue delays. Furthermore, the new rules, whether an Act of Parliament or administrative Acts, should aim to provide legal certainty and reduce unnecessary complexity, ie avoid fragmentation in the domestic system.

11

Bioprospecting in the Arctic and Indigenous Peoples' Rights

VALERIA EBOLI*

I. INTRODUCTION

THIS CHAPTER EXPLORES some legal implications of biodiversity prospecting (or bioprospecting) in the Arctic from the perspective of indigenous peoples. In the Arctic Circle, there is an estimated population of around four million people, about 10 per cent of which belong to indigenous communities.[1] This makes it highly relevant to look at the rights or interests of these communities in relation to marine genetic resources (MGRs) and how far they are entitled to participate in the decision-making processes related to the exploitation of MGRs in the Arctic and to bioprospecting activities.

In order to set the scene, the analysis will begin by focusing on some preliminary issues, such as the human settlements in the Arctic and the specificities of indigenous peoples' rights from a legal perspective. Then their role in relation to bioprospecting activities will be examined, bearing in mind the legal regime of the maritime zones of the Arctic and indigenous peoples' interests in relation to them.[2] Finally, some concluding remarks will be offered, placing the above-mentioned issues into perspective with regard to the international legally binding instrument, the 2023 Agreement under the United Nations Convention on the Law of the Sea on the conservation and sustainable use of marine biological diversity of areas beyond national jurisdiction (BBNJ Agreement).

* The views and opinions expressed are solely by the author.

[1] See Larsen and Fondahl (eds), *Arctic Human Development Report* (Nordic Council of Ministers, 2015) http://norden.diva-portal.org/smash/record.jsf?pid=diva2%3A788965&dswid=-5251.

[2] Khan, 'Rebalancing State and Indigenous Sovereignties in International Law: An Arctic Lens on Trajectories for Global Governance' (2019) 32 *Leiden Journal of International Law* 675; Beckman, Henriksen, Dalaker Kraabel, Molenaar and Roach, *Governing of Arctic Shipping. Balancing Rights and Interests of Arctic States and User States* (Brill Nijhoff, 2017); Koivurova, Molenaar and Vander Zwaag, 'Canada, the EU, and Arctic Ocean Governance: A Tangled and Shifting Seascape and Future Directions' (2009) 18 *Journal of Transnational Law & Policy*.

II. PRELIMINARY ISSUES

A. Indigenous Peoples in the Arctic

As is well known, humans have inhabited the Arctic for several thousand years, and the Arctic region[3] is home to several indigenous peoples.[4] However, both 'indigenous people' and 'the Arctic' can be subject to different interpretations. Here, 'indigenous people' is used to refer to groups of people having a historical existence and identity that is separate from and independent of the states now enveloping them.[5] 'The Arctic' is used here in the same way as it is used by the Arctic Council,[6] to denote the area that falls within the Arctic Circle, identified as the area north of the parallel of latitude 66 degrees, 32 minutes north.[7] This region includes the Arctic Basin, the northern parts of Scandinavia, Russia, Canada and Greenland, and the US state of Alaska. The Arctic also includes parts of Iceland, Sweden and Finland, which do not have coastlines on the Arctic Ocean, which is the shallowest of the five ocean basins on Earth.[8] Insofar as marine resources are concerned, the former group of states is of primary interest.

Some indigenous peoples live along the coasts and their subsistence is strictly related to the exploitation of marine resources. A wide spectrum of cultures, identities and historical experiences characterise Arctic peoples.

The Sámi people live in Northern Europe. The Sámi have historically lived in Fennoscandia, including the Kola Peninsula.[9] It is estimated that nowadays

[3] See Larsen and Fondahl (n 1) 53.

[4] O'Sullivan, '*We Are All Here to Stay*': *Citizenship, Sovereignty and the UN Declaration on the Rights of Indigenous Peoples*, 1st edn (ANU Press, 2020) https://doi.org/10.2307/j.ctv186grnt.

[5] See Byers, *International Law and the Arctic* (Cambridge University Press, 2013) 216–44; Anaya, *Indigenous Peoples in International Law* (Oxford University Press, 2004); Castellino and Walsh, *International Law and Indigenous Peoples* (Martinus Nijhoff, 2005). A definition is also contained in Art 1 of the ILO Convention No 169, formulated as follows: 'This Convention applies to … people in independent countries who are regarded as indigenous on account of their descent from the populations which inhabited the country, or a geographical region to which the country belongs, at the time of conquest or colonisation or the establishment of present State boundaries and who, irrespective of their legal status, retain some or all of their own social, economic, cultural and political institutions.' International Labour Organization, Convention (No 169) Concerning Indigenous and Tribal Peoples in Independent Countries, 27 June 1989, 1650 UNTS 383 (ILO Convention); GA Res 61/295, annex (17 September 2007) Art 1b. See also www.arcticcentre.org/EN/arcticregion/Arctic-Indigenous-Peoples/Definitions.

[6] See Koivurova and Molenaar, *International Governance and Regulation of the Marine Arctic: Three Reports Prepared for the WWF International Arctic Programme* (Oslo, 2010) 15.

[7] For a definition and the related bibliography, see 'Arctic Circle', www.geographyrealm.com/arctic-circle/.Other relevant global international organisations have opted either explicitly or implicitly for different definitions of the Arctic or marine Arctic. For instance, the International Maritime Organization (IMO) has done so by means of its Arctic Shipping Guidelines and the United Nations Food and Agriculture Organization (FAO) has done so by means of its definition of FAO Statistical Area No 18: Arctic Sea.

[8] 'Arctic states' are the states that are members of the Arctic Council, namely Canada, Denmark (in relation to Greenland) Finland, Iceland, Norway, the Russian Federation, Sweden and the USA. See https://education.nationalgeographic.org/resource/arctic.

[9] Larsen and Fondahl (n 1) 111.

between 50,000 and 60,000 live in Norway, between 15,000 and 20,000 live in Sweden, about 8000 live in Finland and around 2000 are in Russia.[10] There are also indigenous peoples living in the Arctic parts of North America, with around 60,000 estimated to live in Canada and around 100,000 in Alaska.[11] They mainly belong to the Gwich'in, Athapaskan and Inuit groups.[12] The first two groups are mainly settled in the Subarctic area,[13] while along the coast there are mainly Inuit. The Inuit belong to the so-called Thule culture[14] and possess a sophisticated technology enabling them to hunt whales.[15] The indigenous peoples of Alaska are generally divided into six major groupings: Unangan (Aleut), Sugpiaq (Alutiiq), Yupik (Central Yup'ik and Siberian Yupik), Iñupiaq (northwest Alaskan Inuit), Athabaskans (Interior Indians), and Tlingit and Haida (Southeast Coastal Indians). They share some common traditions.[16] In Canada, they are divided into nine bands.[17]

Greenland was first populated by Palaeo-Eskimo groups of nomadic migrants who arrived around 4500 years ago, from the Canadian High Arctic.[18] Today, there is an estimated population of 50,000 Inuit in Greenland.[19]

Approximately 850,000 individuals,[20] belonging to different ethnic groups, such as those of Chukchi, Even, Evenki, Nenets and Yukaghir origin, live in the extreme northern part of Russia. They traditionally led a nomadic life and were organised in autonomous clans. Russia recognises these individuals as

[10] For statistics, see https://nordregio.org/maps/indigenous-population-in-the-arctic/. See also Young, Kue and Bjerregaard, 'Towards Estimating the Indigenous Population in Circumpolar Regions' (2019) 78 *International Journal of Circumpolar Health*.

[11] See Young et al (n 10).

[12] For data, see https://gwichin.ca/about-the-gwichin.

[13] For data, see www.history.com/topics/native-american-history/native-american-cultures#section_1.

[14] For the genetic differences among the diverse groups, see Dulik et al, 'Y-Chromosome Analysis Reveals Genetic Divergence and New Founding Native Lineages in Athapaskan- and Eskimoan-Speaking Populations' (2012) 109 *Proceedings of the National Academy of Sciences* 8471.

[15] See Larsen and Fondahl (n 1) 109.

[16] See ibid 107. In Alaska, there are about 35,000 Inuit out of an indigenous population of about 90,000 Alaska Natives. For data, see www.alaskool.org/resources/anc/anc07.htm and at www.worldatlas.com/articles/who-are-the-eskimo-people-where-do-they-live.html. For more detailed data about the composition of Alaska Native population, see www.alaskool.org/resources/anc/anc07.htm.

[17] Labradormiut (Labrador Inuit), Nunavimmiut (Nunavik Inuit or Ungava Inuit), Nunatsiarmiut (Baffin Island Inuit), Iglulingmiut (Iglulik Inuit), Kivallirmiut (Caribou Inuit), Netsilingmiut (Netsilik Inuit), Inuinnait (Copper Inuit), Qikirtamiut (Sanikiluaq Inuit) and Inuvialuit (Western Arctic Inuit or Mackenzie Delta Inuit). For data, see www.thecanadianencyclopedia.ca/en/article/aboriginal-people-arctic. In Canada, Inuit comprise only 4% of the total Indigenous population. The majority (73%) of Inuit live in Inuit Nunangat, which means 'the homeland' and represents 50% of Canada's coastline. Inuit Nunangat comprises 51 communities across four regions: Inuvialuit Settlement Region (Northwest Territories and Yukon), Nunavut, Nunavik (northern Quebec) and Nunatsiavut (Labrador). See official data of the Government of Canada, www.sac-isc.gc.ca/eng/1602010609492/1602010631711.

[18] www.sac-isc.gc.ca/eng/1602010609492/1602010631711.

[19] See Young et al (n 10).

[20] ibid.

'indigenous small-numbered peoples of the North',[21] comprising some 40 different indigenous groups. Overall, it is estimated that there are about 1.13 million indigenous people in the northern regions of the eight member states of the Arctic Council, even if an accurate estimate of their number and distribution remains elusive.[22]

Historically, their economy has been based on hunting, fishing and the exploitation of natural resources.[23] The natural resources may include both mineral and living resources, and can be located either on land or at sea.

B. Exploitation of Marine Resources and Bioprospecting in Areas Traditionally Used by Indigenous Peoples

The Arctic is rich in natural resources, including roughly 13 per cent of the world's oil reserves and as much as 30 per cent of the world's gas reserves, as well as significant deposits of minerals such as tin, manganese, gold, nickel, zinc, lead, platinum and uranium, along with MGRs.[24]

MGRs from the polar regions are of particular importance, since this area is home to a range of organisms with unique adaptive properties for extreme conditions, many of them being the result of biochemical processes.[25] For instance, mention can be made of krill, microorganisms, yeasts, moulds and other fungi, lichen, invertebrates (mainly sponges and tunicates), grasses and other plants, fish (mainly antifreeze proteins) and other vertebrates, algae and unidentified sources.[26] As a result, the polar regions are considered a global hotspot for biological prospecting, or 'bioprospecting', which involves developing products from the compounds obtained from living organisms. In order to understand the relationship between indigenous peoples and such activity related to MGRs, a brief description is needed to set the scene.

There is as yet no agreed legal definition of the term 'bioprospecting'. However, it is usually used to refer to the collection, research and use of biological and/or genetic material for purposes of applying the knowledge derived

[21] For more details, see https://en.raipon.info/.

[22] https://en.raipon.info/.

[23] See Larsen and Fondahl (n 1) 164.

[24] Leary, *Bioprospecting in the Arctic*, UNU-IAS Report (United Nations University, Institute of Advanced Studies, 2008) 12ff.

[25] ibid.

[26] Pharmaceuticals is the main industry benefiting from the use of Antarctic-derived products. For instance, some cancer therapies are derived from microorganisms found in the lakes of East Antarctic Dronning Maud Land and fungi with anti-inflammatory compounds and lichens with antibiotic properties are from King George Island. Patents relating to krill have included nutritional supplements such as krill oil, pharmaceuticals treating inflammation and applications in aquaculture. See Resolution 5 (2015) – ATCM XXXVIII – CEP XVIII, Sofia, www.ats.aq/devAS/Meetings/Measure/616; Guyomard, 'Bioprospecting in Antarctica: A New Challenge for the Antarctic Treaty System' in Francioni and Scovazzi (eds), *Biotechnology and International Law* (Hart Publishing, 2006) 147.

therefrom for scientific and/or commercial purposes.[27] It entails the search for economically valuable genetic and biochemical resources from nature, including in marine areas. Several activities may be performed to this end, in particular onsite research, collection of samples, and the identification and isolation of the genes that code them.[28] They are usually referred to as in situ, ex situ and in silico research activities, and may be subject to different legal regimes.[29]

The economic value of MGRs can be significant, as different products can be derived from genetic resources[30] (eg compound products for the pharmaceutical,[31] biotechnology, agricultural, personal care, botanical, and food and beverage sectors), and such compounds or the derived products can also be patented.[32]

From a legal point of view, a key issue is that of national jurisdiction, which defines who has rights in relation to the MGRs. The norms for this may vary depending on where the activities are performed. As will be further explained below, areas within and beyond national jurisdiction are subject to different legal regimes.

Indigenous peoples may be involved in such activities in different ways in relation to the legal regime of the area from which the MGRs are extracted, depending on whether it is within or beyond national jurisdiction and also depending on under whose national jurisdiction the extraction takes place (as some obligations arise from treaty law only and do not apply to all states).

III. INDIGENOUS PEOPLE: LEGAL REGIME, RIGHTS, OBLIGATIONS

As a preliminary issue, the legal qualification of indigenous people needs to be considered, as consequent rights and duties can be assessed only in accordance

[27] United Nations University, *Access to Genetic Resources, Benefit Sharing and Bioprospecting* (2007) 10, www.unenvironment.org/resources/report/unu-ias-pocket-guide-access-genetic-resources-benefit sharing-and-bioprospecting.

[28] Krabbe, *Bioprospecting and Deep-Sea Genetic Resources in a Fragmenting International Law* (School of Business, Economics and Law at University of Gothenburg, 2021) Juridiska institutionens skriftserie Skrift 038, 41ff.

[29] According to UNCLOS, in situ access refers to 'access to/collection of samples of marine organisms (containing MGR) within their natural surroundings, such as ecosystems and habitats in the high seas or the Area'; ex situ access means 'access to MGR outside of their natural habitats, which involves transfer of samples previously collected from ABNJ that have been analysed and kept in bio repositories'; and in silico access refers to 'access to information, data and research results for in silico testing and the results therefrom'. See Chuxiao Yu, 'Implications of the UNCLOS Marine Scientific Research Regime for the Current Negotiations on Access and Benefit Sharing of Marine Genetic Resources in Areas Beyond National Jurisdiction' (2020) 2 *Ocean Development and International Law* 10. See Glowka, 'The Deepest of Ironies: Genetic Resources, Marine Scientific Research, and the Area' (1996) *Ocean Yearbook* 169.

[30] Leal, Madeira, Brandã, Puga and Calado, 'Bioprospecting of Marine Invertebrates for New Natural Products: A Chemical and Zoogeographical Perspective' (2012) 17 *Molecules* 9842.

[31] Ibata-Arens, *Pandemic Medicine: Why the Global Innovation System Is Broken, and How We Can Fix It* (Lynne Rienner Publishers, 2021).

[32] Krabbe (n 28) 115ff; Francioni, 'Genetic Resources, Biotechnology and Human Rights: The International Legal Framework', EUI Working Paper LAW No 2006/17.

with a definition.[33] The United Nations Declaration on the Rights of Indigenous Peoples (UNDRIP)[34] of 2007 makes reference to a number of criteria used to identify an indigenous people, such as the historical continuity with pre-invasion and/or pre-colonial societies that developed on their territories; distinctiveness; non-dominance; and a determination to preserve, develop and transmit to future generations their ancestral territories and identity as peoples in accordance with their own cultural patterns, social institutions and legal system.[35] In addition to these, the United Nations Permanent Forum on Indigenous Issues[36] has stressed some additional criteria, such as a strong link to territories and surrounding natural resources; a distinct social, economic or political system;[37] and a distinct language, culture and beliefs.

UNDRIP is now the most comprehensive instrument detailing the rights of indigenous peoples in international law and policy.[38] Although it is a soft law instrument, not in itself entailing legal obligations, it nevertheless provides important guidance. It contains minimum standards for the recognition, protection and promotion of the rights of indigenous peoples, and it makes reference to rights and freedoms, such as self-determination and non-discrimination, set out in binding international human rights treaty law, some of which may also be considered as a part of customary international law.

One of the main rights recognised in UNDRIP in relation to indigenous peoples by is the right to lands, territories and resources, including those traditionally held by indigenous peoples but now controlled by others as a matter of fact and of law.[39] The recognition of such rights is based on the assumption that for many indigenous peoples, their relationship to their lands, territories and resources is a defining feature.[40] The close ties of indigenous peoples with the land has to be understood not merely as a matter of possession and production,

[33] From a legal point of view, a social group can be qualified in various ways. For instance, it can be qualified as a people, a minority or an indigenous people, with following different rights and duties. The legal status of indigenous peoples is distinct from that of minorities. See Vukas, *States Peoples and Minorities* (Nijhoff, 1991) 263; Shrinkhal, '"Indigenous Sovereignty" and Right to Self-Determination in International Law: A Critical Appraisal' (2021) 17 *AlterNative* 71.

[34] For the text, see www.un.org/development/desa/indigenouspeoples/declaration-on-the-rights-of-indigenous-peoples.html.

[35] O'Sullivan (n 4).

[36] For further details, see www.un.org/development/desa/indigenouspeoples/.

[37] Many indigenous peoples populated areas before the arrival of others and often retain distinct cultural and political characteristics, including autonomous political and legal structures.

[38] UNDRIP was adopted by the United Nations General Assembly (UNGA) on 13 September 2007, with 144 votes in favour, 11 abstentions and four states against (Australia, Canada, New Zealand and the USA). For further details, see www.un.org/development/desa/indigenouspeoples/declaration-on-the-rights-of-indigenous-peoples.html.

[39] Vierros et al, 'Considering Indigenous Peoples and Local Communities in Governance of the Global Ocean Commons' (2020) 119 *Marine Policy* 104039.

[40] Geary et al, 'Access and Benefits Sharing of Genetic Resources and Associated Traditional Knowledge in Northern Canada' (2013) 72 *International Journal of Circumpolar Health* 351.

but as the fundamental basis of their cultures, their spiritual life, their integrity and their economic survival.[41]

The Declaration refers to the lands, territories and resources that indigenous peoples have traditionally owned, occupied or otherwise used and that they possess under customary indigenous conceptions of 'ownership'.[42] The states are called on to give legal recognition and protection to these lands, territories and resources. As far as economic, social and cultural rights are concerned, the provisions of the Declaration can be read together with Convention No 169 of the International Labour Organization (ILO) Concerning Indigenous and Tribal Peoples in Independent Countries, adopted in 1989 (Indigenous and Tribal Peoples Convention).[43] Article 14 of this binding international instrument recognises indigenous peoples' ownership of the land they occupy as well as lands they share and have 'traditionally had access [to] for their subsistence and traditional activities'. It protects the rights of indigenous peoples to the natural resources on their lands and establishes procedures of consultation. Countries that retain ownership of such natural resources should consult with indigenous peoples. Furthermore, the Convention mentions benefit-sharing principles in connection with the indigenous peoples' rights to the protection of their cultural traditions.

The Indigenous and Tribal Peoples Convention is binding only to its parties, ie those states that have ratified it. As of early 2022, among the circumpolar states, only Denmark and Norway had done so.[44] Hence, the rights enjoyed by indigenous peoples may vary depending on in which state they live.

In line with the framework of the Convention and UNDRIP, the Convention on Biological Diversity (CBD)[45] and its Nagoya Protocol include the right of free, prior and informed consent, as well as the principle of benefit sharing. The Nagoya Protocol requires its contracting parties to respect, preserve and maintain knowledge, innovations and practices of indigenous and local communities embodying traditional lifestyles relevant for the conservation and sustainable use of biological diversity; to promote their wider application with the approval and involvement of the holders of such knowledge, innovations and practices; and to encourage the equitable sharing of the benefits arising from the utilisation of the knowledge, innovations and practices. In addition, to complement the provisions in the CBD, the Nagoya Protocol has been adopted.[46] Of the five

[41] Morgera and Tsioumani, 'The Evolution of Benefit Sharing: Linking Biodiversity and Community Livelihoods' (2010) 19 *Review of European, Comparative & International Environmental Law* 150.

[42] UN Declaration on the Rights of Indigenous Peoples, Art 26, para 2.

[43] ILO Convention (n 5); GA Res 61/295, annex (n 5).

[44] See www.ilo.org/dyn/normlex/en/f?p=1000:11300:0::NO:11300:P11300_INSTRUMENT_ID:312314.

[45] For more details, see s III below.

[46] Nagoya Protocol on Access to Genetic Resources and the Fair and Equitable Sharing of Benefits Arising from their Utilisation (adopted 29 October 2010, entered into force 12 October 2014) 3008 UNTS No 30619.

coastal Arctic countries, only Norway and Denmark are parties to the Nagoya Protocol, while Canada, the USA and Russia are not.[47]

All the above-mentioned legal frameworks and principles have been designed mainly in relation to areas falling under the jurisdiction of the contracting parties. However, they may also be applicable in relation to activities related to areas beyond national jurisdiction, such as the Central Arctic Ocean.[48]

IV. THE LEGAL FRAMEWORKS RELEVANT TO BIOPROSPECTING IN THE ARCTIC

Different areas of law overlap with respect to bioprospecting in the Arctic.[49] Some norms arise from the law of the sea, others from the regime related to the utilisation of genetic resources, including the CBD[50] and its Nagoya Protocol.[51] In this regard, the rights of indigenous peoples may be at stake because their resources or traditional knowledge are mentioned in the text of the CBD. Furthermore, the protection of some indigenous rights may be deemed an obligation arising from international human rights law. Both under the United Nations Convention on the Law of Sea (UNCLOS)[52] and the CBD, rules vary considerably between areas within national jurisdiction and those beyond it.[53] The norms of UNCLOS vary according to different marine zones, while those of the CBD and its Protocol may apply to areas under state jurisdiction and only partially to areas beyond national jurisdiction (ABNJ), as further explained below.

With regard to ABNJ, it is interesting to note the new BBNJ Agreement.[54] A number of issues that are not fully covered by the current legal instruments are addressed and regulated in this framework, under an internationally agreed regime, applicable also in the polar regions. In this context, some attention is paid to indigenous peoples' rights.

In this chapter, the current legal regime will be examined first, in order to assess the existing norms for bioprospecting activities in the Arctic, taking into account UNCLOS, the relevant international human rights instruments and the

[47] For the status of the treaty, see www.cbd.int/abs/nagoya-protocol/signatories/.

[48] See s V below.

[49] Krabbe (n 28) 130ff.

[50] Convention on Biological Diversity (adopted 5 June 1992, entered into force 29 December 1993) 1760 UNTS 79.

[51] Above n 46.

[52] UN Convention on the Law of the Sea (adopted 10 December 1982, entered into force 16 November 1994) 1833 UNTS No 31363.

[53] Molenaar and Oude Elferink, 'Marine Protected Areas in Areas Beyond National Jurisdiction: The Pioneering Efforts Under the OSPAR Convention' (2009) 5 *Utrecht Law Review*.

[54] Resolution adopted by the General Assembly on 19 June 2015, UN Doc A/RES/69/292; Resolution adopted by the General Assembly on 24 December 2017, UN Doc A/RES/72/249; Resolution adopted by the General Assembly on 30 December 2022, UN Doc A/RES/72/248.

CBD with its additional Nagoya Protocol.[55] In particular, the specific rights of indigenous peoples will be analysed in relation to bioprospecting in the Arctic. Finally, the challenges and opportunities relating to the Arctic arising from the BBNJ Agreement[56] will be examined.

A. The Law of the Sea: Exploitation of Resources and Marine Research under UNCLOS and Indigenous Peoples

The first body of law to take into consideration is the law of the sea. The Arctic Circle is mainly composed of iced waters, meaning that UNCLOS is applicable. With the exception of the USA, all Arctic states are contracting parties of UNCLOS.[57]

Both the UNCLOS provisions on the exploration and exploitation of marine resources and those on scientific research may be relevant to bioprospecting activities.[58] UNCLOS does not contain specific provisions on marine *genetic* resources, but it does contain more general provisions on marine *living* resources. Marine genetic resources can be deemed as belonging to the broader category.

It is also noteworthy that all the aforementioned activities are regulated in different ways depending on the maritime zone in which they are performed. In general terms, a demarcation line can be drawn between areas subject to national jurisdiction and those beyond such jurisdiction. UNCLOS's provisions concerning resource extraction, whether relating to living or other resources, make reference to the sovereign or exclusive right of a coastal state to exploit such resources in the maritime zones where it exercises jurisdiction.[59] These provisions were mainly designed for conventional fisheries, and it is questionable whether they can be deemed applicable to other kinds of living resources, such as MGRs. While the former usually require large quantities of organic material, the latter is usually a matter of sampling activities.[60] Indigenous peoples may be involved not only as potential owners of natural resources, but also in relation to their traditional knowledge of such resources.

UNCLOS also contains provisions on marine scientific research. The first point to clarify is how far these may be applicable to bioprospecting. The

[55] Koivurova and Molenaar (n 6); Rochette, Billé, Molenaar, Drankier and Chabason, 'Regional Oceans Governance Mechanisms: A Review' (2015) 60 *Marine Policy* 9.

[56] Agreement under the United Nations Convention on the Law of the Sea on the Conservation and Sustainable Use of Marine Biological Diversity of Areas beyond National Jurisdiction (adopted 19 June 2023) www.un.org/bbnj/ (BBNJ Agreement).

[57] For the status of the Convention, see https://treaties.un.org/pages/ViewDetailsIII.aspx?src=TREATY&mtdsg_no=XXI-6&chapter=21&Temp=mtdsg3&clang=_en.

[58] Krabbe (n 28) 198–99.

[59] Enyew, 'Application of the Right to Permanent Sovereignty Over Natural Resources for Indigenous Peoples: Assessment of Current Legal Developments' (2017) 8 *Arctic Review on Law and Politics* 222.

[60] Krabbe (n 28) 198.

physical operation of marine bioprospecting is similar to the exploration of the seas as pure scientific research. A significant difference lies in the commercial element that is present in bioprospecting.[61] In fact, in the case of bioprospecting, the final aim is to patent, develop products or make profits from innovations based on findings.[62]

If an activity is driven mainly by a view to increasing knowledge about the marine environment, it may be classified as marine scientific research. If commercial gain is the primary purpose for conducting the sampling activity, different views have been expressed on whether it could still be considered marine scientific research.[63] Taking into account that no definition is provided within the framework of Part XIII of UNCLOS, one of the main accepted definitions of marine scientific research is that summarised by the former judge of the International Tribunal for the Law of the Sea, Tullio Treves, namely: 'those activities undertaken in ocean space to expand scientific knowledge of the marine environment and its processes'.[64] In practice, an activity can serve multiple purposes. A resource may, for instance, be collected for scientific aims but at a later stage some commercially valuable information is found. In this case, the character of the activity as marine scientific research should not be compromised.[65] The decisive factor to distinguish marine scientific research from other activities is the main purpose of conducting the activity. If a sampling activity is conducted not in order to increase general scientific knowledge but, rather, for commercial ends, it could hardly be regarded as marine scientific research.[66]

UNCLOS makes no explicit reference to genetic resources.[67] Even if UNCLOS contains some norms related to marine scientific research, there is no specific provision mentioning bioprospecting and the commercial use of marine resources.[68] It is also important to note in which marine area such activities are deployed. They may be deployed in areas within national jurisdiction, such as states' territorial waters, continental shelves or exclusive economic zones (EEZ), but they may also occur in ABNJ, comprising the high

[61] ibid 198.

[62] ibid 84ff.

[63] See Womersley, 'What Is and What Is Not Covered by Part XIII of UNCLOS?' in Zou and Telesetsky (eds), *Marine Scientific Research, New Marine Technologies and the Law of the Sea* (Brill, 2021) 27ff; Krabbe (n 28) 200ff.

[64] Treves, 'Marine Scientific Research' in *Max Planck Encyclopedia of Public International Law* (2008).

[65] Yu (n 29) 10.

[66] Gragl, 'Maritime Scientific Research' in Attard et al (eds), *The Law of the Sea*, IMLI Manual on International Maritime Law vol 1 (Oxford University Press, 2014) 13.

[67] For the purposes here, the term is taken to generally denote any material of plant, animal, microbial or other origin containing functional units of heredity that is of actual or potential value, as defined in the CBD.

[68] Bonfanti and Trevisanut, 'Trips on the High Seas: Intellectual Property Rights on Marine Genetic Resources' (2011) 37 *Brooklyn Journal of International Law* 188, 206.

seas water column and the seabed, ocean floor and subsoil below the high seas water column (the Area). MGRs are the biological building blocks for biodiversity in all of these areas.[69]

According to Article 240 UNCLOS, marine scientific research, in general terms, has to: be conducted exclusively for peaceful purposes; be conducted with appropriate scientific methods and means compatible with the Convention; not interfere with other legitimate uses of the sea compatible with the Convention itself; and be conducted in compliance with all relevant regulations adopted in conformity with the Convention, including those for the protection and preservation of the marine environment.

Articles 246 and 56 specifically deal with marine scientific research activities undertaken in the EEZ and on the continental shelf, respectively. In its EEZ, a coastal state has sovereign rights for the purpose of exploring and exploiting, conserving and managing the natural resources, and with regard to other activities for the economic exploitation and exploration of the zone; and it has jurisdiction with regard to marine scientific research.[70]

While UNCLOS does not directly provide a framework for MGR governance in ABNJ,[71] its vision for a legal order for the seas and oceans includes the 'equitable and efficient utilisation of the ocean's resources'.[72] In relation to the Area,[73] which is subject to the special regime of common heritage of mankind, marine scientific research is, according to Article 143 UNCLOS, to be carried out 'for the benefit of mankind as a whole'.[74]

Part XIII of UNCLOS, relating to 'marine scientific research', could be seen as providing an access and benefit sharing system also for genetic resources, as it requires information on scientific programmes and their objectives and knowledge from marine scientific research to be published and disseminated, along with the promotion of data and information flow (especially to developing countries) and international cooperation. However, it could also be argued that marine scientific research does not equate to 'bioprospecting', so this system may not be applicable. As UNCLOS norms are limited to scientific research purposes, if bioprospecting also involves some kind of commercial activity, those norms may not be deemed completely apt to regulate it.

[69] Morris-Sharma, 'Marine Genetic Resources in Areas Beyond National Jurisdiction: Issues With, In and Outside of UNCLOS' [2017] *Max Planck Yearbook of United Nations Law* 71.

[70] UNCLOS, Art 246.

[71] Proelss, 'Marine Genetic Resources Under UNCLOS and the CBD' (2009) *German Yearbook of International Law* 417.

[72] See Van Dyke et al (eds), *Governing Ocean Resources: New Challenges and Emerging Regimes: A Tribute to Judge Choon-Ho Park* (Martinus Nijhoff, 2013); Scheiber, Oral and Kwon (eds), *Ocean Law Debates: The 50-Year Legacy and Emerging Issues for the Years Ahead* (Brill Nijhoff, 2018).

[73] Banet (ed), *The Law of the Seabed: Access, Uses, and Protection of Seabed Resources* (Brill Nijhoff, 2020).

[74] Scovazzi, 'The Concept of Common Heritage of Mankind and the Genetic Resources of the Seabed Beyond the Limits of National Jurisdiction' (2007) 14 *Agenda Internacional* 11.

According to another view, in the absence of a formal definition, marine scientific research under UNCLOS encompasses both pure and applied research.[75] The former is the study of the marine environment and its resources with a view to increasing humankind's knowledge ('pure' or 'fundamental' research), while the latter is aimed at a subsequent exploitation of resources.[76]

UNCLOS is mainly related to in situ access to MGRs. Based on the marine scientific regime on the high seas and in the Area, in situ access to MGRs that is not exclusively for commercial purposes can be carried out without notification or consent. There is no specific provision explicitly dealing with ex situ access concerning the use of samples that have already been collected. It is questionable whether the marine scientific research regime of UNCLOS may cover not only sampling and data collection activities in the marine environment, but also the subsequent research and analysis of the samples and data retrieved in laboratories. It may be argued that access to ex situ MGR samples is or may be subject to the consent of the researching state that collected the samples, and there is no obligation upon that state to share them.

Insofar as in silico access[77] is concerned, ie access to collected data, paragraph 2 of Article 244 UNCLOS should be recalled. It refers to access to information, data and research results concerning MGRs, and states that the contracting parties shall 'actively promote the flow of scientific data and information and the transfer of knowledge resulting from marine scientific research, especially to developing States, as well as the strengthening of the autonomous marine scientific research capabilities of developing States'. This Article can be argued to relate to in silico resources, granting access to data, information and research results concerning MGRs also in ABNJ.

Even though UNCLOS is deemed applicable, there is nevertheless currently disagreement over the legal regime for MGRs in ABNJ.[78] The legal regime applicable to some areas is also uncertain as a consequence of overlapping claims for jurisdiction. The Arctic states tend to territorialise the area, ie bring under their own jurisdiction larger and larger maritime zones.[79]

[75] UN Secretary-General Report on the Oceans and the Law of the Sea, www.un.org/Depts/los/general_assembly/general_assembly_reports.htm.

[76] Attard et al (n 66).

[77] See s IIIB below.

[78] Park, 'Changes in the Law of Marine Genetic Resources in the ABNJ and Under UNCLOS' in Scheiber et al (n 72) 419.

[79] Several claims over the Arctic are pending. Russia was the first state to submit its extended continental shelf claim, declaring 1.2 million square kilometres of Arctic territory stretching through the North Pole, including the potentially oil- and gas-rich Lomonosov and Alpha-Mendeleev Ridges. It used the mechanisms provided in UNCLOS (Art 76) for claiming an extended continental shelf. See CLCS, 'Commission on the Limits of the Continental Shelf Receives Its First Submission: Russian Federation First to Move to Establish Outer Limits of Its Extended Continental Shelf' Press Release (21 December 2001) UN Doc SEA/1729, www.un.org/News/ Press/docs/2001/sea1729.doc.htm. The other polar states, and in particular USA and Norway, firmly contested this declaration of extension. Furthermore, in the summer of 2007, Russia sent an expedition to plant its flag deep in the seabed of the North Pole, affirming that the Arctic is Russian. See Falconbridge, 'Russian Sub Plants Flag

B. Genetic Resources and their Legal Regime

As the object of bioprospecting is mainly constituted by genetic resources, the legal regime for such resources needs to be accounted for. Genetic resources represent a very special kind of material that is regulated by specific norms. The main treaty regime for this purpose is the CBD and its additional protocols, most notably the 2010 Nagoya Protocol. The CBD is applicable to all terrestrial and marine environments under the national jurisdiction of the states that have ratified it,[80] so it could hardly be implemented within ABNJ.

Under North Pole' (Reuters, 2 August 2007) www.reuters.com/article/idINIndia-28784420070802. In November 2006, Norway declared the extension of its continental shelf by 250,000 square kilometres. The Kingdom of Norway made its submission for three separate areas: one, called the Loop Hole, in the Barents Sea; one in the Arctic Ocean; and one, called the Banana Hole, in the Norwegian Sea. See European Parliament, *Arctic Continental Shelf Claims: Mapping Interests in the Circumpolar North* (January 2017) 6, www.europarl.europa.eu/RegData/etudes/BRIE/2017/595870/EPRS_BRI(2017)595870_EN.pdf, https://perma.cc/P8GY-DM4U. After the aforementioned Norwegian submission, Denmark and Iceland submitted official statements to the UN stating that they did not object to Norway's claim regarding the Banana Hole region. By contrast, Russia contested the Norwegian claims regarding the region of the Barents Sea, including the Loop Hole, so that a dispute began between the two states, which is still unresolved (ibid). Denmark presented submissions for the extension of its continental shelf, for two areas of its concern: the Faroe Islands and Greenland. It claims, among others, that the Alpha-Mendeleev ridge complex and Chukchi Borderland are morphologically continuous with the land mass of Greenland. On 20 February 2006, the Government of the Kingdom of Denmark, together with the Government of Greenland and the Kingdom of Norway, signed an agreement concerning the delimitation of the continental shelf and the fisheries zones in the area between Greenland and Svalbard. The Government of the Kingdom of Denmark, together with the Government of the Faroes, made its first and second partial submissions, regarding the northern and southern continental shelf of the Faroe Islands, on 29 April 2009 and 2 December 2010, respectively. The Government of the Kingdom of Denmark, together with the Government of Greenland, made its third and fourth partial submissions, regarding the southern and north-eastern continental shelf of Greenland, on 14 June 2012 and 26 November 2013, respectively. On 15 December 2014, Denmark/Greenland filed a submission to define the outer limits of its continental shelf in the Arctic Ocean with the Commission on the Limits of the Continental Shelf (CLCS), claiming that the Lomonosov Ridge is a continental extension of its landmass (www.un.org/depts/los/clcs_new/submissions_files/submission_dnk_76_2014.htm). Canada asked the UN for the extension of its continental shelf in both the Atlantic and Arctic oceans. The federal government submitted two claims with the UN Commission on the Limits of the Continental Shelf, one adding about 1.2 million square kilometres to the east coast offshore boundaries and another application for the Arctic. The main area concerning Canada is the 1700-km-long underwater Lomonosov Ridge, which runs from Ellesmere Island towards Siberia. Some issues regarding the Arctic are regulated by circumpolar states through bilateral agreements between them. For instance, on 27 March 2014, the Kingdom of Denmark, together with the Government of Greenland and the Russian Federation, entered into the following understanding by exchange of notes. They agreed that each of them will not object to any submission to the Commission on the Limits of the Continental Shelf made by the other. Any submission or recommendation by the Commission will respect such agreement and will not prejudice the delimitation of the continental shelf between them. They asked the UN Secretary General to make this agreement known to other parties to UNCLOS, as well as to all other states. Since the issue was regulated in a conventional manner, no dispute arose in this case. See Byers (n 5) on 'Maritime boundaries'. Bearing in mind the aforementioned controversial issues, it seems that the legal status of large areas is unclear, with the consequent incertitude about the applicable law.

[80] Article XX of the CBD.

As discussed above, MGRs can be used either for commercial purposes or for scientific (non-commercial) purposes. Furthermore, the commercial utilisation of MGRs can be classified into two subcategories: they can be used as commodities, ie goods to exploit, such as fish, or for other commercial purposes.[81] Collecting or using MGRs as a commercial commodity is not usually deemed to fall within the category of marine scientific research under UNCLOS, because it does not benefit scientific progress.[82] The distinction between utilisation for commercial purposes other than as commodities and utilisation for scientific purposes is more complex. For instance, some genetic material collected for scientific purposes can *also* be exploited for commercial aims. This can be the case, for instance, when collected samples are stored in ex situ biobanks and later used for other aims.

The Nagoya Protocol provides the basis for the international framework for access and benefit sharing within national jurisdictions. It recognises sovereign rights over genetic resources and encourages countries to provide access to their genetic resources in return for a share in the monetary or non-monetary benefits from their use.[83] The Protocol has attracted quite a large number of contracting states.[84]

According to its Article 17 ('Monitoring the Utilization of Genetic Resources'), checkpoints should be relevant to the utilisation of genetic resources, or to the collection of relevant information at, inter alia, any stage of research, development, innovation, pre-commercialisation or commercialisation. Commercialisation of genetic resources usually takes place at the final stage of their utilisation, following previous steps including research and development.

In relation to access, the first principle is that it should be subject to 'prior informed consent' by those who provide genetic resources and traditional knowledge, for example developing countries or indigenous communities. According to the second principle of equitable benefit sharing, those providing the genetic resources and traditional knowledge[85] are entitled to obtain benefits from the sharing of their knowledge with other users. The third principle is about the promotion of fair access to genetic resources in order to promote research and development.[86]

[81] Yu (n 29) 10. De Lucia, 'The Concept of Commons and Marine Genetic Resources in Areas Beyond National Jurisdiction' (2018–19) 5 *Maritime Safety and Security Law Journal* 1.

[82] De Lucia (n 81).

[83] Nagoya Protocol, Art 15.

[84] For a list of the parties to the Nagoya Protocol, see www.cbd.int/abs/nagoya-protocol/signatories/.

[85] Mulalap et al, 'Traditional Knowledge and the BBNJ Instrument' (2020) 122 *Marine Policy* 104103.

[86] Morgera, Tsioumani and Buck, *Unraveling the Nagoya Protocol: A Commentary on the Nagoya Protocol on Access and Benefit-Sharing to the Convention on Biological Diversity* (Brill, 2014); Oberthür and Rosendal (eds), *Global Governance of Genetic Resources: Access and Benefit Sharing After the Nagoya Protocol* (Routledge, 2014).

According to Article 8(j) of the CBD, the principle of access and benefit sharing requires that parties seeking to use marine resources should obtain the approval and involvement of local holders or providers of knowledge and resources and share the benefits arising out of the use of these resources. Prior informed consent for access to the resources is supposed to be given before they are collected. This refers to the consent of the relevant competent national authority in the provider country as well as that of relevant stakeholders, such as indigenous and local communities. Hence, both the CBD and the Nagoya Protocol make reference to indigenous people.

V. INDIGENOUS PEOPLES AND BIOPROSPECTING

Obligations relating to the rights of indigenous peoples are clearly relevant in relation to the Arctic. In fact, as noted above, within the Arctic Circle there is an estimated population of around four million people, of whom about 10 per cent are members of indigenous communities.[87] There is thus a need to investigate how far they are entitled to participate in the decision-making process related to the exploitation of Arctic MGRs and bioprospecting activities.

Insofar as bioprospecting is focused on the MGRs found within the territorial waters or on the continental shelves of coastal countries, both the principle of access and fair and equitable benefit sharing and the principle of free, prior and informed consent should fully apply.

Arctic MGRs that may be found in the high seas or on the seabed and ocean floor and subsoil thereof, such as those of the so-called Arctic Donut Hole (Central Arctic Ocean Hope Spot, at the centre of the Arctic Ocean), are instead in an area beyond the limits of any country's national jurisdiction. According to the CBD legal regime, there is no application of free, prior and informed consent in ABNJ since no country may exercise sovereignty. The BBNJ Agreement, however, makes clear in Article 13 that such consent is always needed.[88]

VI. INTERESTS AND RIGHTS RELATED TO THE USE AND EXPLOITATION OF MARINE GENETIC RESOURCES

Since indigenous peoples are supposed to be consulted in relation to the exploitation of MGRs, an analysis of the legal nature of such involvement is called for. According to the main legal instruments, ie the CBD, its Nagoya Protocol and the ILO Convention on Tribal and Indigenous Rights, states should ensure that

[87] See Eritja, 'Bio-prospecting in the Arctic: An Overview of the Interaction Between the Rights of Indigenous Peoples and Access and Benefit Sharing' (2017) 44 *Boston College Environmental Affairs Law Review* 223, 225, http://lawdigitalcommons.bc.edu/ealr/vol44/iss2/3.

[88] See s V below.

the prior informed consent or approval and involvement of indigenous peoples concerned is obtained before accessing such resources and/or their associated knowledge. Furthermore, indigenous peoples are entitled to participate in the benefit-sharing process. The benefits to be shared can be monetary, such as royalties when the resources are used to create a commercial product, or non-monetary, such as the development of research skills and knowledge.

According to Article 6 of the ILO Convention, states have a general obligation to consult with indigenous peoples before taking legislative or administrative action. National governments must engage in good faith and in a form appropriate to the circumstances seeking to obtain consent or agreement. Such consultation is mandatory, but it is not required to obtain indigenous people's consent. Indigenous people can influence the decision-making process in relation to any restriction of rights to land and resources.[89] On the other hand, indigenous peoples only have the right to participate in the formulation, application and evaluation of plans that may directly affect them and the right to participate in using the natural resources on their lands.[90]

According to Article 15 CBD, any country has the sovereign right to determine access to genetic resources and has discretion in determining the appropriate way to take action with the goal of an equitable sharing structure. Article 15 does not grant this right to the indigenous peoples in whose territory genetic resources are located. The state is responsible for adopting the necessary measures to share benefits with the local communities. So even if indigenous people are involved, they are entitled to participate only in an indirect way. They are recognised as custodians of genetic resources and their associated traditional knowledge, but the contracting states are the main actors in the access and benefit-sharing procedure.

The Nagoya Protocol is of utmost importance as it addresses the connection of benefit sharing for indigenous peoples to prior, free and informed consent as a condition for granting access to genetic resources. According to its Article 6, each party has to obtain prior informed consent from indigenous peoples and local communities in order to access genetic resources. In particular, the Article distinguishes between consent from the state and consent from the local communities and indigenous peoples, establishing the goal of consent from all parties that possess a *right* to the resources. According to this instrument, indigenous peoples seem to be granted a veritable right to the resources.[91]

It can be seen from practice that in some cases indigenous peoples are themselves contracting parties of international agreements. Sometimes they are allowed to perform all the activities related to the interests of which they are holders. The Land Claims Agreement between the Inuit of Labrador and Canada provides an example of a treaty to which an indigenous people is a contracting party.[92]

[89] See Eritja (n 87) 240.
[90] ibid 240.
[91] See below.
[92] www.gov.nl.ca/exec/iias/files/January212005AgreementComplete.pdf.

Indigenous peoples can also play another important role in international law when they are able to influence the decisions of states. For instance, they influenced negotiations on international agreements related to climate change and, in particular, in relation to policy and international law to reduce the impact of deforestation and environmental degradation.[93]

In the framework of the UN General Assembly and the Human Rights Council, the specific post of Special Rapporteur on the rights of indigenous peoples has been constituted.[94] The Special Rapporteur is mandated to: examine ways and means of overcoming existing obstacles to the full and effective protection of the rights of indigenous peoples; identify, exchange and promote best practices; receive and exchange information and communications on alleged violations of the rights of indigenous peoples; and formulate recommendations and proposals on appropriate measures and activities to prevent and remedy violations of the rights of such peoples. Among its activities, the Special Rapporteur is continuously monitoring the situation of indigenous peoples around the world. It issues reports on specific areas or specific topics. One of the reports most relevant to the present analysis is that on extractive industries and indigenous peoples, issued in 2013.[95] It provides an interesting example of the rights of indigenous peoples in relation to natural resources. The principles set forth in the report could also be applicable to the use and commercial exploitation of MGRs.

In the report, the Rapporteur points out that indigenous peoples around the world have suffered negative, even devastating, consequences from extractive industries. In fact, many natural resources, such as minerals and fossil fuels (oil, gas, and coal), are situated on the lands of indigenous peoples, so that their exploitation results in increasing and ever more widespread effects on indigenous peoples' lives. According to the report, a preferred model for natural resource extraction within indigenous territories is one in which indigenous peoples themselves control the extractive operations, through their own initiatives and enterprises. It is affirmed that indigenous peoples should benefit from partnerships with responsible, experienced and well-financed non-indigenous companies to develop and manage their own extractive enterprises.[96]

[93] The United Nations Environment Programme is the principal United Nations environmental body and helps governments to address global, regional and national environmental challenges. As in 1992 during the United Nations Conference on Environment and Development, which produced the Rio Declaration on Environment and Development and Agenda 21 – the United Nations action plan on sustainable development – indigenous peoples' issues were a significant subject of discussion at the United Nations Conference on Sustainable Development (Rio+20) in 2012. For further details, see https://sustainabledevelopment.un.org/outcomedocuments/agenda21.

[94] The UN Office of the High Commissioner for Human Rights (OHCHR) www.ohchr.org/EN/Issues/IPeoples/SRIndigenousPeoples/Pages/SRIPeoplesIndex.asp. At the present time,the person is MrFrancisco Cali Tzay.

[95] For text, see http://unsr.jamesanaya.org/docs/annual/2013-hrc-annual-report-en.pdf.

[96] http://unsr.jamesanaya.org/docs/annual/2013-hrc-annual-report-en.pdf.

Furthermore, when indigenous peoples choose to pursue their own initiatives for natural resource extraction within their territories, states and the international community should help them to build the capacity to do so, and states should privilege indigenous peoples' initiatives over non-indigenous initiatives. Such initiatives have to be qualified as part of indigenous peoples' right to self-determination and to set their own strategies for development. They have the right to decline to pursue such initiatives in favour of other initiatives for their sustainable development, and they should be supported in such other pursuits as well. This includes the right to oppose extractive projects promoted by the state or third-party business interests.

It is confirmed in the report that the free, prior and informed consent by indigenous peoples is required when extractive activities are carried out within their territories. This serves as a safeguard for the internationally recognised rights of indigenous peoples that are typically affected by extractive activities carried out within their territories (except when those extractive activities are necessary and proportionate with regard to a valid public purpose, defined within the overall framework of respect for human rights). States should ensure consultations with indigenous peoples on extractive activities that would affect them and engage in efforts to reach agreement or consent. Extractive companies should also adopt policies and practices to ensure that all aspects of their operations are respectful of the rights of indigenous peoples, in accordance with international standards and not just domestic law, including with regard to requirements of consultation and consent.

Therefore, agreements should be achieved between states and indigenous peoples for extractive projects. Such agreements allowing for extractive projects within indigenous peoples' territories should be

> crafted on the basis of full respect for their rights in relation to the affected lands and resources and, in particular, should include provisions providing for impact mitigation, for equitable distribution of the benefits of the projects within a framework of genuine partnership, and grievance mechanisms.[97]

This approach calls for a more direct involvement of indigenous people also in the case of bioprospecting activities.

As discussed above, Arctic genetic resources can be especially important for the production of new drugs, due to their specific properties. The role of indigenous peoples' traditional medicine and its associated knowledge has proved to be valuable in this regard.[98] The involvement of local communities also requires their participation in the benefit sharing, in order to reach an equitable solution.

[97] ibid.

[98] See Ibata-Arens (n 31) 51.

VII. INDIGENOUS PEOPLES AND THE BBNJ AGREEMENT

Bioprospecting in ABNJ remains a controversial issue, as there is less clear and elaborate regulation of activities in such areas. This is relevant to the parts of the Arctic, such as the Arctic Central Ocean, that constitute ABNJ. In 2019, UN member states agreed to negotiate an international legally binding instrument under UNCLOS on the conservation and sustainable use of marine biological diversity of areas beyond national jurisdiction.[99]

Indigenous peoples might be affected by the new instrument, as the overall objective of the BBNJ Agreement is to 'ensure the conservation and sustainable use of marine biological diversity of areas beyond national jurisdiction, for the present and in the long term, through effective implementation of the relevant provisions of the Convention and further international cooperation and coordination'.[100] To this aim, reference is made to four elements of governance: MGRs, including benefit sharing; environmental impact assessments; area-based management tools (including marine protected areas); and capacity building and transfer of marine technology. All of them are of interest to indigenous peoples, but especially MGRs and benefit sharing.

The draft BBNJ Agreement makes reference to indigenous peoples and their traditional knowledge in several provisions.[101] A challenge in developing this instrument was to find a middle ground between negotiating countries' positions on access and benefit sharing. It aims to promote scientific research on samples and data, protect traditional and local knowledge, and encourage consistency with existing access and benefit-sharing frameworks within national jurisdiction. Furthermore, it aims to address a number of gaps, such as the absence of a biosafety framework.

ABNJ pose specific challenges, not least in the Arctic, prompting proposals for the introduction of detailed provisions on this matter or even an annex regulating this area.[102] Most of the deep ocean is located in ABNJ. This is an environment characterised by stable low temperatures and low oxygen concentrations as well as high pressures, making organisms grow very slowly and develop very specific features.[103] The majority of Arctic MGRs can be found

[99] UN General Assembly, Revised Draft Text of an Agreement under the United Nations Convention on the Law of the Sea on the Conservation and Sustainable Use of Marine Biological Diversity of Areas beyond National Jurisdiction, 18 November 2019, A/CONF.232/2020/3.

[100] See BBNJ Agreement, Art 2.

[101] See below.

[102] De Lucia, 'The Arctic Environment and the BBNJ Negotiations: Special Rules for Special Circumstances?' (2017) 86 *Marine Policy* 234, 236. The author supports his view by making reference to the so-called Arctic article contained in the UNCLOS. In fact, Art 234 of Part XII allows coastal states to adopt their own laws and regulations within their EEZ in relation to ice-covered area, functioning as *lex specialis* vis-à-vis Art 211(6).

[103] Zentner et al, 'Ignoring Indigenous Peoples: Climate Change, Oil Development, and Indigenous Rights Clash in the Arctic National Wildlife Refuge' (2019) 155 *Climatic Change* 533.

in the so-called Arctic Donut Hole, an area located at the centre of the Arctic Ocean, beyond the limits of any country's national jurisdiction, which includes the high seas as well as the seabed and ocean floor and the subsoil thereof.[104]

Additionally, in ABNJ, environmental damage could take decades or centuries to repair. Some isolated ecosystems, such as trenches, host unique life forms that may have evolved over millions of years. ABNJ hold an extraordinarily high diversity of marine macro- and microorganisms.[105] The marine biotechnology industry is particularly interested in these unique organisms as they may lead to the development of new products and processes.[106]

According to the CBD regime, the 'provider'[107] is entitled to give its prior informed consent and to conclude bilateral arrangements to share the benefits from genetic resources.[108] Genetic resources are subject to the national sovereignty of the country where they are located, so that the specific legal regime of any marine area has to be taken into account. As far as MGRs are concerned, Article 22 of the CBD maintains that the CBD should be applied together with UNCLOS in relation to the marine environment. There is also a reference made in the Nagoya Protocol's Preamble that seems to support the inclusion of MGRs in ABNJ within the CBD's material scope when it concerns transboundary situations or for which it is not possible to grant or obtain prior informed consent.[109]

As has been pointed out, in principle, states have the sovereign right to exploit natural resources within their territorial jurisdiction, including genetic resources, and to regulate foreign access to these resources.[110] As far as ABNJ are concerned, on the one hand, the CBD seems not to be applicable to bioprospecting of genetic resources in such areas since, according to Article 4(a), its territorial application is limited to the national jurisdiction of its parties, at least as regards the components of biological diversity.[111] On the other hand, bioprospecting may also relate to processes and activities taking

[104] Eritja (n 87) 234.

[105] Prip, 'Arctic Ocean Governance in Light of an International Legally Binding Instrument on the Conservation and Sustainable Use of Marine Biodiversity of Areas Beyond National Jurisdiction' (2022) 142 *Marine Policy* 2.

[106] Krabbe (n 28) 84ff.

[107] As far as 'providers' of genetic resources are concerned, 'States have sovereign rights over natural resources under their jurisdiction. They are obligated to put in place conditions that facilitate access to these resources for environmentally sound uses. Providers agree terms, which include prior informed consent and mutually agreed terms, for granting access and sharing benefits equitably. Laws within the provider country may entitle others, such as indigenous and local communities (ILCs) to also negotiate terms of access and benefit sharing. The participation of ILCs is necessary in instances where traditional knowledge associated with genetic resources is being accessed.' See Convention on Biological Diversity: ABS, 'Introduction to Access and Benefit Sharing', www.cbd.int/abs/infokit/revised/web/all-files-en.pdf.

[108] Eritja (n 87) 233.

[109] ibid 245.

[110] Krabbe (n 28) 241–42. See also Sulyandziga, 'Indigenous Peoples and Extractive Industry Encounters: Benefit-Sharing Agreements in Russian Arctic' (2019) 21 *Polar Science* 68.

[111] Krabbe (n 28) 245.

place somewhere else[112] under the control or jurisdiction of the parties. In this case, bearing in mind Article 4(b), the convention may be applicable 'in the case of processes and activities, regardless of where their effects occur, carried out under its jurisdiction or control, within the area of its national jurisdiction or beyond the limits of national jurisdiction'.[113]

It would thus be necessary to identify the role of indigenous peoples in these cases and how far they could be involved in an eventual benefit-sharing process. As the CBD regime and the law of the sea interplay, a distinction could also be drawn between resources of the high seas and those of the Area.

In principle, it is up to the state to identify and involve any indigenous people concerned. Nevertheless, according to a different view, some observers have noted that 'International law guarantees the right to consultation and participation as well as the right to free, prior, and informed consent for indigenous peoples, regardless of domestic law or a countries' ratification of the instruments'.[114]

The *Bonn Guidelines on Access to Genetic Resources and Fair and Equitable Sharing of the Benefits Arising Out of Their Utilization*[115] recommend that a benefit-sharing system be developed on a regional and national level. This would guarantee the protection of indigenous peoples' environmental, social and economic interests.[116] For instance, some Arctic countries, such as Norway, Greenland and, to some extent, Iceland, have adopted specific domestic regulations on access and benefit sharing in order to implement their international obligations, while others, such as Sweden and Denmark, have not.[117]

Another initiative aimed at dealing with the specificities of the Arctic environment in order to address issues related to the livelihoods of local inhabitants and indigenous communities, and the potential exploitation of natural resources, is the Ilulissat Declaration.[118] Within this framework, too, the Arctic Ocean coastal states commit themselves to cooperate and take steps to involve indigenous peoples in the exploitation of natural resources. Even if indigenous peoples' representatives were not involved when the declaration was initially signed, they were invited to do so at the Conference convened for its 10-year anniversary.[119] The negotiating parties of the BBNJ Agreement recognised that ABNJ is a unique jurisdictional area and imported some concepts from the CBD, such as that of access and benefit sharing, originally conceived for transactions

[112] For instance, in relation to the use of ex situ resources.
[113] CBD, Art 4(b).
[114] Eritja (n 87) 250–51.
[115] Secretariat of the Convention on Biological Diversity (2002) 9, www.cbd.int/doc/publications/cbd-bonn-gdls-en.pdf.
[116] See PAME, 'Meaningful Engagement of Indigenous Peoples and Local Communities in Marine Activities. A Reference Guide' (May 2021).
[117] See Eritja (n 87) 245.
[118] The Ilulissat Declaration, Arctic Ocean Conference, Ilulissat, Greenland, 27–29 May 2008, https://cil.nus.edu.sg/wp-content/uploads/2017/07/2008-Il ulissat-Declaration.pdf.
[119] Prip (n 105) 3.

within national jurisdictions. The objectives of the BBNJ Agreement focus more on access, benefit sharing and technology transfer than on goals for ensuring the long-term conservation of marine biological diversity. Access and benefit sharing are considered to be means for achieving MGR governance in ABNJ.

The new BBNJ Agreement is supposed to be applicable to the polar regions in relation to those areas that are beyond national jurisdiction, such as the Arctic Central Ocean.[120] As noted, the BBNJ Agreement imports the CBD's concept of benefit sharing, which presupposes a transaction between provider and user of a particular resource within national jurisdiction.[121] It remains unclear who is the 'provider' of MGRs in ABNJ, and hence with whom to negotiate and share benefits or establish a contractual mechanism for achieving benefit sharing. The role of stakeholders, local communities and traditional knowledge holders (such as indigenous people) is still undefined. Nevertheless, they are mentioned, for instance, in Article 13 concerning access to marine genetic resources of ABNJ, Article 14 on fair and equitable sharing of benefits and Article 19 on the identification of areas requiring protection. Article 21 also mentions them in relation to some obligations of consultation.

The issue of access to traditional knowledge associated with (or useful for unlocking the value of) MGRs of ABNJ would require the prior informed consent or approval and involvement of those holding this knowledge on mutually agreed terms. In this regard, local communities and indigenous people would be parties to this kind of agreement.[122]

As discussed above, particularly in the Arctic, many indigenous peoples have a strong relationship with the sea and sea-ice.[123] Both the ILO Convention and UNDRIP 'recognize indigenous people's rights over their land as well as over the resources in their ancestral domain, particularly as those resources are tied to their subsistence and traditional life, including those found on the coastal seas and sea-ice'.[124] In line with this, indigenous peoples can be deemed the owners of the natural resources, including genetic ones, even beyond the national boundaries of a state. In particular, it is likely that they might be the only ones entitled to share traditional knowledge associated with such resources, thus necessitating their involvement in any agreement concerning it. Article 6 of the

[120] See s I above.

[121] Humphries et al, 'A Tiered Approach to the Marine Genetic Resource Governance Framework Under the Proposed UNCLOS Agreement for Biodiversity Beyond National Jurisdiction (BBNJ)' (2020) 122 *Marine Policy* 3.

[122] The absolute need to involve indigenous peoples and get their prior and informed consent in the processes about activities of their concern has also been stressed by the EU. See European Commission and High Representative of the Union for Foreign Affairs and Security Policy, Joint Communication to the European Parliament, the Council, the European Economic and Social Committee and the Committee of the Regions, 'A Stronger EU Engagement for a Peaceful, Sustainable and Prosperous Arctic', JOIN(2021) 27 final, 15.

[123] Eritja (n 87) 237.

[124] ibid 237. Chircop, Koivurova and Singh, 'Is There a Relationship Between UNDRIP and UNCLOS?' (2019) 33 *Ocean Yearbook* 90.

Nagoya Protocol also 'distinguishes between the consent from the country and the consent from the local communities and indigenous peoples, establishing the goal of consent from all parties that possess a right to the resources'.[125] The consent requirement also extends to access to traditional knowledge of indigenous peoples relating to resource use.[126]

The BBNJ Agreement outlines an access and benefit-sharing system modelled on the CBD and the Nagoya Protocol that were designed for accessing genetic resources within national jurisdictions. There is, however, also a need to clarify how to identify the indigenous peoples entitled to take part in the process, regardless of their relationship with a particular state.

VIII. FINAL REMARKS

In the Arctic, bioprospecting promises potential benefits for biotechnology companies, but questions of equity and fairness remain when such activities affect indigenous populations. Their involvement is key to ensuring that the benefits derived from the exploitation of genetic resources are shared fairly and equitably, and that the traditional knowledge and values of these peoples are respected.

The regulation of these issues is affected by legal gaps. The CBD works on the assumption that genetic resources are subject to the national sovereignty of the country where they are located. Areas beyond national jurisdiction remain unregulated and areas within national jurisdiction may be regulated in different ways, as the norms are treaty-based and binding only for the contracting parties.

At present, three main legal international frameworks overlap in the regulation of these activities, especially as far as indigenous peoples are concerned: the law of the sea, the CBD regime and human rights law. The fundamental principles of free, prior and informed consent, as well as of access and fair and equitable benefit sharing, have been introduced, but mainly in relation to resources under national jurisdiction. These principles also affect MGRs, usually exploited by biotechnology companies.

The right of participation in access and benefit sharing of indigenous people is undermined by several factors. First, bioprospecting is not subject to specific regulation under international law. Even though there are some norms related to either scientific research or genetic resources that can be deemed applicable, they are strictly related to the areas under national jurisdiction and binding only for those states who have ratified the relevant treaties. Therefore, the result is a quite fragmented legal framework, which does not guarantee a proper involvement of the local communities.

[125] Eritja (n 87) 248.
[126] Nagoya Protocol, Art 7.

Second, it is unclear which is the applicable law. There are different norms for each maritime zone, and in the Arctic there are also several competing claims, such as those related to the continental shelf, creating uncertainty about which is the legal regime of some areas.

Finally, a legal framework for the exploitation of resources located beyond national jurisdiction, such as in the Central Arctic Ocean, is not yet in force. It would thus be suitable to promptly clarify the situation and the nature of bioprospecting activities in the Arctic. The BBNJ Agreement would appear to offer a good opportunity to do this, especially since norms about the rights of indigenous peoples are contained within it.[127] At the same time, it would be preferable to find a regional solution that grants the same rights to all the indigenous peoples involved, in order to avoid any discrimination due to the different treaty obligations of the Arctic states.

Indigenous peoples should be involved through the exchange of scientific and other information, by being ensured of access to consultation and consent procedures, and being provided with the capacity to effectively participate in them. Currently, the form, scope and procedure whereby free, prior and informed consent is obtained are governed by the country in which the resources are located. A common and shared system would provide indigenous peoples with a more uniform way of exercising their rights. The BBNJ Agreement provides a chance to fully recognise and guarantee the rights of indigenous peoples in relation to bioprospecting, and this chance must not be squandered.

[127] See BBNJ Agreement, Art 13.

12

Changing Human Uses of Marine Resources and International Law: Looking Ahead

NIELS KRABBE AND DAVID LANGLET

THE CONTRIBUTIONS TO this volume chart in different ways how humankind's relationship to the oceans is currently undergoing a transformation. Scientific breakthroughs and cheaper technology are making distant areas of the oceans more accessible, enabling us to analyse the functions of the oceans and marine life at a rapidly increasing pace and an increased level of detail. Coupled with the rising awareness of the threats of climate change, biodiversity loss and overfishing, this development is shifting our perspective of the seas and what services the oceans can provide for humans. While traditional uses of the oceans, such as shipping, fisheries and offshore drilling, remain as economically important as ever, other uses are increasing in relevance. As shown in the preceding chapters, dramatic developments in international law and policy are also linked to this. Suddenly, after decades of negotiation, agreements are being reached which alter the playing field by not only bringing novel rules on the use of marine resources, but also introducing entirely new concepts to the management of the oceans.

While fish and other living marine organisms have always been important sources of food, marine species are now becoming sampled in order to decipher their genomes and explore how their properties and functions can be mimicked and reproduced to develop biotechnological products. Even if both these uses may relate to the same species, fish for food and as genetic resource have been considered separately in policy and regulation. As described by Scotcher (in chapter eight), there are institutional tensions between structures governing fisheries and marine biodiversity, not least in areas beyond national jurisdiction. While these are largely related to the notion of sovereignty and the implications it has for the management and protection of the marine environment, there are also encouraging signs that multilateral efforts can address such tensions and that there is increasing convergence in the management of fish, fisheries and marine biodiversity. Not least, the 2023 Agreement under the United Nations Convention on the Law of the Sea on the conservation and sustainable use of marine biological diversity of areas beyond national jurisdiction (BBNJ Agreement)[1] holds promising potential in this respect. With particular refence to marine bioprospecting, Gottschalk has analysed (in chapter nine) how Sustainable Development Goals can be used to support such convergence in the form of increased consistency across different legal regimes.

Particularly high expectations have been set for using bioactive properties of marine flora and fauna as sources for pharmaceutical development. This is directly connected to the essential quality of biological diversity. The genetic diversity of life in the seas is much richer than that of life on land, not only in terms of the number of species, but also with respect to differences between the genomes across species. Partly as a result of this endemism, many marine ecosystems are also highly vulnerable to human interference. Antsygina has described (in chapter seven) how governance gaps in the protection of sedentary species may impact detrimentally on dependent ecosystems, including corals and sponges, but also how individual coastal states have the legal capacity to take protective measures.

The regulation of human interference with species that contain genetic resources of scientific and commercial interest raises a multitude of questions on the relationship between humans and nature. Barnes has explored (in chapter two) how the emerging notion of stewardship potentially indicates a new perspective of responsibility in relation to nature as well as to present and future generations. Potentially, the further elaboration of stewardship as a legally important notion in relation to areas beyond national jurisdiction will gain traction by its mentioning, albeit briefly, in the BBNJ Agreement.

States have held widely differing opinions on the legal implications of harvesting marine organisms for their genetic properties. As discussed by Stöfen-O'Brien (in chapter four), opinions have also differed on the relationship between the law of the sea, international environmental law and trade law in the regulation of the use of genetic resources. In some instances, rights of indigenous peoples are an important further dimension and represent an additional layer of complexity, as shown by Eboli (in chapter eleven).

Since the adoption of the Nagoya Protocol under the Convention on Biological Diversity,[2] it is undisputed that coastal states can regulate the access and use of genetic resources within their maritime zones as part of their sovereign rights. The legal status of genetic resources in the high seas and the deep seabed, on the other hand, has remained highly contentious. Some states and

[1] Certified True Copy of the Agreement under the United Nations Convention on the Law of the Sea on the conservation and sustainable use of marine biological diversity of areas beyond national jurisdiction, 21 July 2023, www.un.org/bbnj/ (BBNJ Agreement).

[2] Nagoya Protocol on Access to Genetic Resources and the Fair and Equitable Sharing of Benefits Arising from their Utilization to the Convention on Biological Diversity, 29 October 2010 (into force 12 October 2014), 3009 UNTS (Nagoya Protocol).

observers have considered the sampling and claiming of property rights in relation to marine genetic resources to be a legitimate exercise of high seas freedoms. Others have argued that any claim for exclusive rights to such resources would violate the principle of common heritage of mankind. Krabbe examined (in chapter three) how the discussion on new rules have centred on pre-existing principles of international law, and how they fall short of addressing fundamental practical aspects of using genetic resources.

A central challenge is that the use of genetic resources requires only limited sampling in the natural environment, while rapidly increasing collections are being stored as digital sequence information. Prip (in chapter five) has shown how the emergence of digital sequence information has affected different international legal instruments and processes, and how obligations to share benefits have developed. As a result of these complex features of marine genetic resources and their exploitation, it has been challenging to develop domestic rules. Many states have so far refrained from or not given priority to the development of specific national rules. How this challenge has been addressed by Iceland, a country where the use of marine genetic resources has developed into a major industry, was analysed by Árnadóttir (in chapter ten).

Although the technology for sampling and analysing genetic resources of the deep seas has been in place for some time, the legal components have been lacking. The 1982 United Nations Convention on the Law of the Sea[3] does not make any reference to genetic resources. For the mineral resources of the deep seabed, the situation has been the reverse. As one of its central themes, UNCLOS established an elaborate multilateral system for the management of deep seabed minerals, headed by the International Seabed Authority (ISA). But it is only now that technology is being developed which can turn deep-seabed mining into practical reality. As this book is being published, commercial operators are for the first time preparing large-scale operations. In 2022, the Metals Company reached a milestone by completing the first successful recovery of polymetallic nodules from the abyssal plain. As metal prices increase, other commercial actors are likely to enter the field. The advent of marine mining raises questions on how this novel use of the seas will coexist with existing uses. Encouragingly, Chircop, Ascencio-Herrera and Haag have found (in chapter six), the competencies of the ISA and the International Maritime Organization (IMO) to be highly complementary as they interface with respect to activities on the seabed and in the subsoil of the areas beyond national jurisdiction. The regulatory overlaps that might emerge as the legal regime for seabed mining develops can be addressed on a case-by-case basis by collaboration between the ISA and the IMO.

What is making the current situation so captivating is that the rapid developments in practical uses and perspectives are matched by an unprecedented pace

[3] Adopted 10 December 1982, entered into force 16 November 1994, 1833 UNTS 3 (UNCLOS).

of development of international law and policy. The early 2020s has seen developments in three different, but partly connected, areas: increasingly polarised views on deep seabed mining; the global agreement on ambitious environmental objectives under the Kunming–Montreal Global Biodiversity Framework; and the adoption of the BBNJ Agreement. Taken together, they provide for a seismic shift in the international legal landscape. This chain of regulatory events started in deep-seabed mining.

In July 2021, the Pacific Island nation of Nauru invoked the so-called 'two-year rule' of the 1994 Implementing Agreement to UNCLOS, in order to enable a private mining company under its sponsorship to apply to the ISA for approval of a plan of work for exploitation of deep-sea minerals.[4] This decision sets a two-year deadline for the ISA Council to finalise the negotiations instrumentalising the rules on deep-seabed mining of UNCLOS. Should the negotiations fail to deliver before this deadline, the ISA must, according to the interpretation of its Secretary-General, give provisional approval to an application based on UNCLOS and the 1994 Implementing Agreement, notwithstanding the fact that the rules and regulations have not been adopted.[5] The assessment that operations can be initiated even if the mining code negotiations have not been finalised is, however, far from uncontested. Many observers contend that the ISA Council can still decide to disapprove applications.[6] An increasing number of states have also called for a moratorium on deep-seabed mining until scientific knowledge of the environmental consequences has been fully assessed.[7] By failing to conclude the negotiations of the rules during the ISA summer session of 2023, the two-year deadline was effectively exhausted and it is unclear how states will react if an application for approval of a plan of work for exploitation is submitted.

A second development with far-reaching implications for marine policy occurred at the Conference of the Parties (COP 15) to the UN Convention on Biological Diversity (CBD)[8] in December 2022. With the adoption of the Kunming–Montreal Global Biodiversity Framework,[9] a number of different environmental objectives have been set,[10] many of which have a direct impact on marine policy and the development of the law of the sea. By requiring that

[4] Agreement Relating to the Implementation of Part XI of the United Nations Convention on the Law of the Sea of 10 December 1982 (1836 UNTS 3), Section 1(15).

[5] Lodge, 'Opening Remarks: Third Annual Consultative Meeting Between Contractors' (10 October 2019) 4, https://isa.org.jm/files/documents/EN/SG-Stats/10 _October_2019.pdf.

[6] Singh, 'The Invocation of the "Two-Year Rule" at the International Seabed Authority: Legal Consequences and Implications' (2022) 37 *International Journal of Marine and Coastal Law* 375.

[7] www.theguardian.com/environment/2023/jul/08/future-of-deep-sea-mining-hangs-in-balance-as-opposition-grows.

[8] Adopted 5 June 1992, entered into force 29 December 1993, 1760 UNTS 79 (CBD).

[9] Kunming–Montreal Global Biodiversity Framework, annexed to Decision 15/4 by the Conference of the Parties to the CBD, 19 December 2022, CBD/COP/DEC/15/4.

[10] Stephens, 'Introductory Note to The Kunming–Montreal Global Biodiversity Framework' [2023] *International Legal Materials* 1.

at least 30 per cent of coastal and marine areas are effectively conserved and managed through systems of protected areas and other effective area-based conservation measures by 2030, Target 3 of the Framework is of particular importance for marine management.[11] The adoption of this ambitious objective was bold, not only in light of the short deadline, but also because states can hardly deliver on it by merely adopting area-based conservation measures in areas within national jurisdiction. Roughly two-thirds of the total surface of the oceans count as high seas, so unless areas beyond national jurisdiction can be protected, the decision would require virtually all of the combined area of all coastal states' maritime zones to be protected. The decision thereby effectively presupposed the development of rules and procedures for establishing marine protected areas in areas beyond national jurisdiction.

Thirdly, the consensus adoption of the Global Biodiversity Framework put pressure on the negotiations on marine biological diversity of areas beyond national jurisdiction, which had been ongoing in different forms for over 15 years. Central components of the negotiation concerned new rules for establishing marine protected areas in the high seas and the deep seabed. With the negotiations dramatically running over time, a consensus agreement on a text was finally reached in March 2023. Adopted only three months after the CBD decision in Montreal, the BBNJ Agreement provides the legal means to achieve the objective of protecting 30 per cent of the seas by 2030 as provided by the Global Biodiversity Framework.[12] Although it may take several years until the BBNJ Agreement enters into force, it represents a major landmark in the history of the law of the sea. Not only does the Agreement provide a structure and procedure for adopting marine protected areas; the BBNJ conference of parties and secretariat have also been constructed as the driving force for cooperation of states parties in taking such decisions, as well as for horizontal cooperation between different sectoral and regional marine institutions. Effective institutional cooperation is crucial for the functioning of this part of the Agreement, since the mandate to set restrictions on impacting activities lies with the relevant sectoral organisation and the restrictions are made on the basis of the sectoral organisations' respective rules. While it remains to be seen how successful the BBNJ Agreement will be in this regard, it has the potential to promote the integration of marine governance, which so far has suffered from a high degree of fragmentation.

The impact of the BBNJ Agreement for marine governance and the law of the sea extends beyond marine protected areas. By providing rules for preventing, mitigating and managing adverse impacts on the marine environment, the

[11] According to the decision, these measures shall especially focus on areas of particular importance for biodiversity and ecosystem functions and services.

[12] Mendenhall et al, 'The Ship Has Reached the Shore: The Final Session of the "Biodiversity Beyond National Jurisdiction" Negotiations' (2023) 155 *Marine Policy* 105686.

chapter on environmental impact assessments establishes a rigorous framework to operationalise the pre-existing rules in UNCLOS. These standards are groundbreaking for international environmental law in general and are likely to become a source of inspiration for regulation beyond the agreement's scope of application. The agreement also aims to promote a more equitable distribution of access to the seas and their resources by providing modalities for capacity building and transfer of marine technology. In part, these issues were already regulated in UNCLOS, but have in principle been left unimplemented.

The conclusion of the BBNJ Agreement does not only provide rules to achieve environmental objectives; it also finally closed the vast divide in legal perspective on genetic resources, as discussed in several chapters of this book (see primarily the contributions by Krabbe, Prip and Stöfen-O'Brien). By adopting mandatory requirements for notification and information on a wide range of aspects both before and after the collection of marine genetic resources, the new rules provide a comprehensive overview of relevant activities, including how genetic resources are used. The Agreement also includes rules on how samples and information of genetic resources should be shared, and how capacity among developing countries should be strengthened. The so-called enabling clause in Article 14.7 also enables the conference of the parties to take a decision by qualified majority to introduce mandatory sharing of monetary benefits from the use of genetic resources, potentially including the taxation of sales.

These developments in international law respond, at least in part, to the new perspectives of the oceans and to the novel uses of marine resources discussed in this volume. But there are also other areas where our understanding of the oceans and their function is undergoing important developments which have yet to be addressed in policy.

One dimension of marine governance that has been much discussed in science,[13] though has arguably not received the attention it deserves in the above-discussed policy developments, is the potential role of marine ecosystems in climate change mitigation. While the importance of minimising the impacts of climate change on biodiversity is clearly recognised in the Kunming–Montreal Global Biodiversity Framework,[14] the role of marine and other ecosystems in mitigating climate change is mentioned more in passing and with little specificity.[15]

By binding carbon and effectively pumping it into the sediments through their life cycles, many marine species play an important role in abating climate change. Some species, due to their function and role in the ecosystem, are

[13] For an overview, see Christianson et al, 'The Promise of Blue Carbon Climate Solutions: Where the Science Supports Ocean-Climate Policy' (2022) 9 *Frontiers in Marine Science* 851448.

[14] Target 8 is to 'Minimize the impact of climate change and ocean acidification on biodiversity and increase its resilience through mitigation, adaptation, and disaster risk reduction actions'.

[15] Target 11 refers to enhancing 'nature's contributions to people, including ecosystem functions and services, such as the regulation of air, water and climate'.

particularly important from a climate perspective, and fishing practices can significantly affect the ability of the ocean to sequester CO_2. As has been discussed by the present authors elsewhere, integrating the climate effects of marine activities in the design of policy measures, not least focusing on how fishing is being conducted, can increase the magnitude of carbon sequestration performed by marine flora and fauna.[16]

Although the importance of ensuring the integrity of ecosystems, including marine ones, when taking action to address climate change was recognised in the 2015 Paris Agreement,[17] the BBNJ Agreement is the first time that the carbon cycling services of the oceans are explicitly referred to in an international agreement. Importantly, the agreement also obliges, in its guiding principles and approaches, its parties to be guided by an approach that builds ecosystem resilience and maintains and restores ecosystem integrity, including the carbon cycling services that underpin the role of the ocean in climate.[18] While seemingly a small step, and of limited practical significance in the short term, these references may serve as a starting point for processes to establish what policy changes may promote climate services and how these can be implemented in the management of the oceans. While these elements of the BBNJ Agreement may appear vague, it is not the first time the law of the sea has included forward-looking references to legal concepts which have not yet been fully conceptualised. In the UN Fish Stocks Agreement of 1995,[19] the ecosystem approach was given a prominent guiding role in the management of transboundary fish stocks. At the time, the idea of managing ecosystems from a more holistic perspective had few precedents in policy.[20] The ideas of how to include impacts across species in fisheries regulation was sketchy at best. However, the inclusion of the concept in the agreement, and the subsequent efforts by states and regional fisheries management organisations to implement the approach, resulted in dedicated research efforts which deepened the scientific understanding.[21] New insights, in turn, prompted policy action that slowly moved fisheries management beyond a single-species focus.[22] Hopefully, the carbon cycling references in the BBNJ

[16] Krabbe et al, 'Reforming International Fisheries Law Can Increase Blue Carbon Sequestration' (2022) 9 *Frontiers in Marine Science* 800972.

[17] Rayfuse, 'Climate Change Impacts in Regional Fisheries Management Organizations' in Cadell and Molenaar (eds), *Strengthening International Fisheries Law in an Era of Changing Oceans* (Hart Publishing, 2019) 247.

[18] BBNJ Agreement, Art 7.

[19] Agreement for the Implementation of the Provisions of the UN Convention on the Law of the Sea of 10 December 1982 relating to the Conservation and Management of Straddling Fish Stocks and Highly Migratory Fish Stocks, 4 August 1995 (into force 11 December 2001) 2167 UNTS 3.

[20] Langlet and Rayfuse, 'The Ecosystem Approach in Ocean Planning and Governance: An Introduction' in Langlet and Rayfuse, *The Ecosystem Approach in Ocean Planning and Governance*, vol 87 (Brill, 2019) 1.

[21] Garcia et al, 'The Ecosystem Approach to Fisheries. Issues, Terminology, Principles, Institutional Foundations, Implementation and Outlook' (FAO, 2003).

[22] Shen and Song, 'Implementing Ecosystem Approach to Fisheries Management in the Western and Central Pacific Fisheries Commission: Challenges and Prospects' (2023) 8(4) *Fishes* 198.

Agreement can initiate a similarly fruitful cross-fertilisation between science and policy that will gradually introduce climate aspects into ocean management.

Climate change also has other implications for marine governance that call for increased discussion. One such area is the increasing risk of conflicts between efforts to reduce climate change and other environmental objectives. For a long time, the challenges of climate change and the loss of biological diversity have been discussed as two separate problems. However, as efforts to reduce emissions and promote the conservation of biological diversity increase, it is becoming apparent that measures which are considered helpful to address one of these problems may have detrimental impacts on the other objective. In scholarship, this has been referred to as problem-shifting, but it has so far been little explored in marine policy.[23]

One example of such a trade-off is how climate interests call for shipping to take the shortest route and thereby reduce emissions. Biodiversity interests, on the other hand, would strive to reduce human stressors in biologically sensitive sea areas and divert shipping lanes to less sensitive areas, thereby potentially making shipping routes longer. While both these objectives are promoted in regulation, guidance on how to make trade-offs and prioritise between biodiversity and climate measures is lacking and the problem has been poorly recognised in policy. The new BBNJ Agreement falls short in this regard. Though it identifies the establishment of marine protected areas as a central measure to conserve biological diversity and references climate change and carbon cycling, the Agreement does not recognise that these interests may come into conflict.

At a more concrete level, the conflict between climate and biodiversity interests is being increasingly discussed in relation to deep-sea mining. The companies which are getting ready to launch commercial operations, as well as their state sponsors, regularly refer to the fact that many of the minerals which are vital for the green transition in the energy production, automotive and other sectors are particularly highly concentrated in polymetallic nodules found on the deep seabed.[24] Citing scientific uncertainty on the impact of mining on biodiversity, most states are reluctant to accept mining operations for the time being. Still, how to handle this potential trade-off between climate and biodiversity interests has so far been little considered in the policy debate on deep-sea mining.

In conclusion, human perspectives of the ocean and the use of its resources are rapidly changing. In order to meet these challenges, impressive efforts have recently been made to reform law and policy. The historic milestone of the new BBNJ Agreement particularly stands out. Once the agreement has entered into force, it should significantly contribute to a more sustainable management of the

[23] Kim and van Asselt, 'Global Governance: Problem Shifting in the Anthropocene and the Limits of International Law' in Morgera and Kulovesi (eds), *Research Handbook on International Law and Natural Resources* (Edward Elgar Publishing, 2016) 473.

[24] Toro, Robles and Jeldres, 'Seabed Mineral Resources, an Alternative for the Future of Renewable Energy; a Critical Review' [2020] *Ore Geology Reviews* 103699.

oceans. However, its scope excludes the marine areas of coastal states and the coastal waters which are most biologically productive and where human impact is most problematic. Ideally, a more intense global cooperation to conserve life in the deep seas will inspire environmental reforms also on the domestic side. It is clear that there are a multitude of challenges facing marine management and the use of marine resources. While this volume has addressed a handful of these problems, many more are calling for scholarly examination and political action.

Index

www.ingramcontent.com/pod-product-compliance
Ingram Content Group UK Ltd.
Pitfield, Milton Keynes, MK11 3LW, UK
UKHW020806290926
15470UKWH00003B/980

9 781509 968275